ST. MARY'S
COLLEGE OF EDUCATION
LIBRARY

942.085

MAC

20,494

X

ST. MARY'S COLLEGE OF EDUCATION

LIBRARY

Date Due	Date Due	Date Due
-2 JUN 1977		
19 APR 1979		

MACMILLAN

Portrait of a Politician

[Barratts]

RIGHT HONOURABLE HAROLD MACMILLAN, PRIME MINISTER

MACMILLAN

Portrait of a Politician

By EMRYS HUGHES

London
GEORGE ALLEN & UNWIN LTD
RUSKIN HOUSE   MUSEUM STREET

20,494

FIRST PUBLISHED IN 1962

This book is copyright under the Berne Convention.
Apart from any fair dealing for the purposes of
private study, research, criticism or review, as per-
mitted under the Copyright Act, 1956, no portion
may be reproduced by any process without written
permission. Enquiries should be addressed to the
publisher.

© George Allen & Unwin Ltd, 1962

REFERENCE LIBRARY

———o———

ST. MARY'S COLLEGE OF EDUCATION
BELFAST

Section ....

942 | 085 | HUG

PRINTED IN GREAT BRITAIN
BY BLACKFRIARS PRESS LTD
LEICESTER

'Theoretically, I have no absolute belief in property at all, and have a sneaking kindness for Communism of the old Platonic or Christian kind. But if we have Property with a big or a small p, do, please, let it be on an *equitable* basis. Why the Duke of Bedford should compel me to pay him certain sums of money annually, because I have built a nice house on a bit of land, which he says is his and Wordsworth's poems should be open to be made money of or mincemeat of, by me or any other publisher, who chooses to be reckless in what he does, provided only he does business, I cannot understand.'— ALEXANDER MACMILLAN (July 30th, 1875) in a letter to Lord Coleridge.

PREFACE

WHEN Bernard Shaw was asked why he had written a play about Saint Joan he replied, 'To save her from John Drinkwater'.

I cannot say that I have written this book about Harold Macmillan to save him from Randolph Churchill. Indeed, knowing how easily Randolph Churchill is provoked it might tempt him to write a biography of Macmillan yet and in that case we might get further light on Suez and we might be treated to more sensational political revelations and more skeletons might be dragged out of the Conservative cupboard. My own view, however, is that by writing his biography of Anthony Eden, Randolph Churchill performed a useful public service and certainly showed that an unauthorized biography could be as useful and informative as an authorized official one. Considering how Tory M.P.s in the House of Commons and in the country reacted to Randolph Churchill's book on Anthony Eden, I hardly think they would show much enthusiasm if it were announced that Randolph was now contemplating a biography in defence of Macmillan. However if Randolph, or any other Tory idolator of Macmillan, now decided to start on him, I can at least claim to have paved the way and done something to make the task of some other biographer a little easier by gathering together some of the facts into one volume even if it may be regarded as mildly controversial.

Any British Prime Minister deserves some kind of biography if even only for reference purposes It is surely unfair to American students who write asking one to recommend a book about Harold Macmillan to tell them that they can choose between *Who's Who* and the *Encyclopaedia Britannica*.

Of course Harold Macmillan is a more difficult character for a biographer than Anthony Eden. He is a more complex personality. When I asked a foreign diplomat what he thought of Macmillan he replied 'Which Macmillan?' There was point in this for at different times, in different situations and to different persons, he is a different Macmillan.

I have, however, tried to simplify things and have reduced him to two, the young pre-war Conservative Party rebel, out of touch with his party and attempting to give it a new programme, policy and outlook and not succeeding very much, and the post-war politician who became its leader and Prime Minister.

For the one I have, being a little of a rebel myself, a certain amount of respect and sympathy. For the other I have rather mixed feelings, which might be termed political prejudices, and which the critics will inevitably discover in the book.

It would, however, be a rather difficult task for an orthodox Conservative to attempt a biography of Harold Macmillan. He might easily end up, after reading the early speeches and reading the early books, by not being a Conservative. Indeed there is a little of a mystery how Macmillan ended by being an orthodox (a Right-wing) Conservative as *The Times* hinted when he became Prime Minister.

What happened? Why did he shy off from the logic of his own arguments. Why did he go Right and not Left and not end up in the Labour Party? If he had done so he might have succeeded in leading the Labour Party! At one time he was very interested in the Labour Party indeed and Left-wing Labour M.P.s thought he might be thinking of coming over. When he addressed the Young Conservatives he explained that he was frightened off by Karl Marx. But Karl Marx was hardly likely to have been the nigger in the wood pile then and not in the running for the leadership of the Labour Party anyway.

When I asked a veteran Labour M.P. why he thought Macmillan, finding it impossible to stay in the middle of the road, had turned right he explained, 'It wasn't really a matter of principle, it was a matter of class; he had got into the wrong class and couldn't get out of it'.

When he ultimately became Prime Minister he was really not the Leader of the Conservative Party; he was its prisoner, the political figurehead, the spokesman, the soothsayer of all the vested interests whose power he had earlier set out to challenge. His speeches became the patter of the politician with his eye on the next General Election and not the reformer thinking of the next generation.

The one really adventurous thing he has done as Prime Minister was to go to Russia. For a time then he raised hopes that the Western world had produced someone who could ease the tension, slow down the arms race and work out an agreement with the Soviet Government which would bring peace.

But the hopes died away when he showed no boldness nor initiative in working out a new international policy and pursuing it
with determination. He found he was as much a prisoner on the
international front as he was in politics at home.

Having strongly opposed a policy of appeasement before the
war he had no hesitation at all, when Prime Minister, to carrying
out a policy of appeasement towards the real enemies of the
British people on the home front, the powerful capitalist, financial and landlord vested interests, the speculators of the Stock
Exchange, the property racketeers, the take-over bidders. By
increasing working-class rents, through the Rent Act, the Tory
Government made Britain the property owners' paradise and
inflicted hardship on millions of poor people.

If any ghost haunted 10 Downing Street, before it was pulled
down, it would have been the wraith of some ancient Scottish
crofter unable to believe that a Macmillan could have been
associated with laws to put up poor folk's rents. By increasing
rents and ending food subsidies and increasing health charges he
compelled the workers to demand higher wages and set in motion
the inflation which made a financial and economic crisis
inevitable.

Macmillan's total surrender to the tax dodgers and the 'free
enterprise' speculators, who made fortunes out of capital gains,
his failure to plan and re-organize British industry to meet the
rapidly changing economic conditions of the modern world,
made it impossible to build up a real sound economy which
would ensure the British people of a steadily rising standard of
living and a really prosperous future.

While we were moving quickly into a world of mergers and
monopolies he continued to babble about 'free enterprise' refusing to assert the authority of the State over the big business
tycoons and assert the rights of the community against the get-
rich-quick vested interests who were out to exploit it.

It would be impossible in one short book to state the case
against Macmillan and his record of servility to his capitalist
masters.

Ultimately he was driven to seek refuge in the Common
Market because of his deliberate neglect to work out anything
like a long-term plan for the future of Britain.

Knowing the huge burden that the arms race was placing on

the British economy, yet he continued it, squandering our money on armaments that were obsolete, gambling on costly ventures like Blue Streak, wasting British labour and technique and the brains of our scientists on the idea of an independent nuclear deterrent which was based on the assumption that we must be prepared in the nuclear age to go it alone in a war with the Soviet Union. At the end of his five years of Premiership it was the military men on his own back benches who were bitterly critical of his defence policy and were demanding that he should introduce conscription in order that he should strengthen armed forces which did not have modern weapons. By his subservience to America he put Britain in the front line in the event of a nuclear war and by making Britain an American base placed the British people in a position of maximum danger with the minimum amount of security. While President Kennedy was telling the American people that they must have air raid shelters in order to survive, Macmillan has had to admit that the British people couldn't have fall-out air raid shelters because we couldn't afford it.

In a paragraph at the end of the 1962 Defence White Paper, as a sort of afterthought, we are casually told that the Government is contemplating a scheme for 'dispersing mothers and children and other people in priority classes from major centres of population'. Where they are to be dispersed to, we do not know.

We have reached the stage when Sir Robert Watson-Watt, the inventor of radar, tells us 'The fairy tale of the Great Deterrent is a menace to our survival, to the survival of the human race'.

This book of course is not the end of the story. More chapters remain to be written for Harold Macmillan is still Prime Minister and the leading actor on Britain's political stage. Indeed these remaining chapters may be the most interesting for successive by elections in March 1962 have shown that Tory majorities, even in safe Tory seats, are slumping and that British politics are in the melting pot. So, indeed, is the whole future of Britain. We are involved in what Macmillan has called 'the terrible nuclear arms race' with no signs that we are winning it or can win it, and in the midst of a financial and economic crisis. We are also negotiating entering the European Common Market which could mean big revolutionary changes in our economy and our national life.

We are all interested in what happens to Macmillan now because it concerns us all.

British politics have become more interesting than they have been at any time since the war.

The concluding chapters in Macmillan's political life may be more fateful for the people of Britain than anything that has gone before.

However they will have to wait for another edition or another volume.

I understand that the Young Conservatives are badly in need of a new text book on modern politics. They are welcome to use this one. They certainly should know as much as possible about the Prime Minister, the story of his political career, how he rose to power and what he did when he got there.

EMRYS HUGHES

Dunure   17.3.62

CONTENTS

ILLUSTRATIONS

CHAPTER I

HIGH ROAD TO ENGLAND

'BUT SIR, let me tell you, the noblest prospect which a Scotch-man ever sees is the high road that leads to England.'

So said Doctor Samuel Johnson to his biographer James Boswell. Had Boswell never taken the high road that leads to England, this much-quoted remark, like many of the other sayings of Doctor Johnson, would probably never have been handed on to posterity.

'My grandfather came to England to earn a living and he had every right to do so,' said Harold Macmillan in the House of Commons when somebody made a reference to his grandfather. He was quite right.

Had the Government, in Dr Johnson's time, introduced a Bill to keep out the Scots as the Macmillan Government did to keep out the Irish, the West Indians and other citizens of the British Commonwealth, the Macmillans would never have been able to settle in England—and it would have been so much the worse for England.

'We need Scots who understand these things, Englishmen are non-adult in politics,' wrote Bernard Shaw to me in a letter in January 1946. As an Irishman he claimed to be objective. Since the beginning of the century five British Prime Ministers had forefathers who came from Scotland. Balfour, Campbell-Bannerman, Bonar Law, Ramsay MacDonald were all Scots. There were others before them. The Macmillans had as much right to take the high road that leads to England as the rest of them.

As a matter of fact the English-speaking peoples of the world are as much indebted to the Macmillans as Dr Johnson was indebted to Boswell. The publishing house of Macmillan not only published the works of many of the great literary figures of the century but they supplied English educational textbooks to half the world and helped greatly to spread literature, culture and civilization all over the globe. There can hardly be a library anywhere where the English language is read and spoken without some books published by Macmillan being on the shelves. Popular editions of the great classics, Shakespeare, Milton, Tennyson, Charles Kingsley, Lewis Carroll, Thomas Hardy, Rudyard Kipling are only a few of the names who figure in the Macmillans' catalogue.

It cannot be denied that the enterprising publishers who came from Scotland did an enormous and invaluable service to the English.

'My brother and I,' said Harold Macmillan to George Moore during a dinner party at the Garrick Club in 1931, 'depend very much upon what our grandfather did. I hope our successors will live by what we are doing now. A publishing house is a long-term business. It doesn't live from hand to mouth.'

Certainly Daniel Macmillan, the founder of the publishing business, was a remarkable and outstanding man. He was born on September 13, 1813 on a small croft in the northern part of the Island of Arran in the Firth of Clyde.

The Macmillans had originally come over to Arran from Kintyre, in Argyllshire, but had been there for several generations.

Malcolm Macmillan, Daniel's grandfather, had been a tacksman, a small farmer who collected the landlord's rent from the other farmers and also supplied them with peat and corn food. There are gravestones of Macmillans in the little churchyard at Lochranza and also plaques on the church walls. They had large families and so did Malcolm's son Duncan. He had four sons and eight daughters and Daniel Macmillan was the tenth child and the third son. Four of the daughters died, like so many children of the poor crowded into small houses, from an epidemic.

They lived in extreme poverty. From passages in Daniel's journal and from his letters it is clear that at times good and sufficient food was scarcely abundant in the household and at others it was near starvation. Burns, shortly before, had written bitterly of the life of a small farmer in Ayrshire as combining 'the cheerless gloom of the hermit with the moil of the galley slave'.

Duncan Macmillan's life was even worse than that of Burns, for he had a larger family to keep. To live at all, it was a grim struggle with nature and the landlord had to be paid his rent as well.

To the tourist and the traveller Arran is the beautiful island in the Clyde with the rugged hills standing out majestically against the skyline, dominated by the peak of Goat Fell and the range which in its outline resembles a sleeping warrior and is called by that name.

But life in the remote corner of the island at the beginning of the last century to the men scratching their living from the land and trudging over the hillsides after their sheep was just slavery and drudgery.

Arran, it has been said, with its hills and glens and burns and moorlands, is Scotland in miniature. Its history at the end of the eighteenth and the beginning of the nineteenth centuries was the history of Scotland too. These were the years of the enclosures and the evictions.

Northern Arran in 1815, the year of Waterloo, as the ruins of many crofts in the glens and the hillsides still show, had quite a large crofting population. But when leases expired in 1815 rents went up and it became impossible for many to live there. So they made their way to the mainland, to the towns where there was a demand for labour, and often from there via Greenock and Glasgow to Canada, the States and other countries overseas.

If you want to know more about the historical background and why so many Macmillans, Curries, Mackelvies left Arran by the score in these years you can study it in books like Macleod's *Gloomy Memories* and Tom Johnston's *History of the Working Classes in Scotland*.

When Daniel was three the family decided to cross over to the mainland and settled down on another small farm near the town of Irvine. The father kept a few cows, pastured on the burgh moor and cultivated a few acres of the town's land. He was a carter too and carried coal from the pits into the town. He died when Daniel was ten years old, 'broken down with trial and care and ill-health', and the son was sent out to work with a local bookseller and bookbinder to whom he was bound to serve faithfully for seven years, for the wage of 1s 6d a week for the first year, with a rise of 1s a week for each of the remaining six years.

ST. MARY'S COLLEGE OF EDUCATION
FALLS ROAD. BELFAST. 12.

When he had finished his apprenticeship he went to work at a bookshop in Stirling and then to another in Glasgow. There, he wrote, 'I worked hard and closely from early till late. I was always at work at seven and never or hardly ever finished before nine; it was often ten, eleven and twelve before I got away.'

Overwork undermined his health at a very early age. The work in the Glasgow shop was too much for him. One of his friends there, James Maclehose, had managed to get a job in far away London, and he wrote inviting him to join him, offering him half his bed until he found work there too. So Daniel Macmillan made his way to London, not by road, but by sea from Leith and tramped around from bookshop to bookshop seeking work.

One bookseller offered him not work but religious advice. 'This advice,' he noted, 'disgusted me—not what he said, but the way he said it. There is a great deal of humbug about religious people.'

He went out into the streets and prayed and wept, bitterly. One bookseller, Mr Marshall of Simpkin and Marshall, offered him a job at £60 a year living in, on condition that he would engage for a year. He found no suitable work in London and went on to Cambridge where he was given a job in Johnson's bookshop at £30 a year. There he stayed for three years and then went to Seeley's bookshop in Fleet Street at £60 a year.

His brother joined him and later they established a business of their own and then borrowed money to buy a bookshop at Cambridge.

Their bookselling business developed into publishing which grew steadily. Daniel Macmillan's life had been one long struggle against poverty and ill health and he had hardly begun to reap the reward for his energies when he died at the age of forty-five.

The letters of Daniel Macmillan, which were edited by Thomas Hughes, Q.C., give us an idea of what this able, courageous, determined man was like. Dogged by periodical illness, most of his life struggling perpetually against poverty, he won through to the success which came to him too late in life to really enjoy.

He was shrewd and sensitive and had acquired a wealth of experience and knowledge without ever having had any school education worth speaking about. He had won the regard of many distinguished literary men who recognized his all-round abilities. Among his greatest friends were the Reverend Frederick Denison Maurice, one of the early Christian Socialists, and Charles Kingsley, with whose literary career he was closely associated.

Daniel Macmillan was such an admirer of the Rev Frederick Denison Maurice that he named one of his sons after him. Maurice Harold Macmillan inherited the name if not the political outlook of the early Christian Socialist. Alexander Macmillan shared this respect for the Rev F. D. Maurice and to some extent his views on social questions, views which he expounded in an unpublished pamphlet.

He was a good literary critic and a gifted descriptive writer himself and an intelligent enlightened man who had suffered greatly and had great sympathy with human suffering. His letters are packed full of wisdom and understanding of humanity and reveal a mind which was able to give a tolerant judgment of his contemporaries and a deep understanding of the life of the times in which he lived.

His brother Alexander was an able man too, and the business carried on and prospered with various members of the family, working hard to continue building up the firm.

The Macmillans found that the antipathy of the English for the Scots had not ended with Dr Johnson.

One of their first publications was a philosophical treatise called *Three Questions* by William H. Millar. The full title was *The Three Questions: 'What Am I?' 'Whence Came I?' 'Where Do I Go?'* When Mr Longman, a rival publisher, saw it, he answered the questions thus: 'A Scot; from the Land of Cakes; to the Devil!'

Maurice Crawford Macmillan, the father of Harold Macmillan, was Daniel's second son. He was largely responsible for building up the firm's business overseas, especially in India.

'As the years passed,' Charles Morgan tells us in his interesting and authoritative book *The House of Macmillan*, 'elementary education was given increasing attention. There were history and geography readers for all seven standards, literary readers from the primary stage upwards, and a mass of apparatus. As well as special editions for Indian schools, there were readers in Afrikaans for South Africa, in Swahili for East Africa, in Arabic for Egypt, Anglo-Chinese readers and Australian readers—which may explain the order of the American general to his troops: that when they went to Australia they were to make themselves familiar with the customs and language of the inhabitants. All these matters, together with the firm's paper supplies, their bindings, their travellers' reports and the business of their depots, fell upon Maurice. No man could have borne it who was not an educational enthusiast. As it was, Maurice Macmillan built up what is perhaps the firm's most solid asset—an educational series which today, under the control of his son Daniel, continuously retains its youth. The benefit of his work to Macmillan must certainly extend far into the future.'

Maurice Crawford Macmillan married Helen Belles, the daughter of an American doctor, who came from Indiana, USA, and Maurice Harold Macmillan was born in London on February 10, 1894.

CHAPTER II

ETON, OXFORD, THE GUARDS
AND POLITICS

YOUNG Harold Macmillan had been born into an entirely different world from that of his grandfather. His parents were rich and could afford to give him the education and the opportunities which were given to the sons of the aristocracy and those of the wealthy middle class.

His father decided to send him to Eton. He spent five years at Eton mixing with the sons of princes, dukes, earls and lords—all the boys came from wealthy families. Otherwise they would not have been there.

At Eton they were taught good manners and they acquired from their teachers and tutors the Oxford accent and received the conventional education given to the boys who by birth and wealth were regarded as being destined to be the ruling class.

Eton, like every other educational institution, could hardly have avoided receiving a part of their education from the educational text books published by Macmillan.

If some superior boy was inclined to look down on him for being the son and grandson of a bookseller he could at least retort that his father and grandfather were capable of earning their own living and had produced something which was of value to the community and the country (which was more than what some of his fellow pupils could say).

He must have been clever and intelligent and from his mother, who could speak French, he learnt to speak the French language fluently.

During his holidays he sometimes went to the Island of Arran where the family used to take the minister's house in the village of Sannox for the summer season.

Young Macmillan tramped the hills as his great grandfather had done. But it was rather different. Arran was a wonderful island for a holiday, as long as you did not have to make your living there on the land.

For the wealthy there is hunting and shooting and fishing, stalking the deer on the hills and the ridges. In the grouse shooting season there are beaters to drive the grouse into the air and gamekeepers to carry the guns and keep away the poachers from the pools in the burns which are preserved for the people rich enough to acquire the sporting and the fishing rights.

One wonders whether the young Macmillan on these holidays in Arran reflected on the changes in the family fortunes.

If his great grandfather Duncan had stayed on there and not departed for the mainland he might have been a gamekeeper working for the estate or a crofter making a little extra by letting his house to summer visitors from Glasgow.

From Eton he went to Oxford, to Balliol. He had a distinguished career at Oxford where he was an Exhibitioner, an award earned by successful students.

Then the First World War came and he joined the Grenadier Guards, became a captain, was wounded three times and received the Military Cross.

When the war was over Captain Macmillan was appointed to the post of *aide de camp* to the Duke of Devonshire, who had become the Governor General of Canada.

In those days these appointments were usually given to dukes. They were sent to the Dominions as representatives of the Crown, were regarded as minor potentates, and were attended with the ceremonies and the concessions associated with monarchy.

Young Captain Macmillan fitted into this routine well. He was tall, good looking and presentable, and Eton and Oxford had given him confidence and poise.

Even if he were not a marquis or an earl or a viscount he at least looked like one. He had the bearing—he carried himself with great assurance and dignity. Even if he had no blue blood in his veins at least he had ability.

It ended up by his marrying one of the Duke's daughters. The wedding was one of the events of the London season. Queen Alexandra and the Princess Louise were among the guests.

Another was Thomas Hardy, the novelist. He had come out of respect for his publishers.

After Eton, Oxford and the Guards, publishing might not be too exciting an occupation, even if there was money in it.

Why not go into politics? He had all the qualifications for a Tory M.P.—the money, the right background, the connections with the aristocracy.

This was just the kind of promising young fellow that the Tory Party Head Office thought might be useful in Parliament. Even if some of the nobility might be a little snooty about the son of a publisher, were not the Tory benches at Westminster crowded with sons of self-made men, the new *nouveau riche*, coalowners, steelowners, brewers, shipowners and people who had made their money by speculating on the Stock Exchange. Compared with the way some of them had made their money, publishing was eminently respectable.

Yes, they would try to find him a seat in Parliament, not one of the safest, perhaps, not one of the hereditary pocket borough county constituencies nor one of the seaside resorts which could be trusted to return anything blue, but one of the more difficult seats in the industrial north.

Why not Stockton-on-Tees?

So at the General Election of December 1923, Captain Harold Macmillan became the Conservative candidate for Stockton-on-Tees. It was a three-cornered fight but the Liberal managed to get in by a narrow majority of seventy-three votes. It was a neck-and-neck finish with Major R. Stewart, the Liberal, polling 11,734 against Macmillan's 11,661, with Labour polling 10,619.

It was obviously worth trying again. The first Labour Government of 1924 did not last the year. There was another General Election in October. This time the Conservatives won the seat. The figures were Macmillan 15,163, Riley (Labour) 11,948, Stewart (Liberal) 8,971.

At the age of thirty Harold Macmillan became a Member of Parliament. His feet were on the first rung of the political ladder.

He had begun his political career.

CHAPTER III

LEFT WING CONSERVATIVE

IT CANNOT be said that the young Harold Macmillan took to politics like a duck takes to water. In fact he showed no great hurry to get into the water at all. It was five months after the opening of the new Parliament and he made his maiden speech in the Budget Debate on April 30, 1925.

Winston Churchill, to everybody's surprise, had been appointed to be Chancellor of the Exchequer in the new Tory Government. He had only recently come over from the Liberals and this was his first Budget.

It had been bitterly criticized by the Chancellor in the Labour Government that had been defeated, Philip Snowden. One of its proposals was a scheme for widows' pensions, which the Labour Government intended to introduce if it had survived. Otherwise it was a typical Tory Rich Man's Budget, the dividend paid to the plutocracy who had subscribed to the Tory Party's Election Funds.

A maiden speech usually attracts a full House and curious Members came in to hear the young Macmillan.

It was very much the usual conventional new Member's maiden speech in which he began by claiming the indulgence of the House on the occasion of addressing it for the first time.

But he was rather more controversial than is usual in a maiden speech. He thought that Mr Snowden's statement that it was a rich man's Budget was 'monstrous' and was due to a certain feeling of disillusionment and disappointment. The remissions in taxation that the Chancellor had given were on the lower scale of income tax and benefited the poorer income tax payers. It was always a proposal that had been made by the Members of the party sitting behind him. 'That is where the shoe pinches. If these proposals had been made when they were still in office all would have been well. . . . They will be remembered far longer than Hon. Members opposite may imagine. Hon. Gentlemen opposite are in a dilemma in this matter. They

28

are not quite certain whether to take the line that we have been stealing their clothing while they very incontinently went to bathe in the muddy waters of Russian intrigue, or whether they are to say the clothes are no good anyway.'

This was a reference to the issue of the Russian Treaty which had been one of the causes of the Labour Government's defeat.

He referred to an appeal Ramsay MacDonald had made to some of the 'younger and more progressive Members of the Conservative Party' to range themselves under his flag. 'I well understand that the general of an army, half of which is reputed to be in mutiny and the other half in a state more or less of passive despair, should wish to find some new recruits, but I can assure him that I belong very much to that body of the younger members of the party, and that, if he thinks that we are either so young or so inexperienced as to be caught by a trap so clumsy as his, it shows that he totally misunderstands the moral principles and ideals of democratic Toryism. He has no conception of what those ideals and principles mean to us if he thinks that he and his party have only to offer to us as the true Socialism a kind of mixture, a sort of horrible political cocktail, consisting partly of the dregs of exploded economic views of Karl Marx, mixed up with a little flavour of Cobdenism, well iced by the late Chancellor of the Exchequer, and with a little ginger from the Member for Gorbals (Mr Buchanan)—if he thinks that this is to be the draught given to our parched throats and that we are ready to accept it, he is very much mistaken. . . . I am sure that for myself, and for many others who have the same views as I have, although we are but young, newly-arrived and inexperienced members of the party, it has been, to have a Budget like this, an immense encouragement, and we claim it as a sign of what Conservatism can do and has always done, when it is true to itself.'

Members trooped out again to wet their 'parched throats'. The old Tory hacks said to one another that they had heard things like this before. 'Younger and more progressive members of the Conservative Party indeed, who do they think *they* are?' Lots of chaps have talked like that when they first came into this place. Joe Chamberlain came in here as a Radical Republican. And look how he ended. Then remember how progressive Winston was in his younger days. But you can't blame this young chap. He's not much more than thirty. What will you have to drink?'

The members of the Clydeside Rebel Group discussed the maiden speech of the new Member over cups of black coffee.

'He's got an Oxford accent and speaks like an Englishman,' said David Kirkwood, 'but his folk must have come frae Scotland.'

'He's no Macmillan the lawyer that acts for Glasgow Toon Council an' advised them that free school meals are illegal?' asked George Buchanan. 'He's too young for that.'

'No,' said Jimmy Maxton, 'he must be the son of Macmillan, the publisher.'

'His grandfather came from the Isle of Arran,' said Campbell Stephen, who had once contested Bute and North Ayrshire. 'He came to London an' made a lot of money oot o' publishing.'

'Och,' said David Kirkwood, 'I remember now, he married the daughter of a dook.'

'Aye,' said Jimmy, 'you couldn't expect him to have much sympathy with Karl Marx. Marx would have expropriated the dook an' the hale lot o' them.'

'We'll see how progressive he is when my next amendment to increase the Unemployment Scale comes to be voted on,' said George Buchanan.

'You chaps must have a little charity,' said Maxton, 'we've heard many worse maiden speeches than that.'

'That's not saying much, Jimmy,' said Davie, 'but we'll see hoo the young fellow gets on. We'd better give him a chance.'

Young Macmillan, however, didn't trouble them for a long time after that. He didn't make many speeches in that Parliament and wasn't seen too often in the House. Publishing had to come before politics.

In his first speech he had tried to say where he stood in politics—if he understood himself. He was not a reactionary Conservative of the old school. He was 'progressive' in his views and outlook. Certainly he did not approve of Karl Marx. One could hardly have expected that. Then he did not approve of Cobden and Free Trade and all that sort of thing which really belonged to the middle of the nineteenth century. He had been immensely encouraged by the fact that Winston Churchill had introduced Widows' Pensions. It showed that the Conservatives could become democratic if they wished. Why couldn't they do more for the unemployed? Stockton-on-Tees was full of unemployed. They came to heckle him at election meetings. Why couldn't the Conservatives have a policy for unemployment? Why couldn't they be more progressive? Why should the Conservative Party be the party of the old-fashioned type of hard-boiled capitalist concerned with making big profits out of the workers and nothing else? There were some other young Conservatives asking these questions and theorizing along these lines too and they formed themselves into a discussion group to think out a new policy.

Macmillan was welcomed. Now they would at least be able to get their views published.

In 1927 they published their views in a book called *Industry and the State—A Conservative View*. It appeared above the names of Robert Boothby, John de V. Loder, Hon. Oliver Stanley and Harold Macmillan, all young Conservative M.P.s, and was published by Macmillan. The book was so full of 'ifs' and 'buts' and vague passages which cancelled each other out that it was difficult to discover exactly what the authors meant. They were of course opposed to Socialism but they stressed that they were also opposed to individualism. They declared in their introduction 'That the Conservative Party stands in need of some definite industrial policy, even if it is to be of complete *laissez faire*, cannot be disputed for the present outlook can only be described as chaotic'.

There were whole pages of the book which might mean anything or nothing. They said, 'In attempting to analyze the principles of Conservatism we must at least avoid the error of too close an approach to precision or to dogma'. They certainly succeeded in avoiding this. Anti-Socialist they certainly were. They wrote 'Socialism in "our time" spells economic disaster. Socialism "at any old time" can safely be left to future generations to discuss if they still have any inclination to do so.'

'A completely salaried industry would be an industry dead,' they asserted, completely oblivious of the fact that even at that time many of the essential services were being run by salaried people, the municipalities, local government services, education, the Post Office, the armed forces, the civil service.

In the very next page it proceeded to say: 'But if we reject

Socialism as antagonistic to Conservative principles we must also
do the same for the other extreme, unrestricted individualism.
That too offends against continuity, for all the Governments
since the Reform Bill have in some way or other interfered with
industry. Conservative Governments and the Conservative Party
have been, or have desired to be, particularly active, witness
Factory Legislation and Tariff Reform; whilst last autumn session
the Conservative majority passed in the space of six weeks an
Electricity Act, a Merchandise Marks Act, a Sale of Food and
Drugs Act, and the supplementary estimate for the establishment of a Broadcasting Corporation.'

The book read as if alternate paragraphs had been written by
members of the Fabian Society and the Anti-Socialist Union.

How much of it was written by Harold Macmillan, or by
Oliver Stanley, or by Boothby was not clear. But it was regarded
as a declaration by the Conservative Left.

One of the Conservative Left might be a fair description of
Harold Macmillan's position in the Parliament of 1924 to 1929.
The difficulty was how to define precisely what this meant.

It can hardly be said that he made any great impression in the
Parliament of 1924-1929 and in the 1929 General Election he
lost his seat at Stockton-on-Tees to the Labour candidate. The
figures were F. F. Riley (Labour) 18,961, H. Macmillan (Conservative) 16,572, J. C. Hayes (Liberal) 10,407.

He was not in Parliament when the second Labour Government was in office between 1929 and 1931 but was re-elected in
the election which followed the formation of the National
Government under Ramsay MacDonald, the figures being:
H. Macmillan (Conservative) 29,199; Riley (Labour) 18,168.

He continued to be Conservative Member for Stockton until
1945.

There is an interesting study of Macmillan at this time in a
book, *One Hundred Commoners,* a collection of Parliamentary
sketches by James Johnston who had watched him from the
Press Gallery in his capacity of Parliamentary correspondent of
the *Yorkshire Post.* Johnston recorded the following impression
of him:

'The young enthusiasts in the Conservative Party who have devoted
themselves to the advocacy of social reform have been called by some

[From 'Farming News']

RUINS OF THE MACMILLANS' OLD HOME IN ARRAN

[Macmillans]

DANIEL MACMILLAN

[Macmillans]

ALEXANDER MACMILLAN

[Barratts]

1926

[Barratts]

1946

humorists the Y.M.C.A., and the name has become a House of
Commons favourite. In the group thus nicknamed Captain Harold
Macmillan is a prominent figure; he is indeed its most frequent and
most efficient spokesman. He is a model Y.M.C.A. man. His correctness of manner and bearing, his moderation of speech, the suggestion
of the "good boy" which he carries about with him are all typical of
the general idea of what a Y.M.C.A. member should be. He has the
external qualities which assist a Parliamentarian's progress. His tall,
debonair figure and his fresh youthful face predispose the House in
his favour. He has charm, marred perhaps by a touch of smugness.
Smugness, however, with him is free from the slightest taint of
insincerity. He is sincere in the fullest sense, earnest with the earnest-
ness of devoted youth, for in years he may still be reckoned among
the young, and in aspect he is essentially youthful, while his devotion
is evident.

'He is an enthusiast who does not enthuse. There is no declamation
in his speeches, no skilful manipulation of voice, no display of studied
gesture; and equally little is there anything which could be called
inspiration. He holds his ideas and is not held by them. They do not
seize him and carry him where they will. He has them always under
control.

'Somehow or other he recalls Mr Bonar Law in his manner of
speech. He pours out his facts with the same undemonstrative fluency
as Mr Bonar Law did; his tall figure and the way he stands are also
reminiscent of him. He has a grace of style, however, after which
Mr Bonar Law never sought. He never glows, but he is never form-
less, or slovenly, or unpolished. He dresses his ideas with the same
taste and care with which he dresses his body. He is one of the best-
tailored men in the House and he is also one of the most polished
speakers in it. Just as in dress he is not a dandy, so in style he is not
an ornamentalist, but he has not the severe tailored chicness of Mr
Runciman. Gracefulness and not mere chicness is the characteristic
of his speech.

'Some enthusiasts for reform deal in vague general phrases, and if
they are challenged to descend into the perilous region of the particular they flounder about in a helpless fashion. They have no detailed
plans for rebuilding the social fabric. They can only denounce the
present system or paint in broad, sweeping outline the ideal kind of
society they would desire to set up; they cannot fill in the multitudi-
nous details of such a picture.

'Captain Macmillan is full of plans for the necessary repair and
reconstruction of society. He has no grandiose ideas; he has a keen
perception of the defects of the social structure, and he seeks to
remedy them. He is not a mere patcher. Where the structure is so
faulty that it requires rebuilding he is not afraid of the venture, and
he sees how it can be successfully carried out. That means he is not
merely an idealist, but that he is also a practical student of social

C

affairs. He is a master of Blue Book knowledge and he is also in personal contact with the realities of life. He is essentially a child of the economic era in politics. The questions which engage his mind and draw him into the discussions of the House are all social, economic questions. Unemployment, the organization of industry, rating in its effects upon social and industrial life, are the matters upon which he speaks, and his interest in them is essentially human. His governing impulse in all these matters is the desire to give to the mass of the people the fullest possible individual life. He is one of the few promising men whom this Parliament has produced. He has the affinity with the spirit of the age and the understanding of Parliamentary ways which guarantee success in the political life of the future.

'Some day he will be one of the guiding forces of the Conservative Party, a capable and persuasive Minister.'

Johnston was a shrewd political journalist. He was of course writing for a Conservative paper circulating in the North of England, but this sketch gives us an idea of how the young Macmillan appeared to a gallery journalist.

Macmillan was obviously then a young innocent in Parliament, very much the young politician as yet unspoiled and uncorrupted by the House of Commons. He was to become less innocent in later years.

In 1933 he published another book, this time under his own name. It was called *Reconstruction—A Plea for a National Policy*.

The first chapter was called 'The Need for a Policy'. He had begun to realize that fundamental changes were needed in society. He declared:

'The great need for the moment is not only for a policy of action to deal with a pressing situation, but for a new theory of social and economic organization which will facilitate the evolution towards a new economic system suitable to the changed circumstances of the modern world.'

He wrote about the development of a revolutionary situation. The World Economic Conference had broken down. What were we drifting to? He wrote:

'Revolutionary movements can only grow with the development of a revolutionary situation. [Had he been re-reading Karl Marx?] So it was in eighteenth-century France; so it has proved in modern Russia, Italy, Germany. The revolutionary situation, however, can only develop as a result of the bankruptcy of statesmanship and the impoverishment and discontent consequent upon a deepening or protracted economic crisis. In Britain we have still time to think. Let us face the fact frankly, however, that we have time only because of the buffers which have been wisely created between the worker and destitution. The cushion of social services on which he is able to fall in times of depression may not be as soft as more prosperous people imagine; but it has served the purpose in recent years of at least assuring a basic minimum of subsistence, while efforts to induce recovery were carried out.'

There was a note of urgency in this book which was not in the previous one. 'The only thing we can conceive of as more dangerous than a mistaken policy is to have no policy at all,' he wrote. 'The machines which enabled man to conquer scarcity now threaten to plunge him deeper and deeper into poverty.' Karl Marx would certainly have endorsed that.

CHAPTER IV

CASE FOR PLANNING

THERE was a chapter entitled 'The Case For Planning'. It opened with the passage: 'The idea of planning is slowly but definitely gaining ground as the real nature of the problem now confronting us is revealed. It is a view which arises out of the realities of industrial and commercial life. It has found its adherents not so much among theorists as among those industrialists who see that it is in harmony with what they find it necessary to aim at in the daily conduct of their businesses.'

He went on to say: 'The reply which must be made to those who dream of a return to the old days and rebel against any suggestion of organization — what they call restriction — is simply that the world has changed and that such a return is technically, politically and economically impossible'.

'Planning,' he concluded, 'is forced upon us. . . . The economic system is out of gear.'

It was not, however, Socialist planning that he was advocating. It was to be centralized planning 'through the intelligent direction of production by a central authority for each industry guaranteed against redundancy, duplication and disorderly competition by the grant of monopoly powers in return for the acceptance of certain social responsibilities'.

He argued that we would not be travelling into an entirely new field. There were the Public Utility industries. The Electricity Board was an example. The London Passenger Transport Act (which had been passed by a Labour Government) was in operation. 'It was forced on us not by theoreticians but by facts. We have now an organization at work eliminating the wasteful redundancy and the competitive confusion of London passenger transport and developing an efficient service in accordance with economic and social requirements.'

He gave other examples, the Marketing Boards.

'Planning,' he concluded, 'has been admitted to be necessary in electricity, coal mining, transport, agriculture. There are few

people who would deny the beneficial effects of the action **taken**
under the Electricity Supply Act or the London Passenger
Transport Act. In coal mining only a very timid and tentative
approach has been made and the insufficiency of the planning
is demonstrated by the insufficiency of the results.' He might
have added: 'We have not yet carried the process to its logical
conclusion and nationalized the mines'. We were to do that
later.

What he wanted was a recognition of the principle of planning with a central authority to survey British industry and
carry it out.

The State was to plan ahead with some industries reorganized
under monopoly powers and others on Public Utility lines.

In those days it was certainly a revolutionary conception, 'half
way to Socialism' a Tory of the old school would have called it.

He thought it necessary to forestall a criticism usually made
against Socialism. 'It may be suggested that what has been
advanced is a bureaucratic structure of organization which
would interfere with every impulse of private enterprise by regulation and restriction of every kind, and that in order to make
the system work it would be necessary to control prices, profits,
wages, salaries, rents, and every other charge now determined
by the free play of competitive forces. The simple answer to this
is that it is not true.'

The last chapter of this interesting little book was called 'The
Threat of Dictatorship: Fascism and Communism'.

It began with the passage: 'The policy which has been advocated in this book will no doubt be described as "Socialism" by
some elements on the right and as Fascism by some elements on
the left. The only importance of the use of these descriptions is
that they are levelled as accusations calculated to arouse opposition by an appeal to passion.'

He strenuously denied that his plans meant any threat at all
to political liberty. He was against revolutionary violence. But
because there had been revolutionary violence in Italy and in
Russia that was no argument against the idea of economic planning. 'The Russian Five-Year Plan was formulated ten years after
the Bolsheviks came to power. The revolutionary movements
existed before their economic policies were even conceived.'

One wonders whether Harold Macmillan, writing this book

in 1933, realized all the implications of these policies that he was advocating. They were certainly revolutionary in the non-violent sense of the word. The Five-Year Plan had originated in Russia. Macmillan was certainly not advocating that we should do it the Russian way but his proposals were for a planned economy in Britain all the same.

When Britain was faced with the financial and economic crisis of 1961 there were ironic cheers from the Labour Benches when Selwyn Lloyd, the Chancellor of the Exchequer, declared that we must go in for economic planning. Conservatives had become used to sneering at the idea of planning and in the Conservative vocabulary it had almost become a dirty word. When Harold Wilson used the word 'planning' and stressed the need for economic planning they jeered and laughed. They had obviously not read what Harold Macmillan had written in a forgotten little book published nearly thirty years before. The book was published in 1933.

In his book *A Diary With Letters*, Thomas Jones, who for many years was secretary to the British Cabinet and met most of the people in the centre of politics in his day, noted under the date February 3, 1933, that he had met Harold Macmillan. 'He, Harold Macmillan, talks very much like a Professor of Economics. He has just returned from Russia much impressed by what he saw.'

It was quite a courageous thing to do for a prominent Conservative to go to Russia in those days.

Did some of his friends think he was moving too far to the Left?

Macmillan delivered a long speech, in which there were many caustic references to the Government, in the Debate on the King's Speech, November 21, 1934.

He was lucky to be called as the last speaker at eleven o'clock in the night and as he had not finished his speech, he had the right to continue it the next day to a larger audience.

He dealt at length with the reports of the Commissioners for Distressed Areas which 'revealed for the first time to many southern readers the full amount of distress and the poignant and sombre picture of these areas which have so long suffered from conditions which were not altogether known to many of the inhabitants of the more prosperous parts of the country'.

He was grateful to the Commissioners for the information they had compiled about the distressed areas in the country.

He said:

'We have the misfortune sometimes either to fight elections or to go about speaking, and within this House itself, to whatever party we belong, there is a very real knowledge of the conditions of the country . . . But in the country as a whole these conditions, which have long been known to Members who have had the duty of representing these areas, have been hidden either purposely or by the mere difficulty of getting knowledge through to public opinion and have not been known to the mass of the English people . . .

'It is a great gain that we have brought in a great State document full of human touches, admirably written, well describing the conditions of the people, and a document which future historians will regard as one of the great State papers of the day. It is a gain that we have presented that picture to the people as a whole, so that when they have to decide as to whether small measures or great measures, whether timid measures or bold measures be taken, they will have been able to consider the reports of these gentlemen who have been asked to undertake these investigations.

'War is not the only operation in which it is sometimes an advantage to have a visitation from general headquarters to the front line trenches. I am glad that there has been on this occasion a visit from Whitehall to the Passchendaele of Durham and South Wales.'

Macmillan wanted to know exactly what the Chancellor of the Exchequer, then Neville Chamberlain, meant in his statement about the measures that were recommended for dealing with the plight of the unemployed. He had said that some of the recommendations 'raise very far-reaching questions of policy . . . others again require further investigation. Still others have been approved, and will in due course be carried out.'

Chamberlain, he said, was 'a master of the art of saying just what he means to say and no more' and a very great deal depended upon the interpretation of the last sentence.

'I have been long enough in the House to know,' he said, 'that when a Minister says that a suggestion carries with it or involves issues of general policy it means that he has made up his mind to do very little about it and that that is a convenient way of saying so.'

Unemployment, Macmillan agreed, could only be dealt with on a national and not a distressed area basis.

'A phrase once used on another subject by a great Tory leader is as

true today as it was then. Speaking of the problem of the Indian
frontier, Lord Beaconsfield used this famous phrase:
    "The keys of India are not in Herat or Kandahar; the keys of
    India are in Whitehall."
So it is with the problem of unemployment. The key lies not in South
Wales or Durham, but in Downing Street and Threadneedle Street.'

He thought that one of the reasons why industry was inclined
to come from the North to the South was that wages were low
and conditions bad, and commented:

'I believe it would do more than anything else to counteract that
movement to the South if a good trade union movement were
organized in the South of England. I believe that the enforcement of
the highest standards of wages and conditions would be a very
effective measure to deter what is at any rate a bad form of attraction
from one part of the country to another.'

Such enthusiasm for the trade union movement was not often
shown from the Tory benches.

He went on to deal with the Gold Standard and the relation
between finance and unemployment, and quoted with approval
a speech that had been made by the Civil Lord of the Admiralty.
He went on:

'The Civil Lord has taken one glance at the economic problems of
the country and he has seen more in those few weeks than the
Government have seen in three years. I do not know what course he
will pursue. I do not know whether he will go through with his
policy, whether he will continue in the Government, but I can
promise him that, if he decides that he can no longer continue in a
Government which rejects his views, he will have such a welcome
and such a backing from the people of England that he will be able
to lead a crusade which will overturn the Government itself.'

These were bold words from a Government back bencher.

Then came a criticism of the role of finance in the capitalist
system:

'We are neither investigating the surplus abroad nor at home. Money
is therefore all dressed up and nowhere to go. The cheaper we make
it, the less of it we use . . . If the system is to go on it must expand
either abroad or at home or both. If it cannot invest its surplus, it
must reduce its surplus, either by more leisure, more wages and
greater social advantages; but if it does none of these things it will
sink of its own weight.'

In his maiden speech Macmillan had scoffed at Karl Marx
but here he was using an argument that Marx would thoroughly
have approved if Marx had put it more colourfully. 'Capitalism

contains within itself the seeds of its own destruction.' And it
looked as if Macmillan had also found this out.

Then he turned scornfully on the Government Front Bench:

Mr Disraeli once said that he saw before him a bench of extinct vol-
canoes. I would not be so rude, but there are a few disused slag heaps
which might well be tidied up.'

There were some passages in the speech which could have
been made about the political situation at the end of 1961:

'What is the position of the ordinary people in this country? I am
convinced that today we have a situation unlike anything our fathers
saw. We have a small body attached to the Conservative Party, a
small body attached to the Labour or Socialist Party and smaller
bodies attached to various sections of the Liberal Party, but the great
mass of middle opinion is still undecided. It does not make up its
mind how it is going to vote, or which way it will throw its force
until perhaps somewhere much nearer the election, and it is faced
with the curious dilemma that it is not given what it wants by any
of the leaders of thought. It does not want to be Socialist. It may have
to vote Socialist for it is the only thing left to it if it wants to oppose
the Government of the day.'

He concluded:

'How many Members are there in this House who know that today
they do not represent accurately the views of their constituents?
What do we suppose, in fact, would be the result, if a Dissolution
were decided today? I say to my friends, many of whom care deeply,
would they rather fight the next election on a record or a programme? If I am beaten on a programme, I have something worth
fighting for. It is in the power of Ministers to give it to us.

'If they do not, they will place such a pressure on the whole
system itself that it may collapse under the strain to which, in the
coming years, it will be inevitably subjected.'

No wonder Neville Chamberlain, when he became Prime
Minister, did not give Macmillan any office. He certainly could
hardly have expected it after a speech like that.

No Prime Minister likes to hear himself and his Front Bench
described as 'disused slag heaps'.

But it was certainly a courageous speech. Macmillan had no
need to be ashamed of this one in later years.

Speaking in the Third Reading Debate of the Distressed Areas
Bill on December 13, 1934, he said that he had no desire to
minimize the importance of the bill but 'compared with the
problems before us this is a mouse, a nice mouse, a good mouse,

a profitable and helpful little mouse, but a ridiculous, micro-scopic, Lilliputian mouse'.

It was just a bill 'to deal in a charitable sense, in the widest sense of the word, with the worst effects of unemployment upon individuals in the worst areas'.

Oliver Stanley, with whom he had collaborated before Stanley had become Minister of Labour, 'had thrilled the House, because he showed that he believed what we all believe, that startling, revolutionary changes are necessary if the system is to be adapted to modern needs, and if the power of Man over Nature is to be exploited not to the detriment but to the benefit of man-kind'. He continued:

'The only thing I am not sure of is whether this revelation was wise. The most successful form of propaganda has always been that of the cell, the nucleus, through which the gospel is spread abroad.'

This sounded as if he had been reading Lenin:

'Some people may have thought that I was performing to some extent the function of the cell, in the private ranks of the party, while he was performing it upon the Front Bench. Perhaps he thinks the time has come to throw off the mask. "We are all planners now," said my Right Hon. Friend. I have one advantage over him. When he speaks I can see the faces of his colleagues. When he made that historic remark there was a look of satisfaction and delight on the faces of some of his colleagues—those in the plot, I suppose; but over the rest stole a kind of sickly and selfconscious smile.

'Mr Beerbohm once wrote a true and witty observation, "Life is a prison without bars". So is a Cabinet. I do not know what will be the history of the next two years of this Parliament. I do not know whether we will drift on without a statement of Government policy, without a formulation of Government policy on a wide scale, but I know a great responsibility lies upon the members of the Govern-ment who remain members of the Government if they are dissatisfied with the scope of its policy. We have freedom of speech, but they have responsibility of silence.

'We have had the lesson of the Parliament of 1924-9. We saw the greatest majority of modern times, up to this Parliament, dissipated, lost. We saw a Government flung from office with contempt because there were a million unemployed in England. Are the Government going to the country without a policy, without a plan; with their tinkerings, with their alleviations—all good—but without a broad, general policy of economic reconstruction and say that the system demands 2,500,000 unemployed? If they do that they destroy the system. Policies take time to work out . . . They need foresight; they need planning ahead. We support this Bill but we want to be assured that the Government are doing more and are going to present to the nation, and to ask it to support, a policy commensurate with the evils and necessities of the hour.'

But all this fell on deaf ears. The Tory Government was not there to bring about 'startling revolutionary changes in the system'. Macmillan sounded far too revolutionary for either the Tory back benches or the Tory Front Bench.

In 1935 Macmillan's published a book called *The Next Five Years—An Essay in Political Agreement*, which took the form of a lengthy discussion on the problems facing Great Britain. Most of the people who put their signatures to it were Liberals or Socialists but among the very few Conservatives who signed it was Harold Macmillan. He was also a member of the Drafting Committee and many of the ideas which he had been advocating were included in it.

Far from showing any prejudices against Socialism or nationalization it had a chapter on 'The Organization of Industry' and a paragraph on 'Socialized Industries' which although carefully worded would have been violently opposed by the official Tory Party.

The authors while avoiding the word 'nationalization' were in favour of 'public corporations'. They said:

'The extent to which public ownership or management is introduced is necessarily limited by the ability of the machine of government— government in the largest sense including Parliament—to undertake additional responsibilities without undue risk of inefficiency or corruption. This may prove to be the most important limiting factor in any immediate programme . . . for there is no lack of spheres of economic activity, which are suitable for socialization on other grounds, provided that they can be organized efficiently.'

Transport, however, was an industry which should be planned in the public interest.

The authors said:

'So far as the railways are concerned, socialization would present few difficulties and few disadvantages.'

Electricity was another 'case for early socialization'. 'There is even less need than usual in this industry,' they continued, 'to fear any lack of enterprise under public control, for the great municipal electricity undertakings have long ago established themselves among the technically most efficient and commercially most enterprising of the country.'

There was a strong case for the nationalization of some forms of insurance.

Later they said:

'The interests of the power consumers might also be greatly advanced by socialization of several branches of the distributive system. Milk and coal would seem to be clearly indicated, since the production of these commodities is already under centralized control. In the case of milk there is the added circumstances of the existence in many parts of the country of what almost amount to local monopolies.'

This went further than the Labour Government which came into power in 1945 was prepared to go.

The paragraph concluded:

'The nationalization of *mining royalties* has become almost an agreed principle, while there is a very large and growing body of support for the nationalization on political rather than on economic grounds of the manufacture of armaments. This list is by no means exhaustive, but when taken with the special treatment recommended for the depressed industries, it would provide quite enough for the labours of one or even two parliaments.'

A Socialist might have agreed to these conclusions but the Tories certainly would have not.

CHAPTER V

MUTINY

AFTER the General Election of 1935 Macmillan became one of the most outspoken critics of the foreign policy of the National Government under Baldwin. After the outbreak of the Italo-Abyssinian War he declared it was possible that the League of Nations in its existing form might fail but that was no reason why we should help to undermine the very structure which a few weeks ago the nation authorized us to underpin.

When sanctions against Italy were abandoned in 1936 he voted with the Labour Opposition against the Government.

To vote against the Government in a Vote of Censure Division and on a Three-Line Whip was regarded as tantamount to high treason in the Whips' office. He was the only Tory Member to go into the Lobby against the Government. The motion that Attlee had moved read:

'That His Majesty's Government by their lack of a resolute and straightforward foreign policy, have lowered the prestige of the country, weakened the League of Nations, imperilled peace and thereby forfeited the confidence of this House.'

It took a good deal of courage for a back bench Tory to go into the Lobby to vote for this wholehearted vote for no-confidence in the Government.

One can assume that after this act of open mutiny and defiance that Macmillan was regarded as a traitor by the Tory Whips' office.

Whether angry words were exchanged between Macmillan and the Chief Whip we do not know, but on June 29, 1936, he wrote to Baldwin, the Prime Minister, the following letter:

Dear Prime Minister,
In view of my vote following the Foreign Affairs Debate on Tuesday, June 23rd, I feel some explanation is due to you, more especially because of the many kindnesses you have shown me personally. At the last General Election I made it quite clear to my constituents that, while I would give general support to the National Govern-

ment, I would also pursue by speech and vote the special policies to which I was personally pledged.

Although I am still in favour of a National Government in these difficult times, and shall probably be found in the great majority of cases in the Government lobby, there are some issues which have arisen, or seem likely to arise, on which I am unable to give the Government the support it has the right to expect from those receiving the Government Whip. It occurs to me, therefore, that it would perhaps be more satisfactory if I was no longer regarded as being one of the official supporters of the present administration.

Yours sincerely,
HAROLD MACMILLAN.

To this Baldwin replied:

My dear Macmillan,

I have received the letter telling me that you feel unable any longer to receive the National Government Whip. I regret the decision which you have thought it necessary to take.

Yours sincerely,
STANLEY BALDWIN.

He remained an independent Conservative for about a year but then accepted the Whip, although he remained one of the group of M.P.s who backed Churchill in his campaign against Chamberlain. The Munich Pact, he said, was not peace by negotiation and it was sheer hypocrisy to describe it so.

In November 1938 he again voted against the Government —with Winston Churchill—when it refused to set up a Ministry of Supply.

As an appendix to his little book *Economic Aspects of Defence* he re-published a memorandum on the policy of Munich which he had circulated privately after the Munich Agreement.

It was a detailed analysis of Neville Chamberlain's policy on Czechoslovakia. In it he wrote:

'When I was asked in the House of Commons to vote for all that, I refused. I would refuse again, for I believe with Mr Duff Cooper that a Member of Parliament has a higher duty to perform than to become a voting machine in favour of his Party, "right or wrong". The action I have taken is in accordance with the mandate I sought from my constituency at the last election. It is not I who have to answer for a dereliction of duty.'

He certainly had little hope of getting office in Neville Chamberlain's Government after that.

Macmillan had become increasingly critical of the Conservative Government not only in the field of foreign policy but on home affairs as well. A speech that he delivered in the House of Commons on June 28, 1938, is interesting as showing the way his mind was reacting to the Government's failure to do enough in the face of the serious unemployment, which sitting as he was for Stockton-on-Tees in the centre of the big industrial area of the North-East of England, was constantly being brought to his attention.

The occasion was the debate on the Ministry of Labour Estimates.

Previous speakers had attacked the Government on the issue of unemployment.

Sidney Silverman, the Member for Nelson and Colne, had spoken movingly about the plight of the unemployed in Lancashire. The increase in the number of unemployed cotton operatives had been 77,734 in the previous twelve months. There were over 18,000 more engineers out of work, 18,000 more in the iron and steel trades, 18,000 in the distributive trades and 25,000 in coal mining.

J. A. Parkinson, of Wigan, opening the debate for the Labour Party, had pointed out that the increase of 382,000 in the number of unemployed during the year had brought the army of unemployed up to 1,750,000.

Even *The Times* had become critical of the Government on unemployment and had said that the country expected Mr Chamberlain to produce:

'a constructive national and imperial policy'

and had added:

'The country will not tolerate the idea that we can have a five years' plan for rearmament but no such comprehensive plan in the more constructive branches of national administration.'

Even Mr Amery, the veteran Tory imperialist from Birmingham, was critical of the policy of the Unemployment Assistance Board. He spoke of the burden of high rents on the unemployed. He said:

'The coming of every additional child is a hardship, not only to the parents but to all the rest of the family and to itself. The larger the family the fewer the rooms they are crowded into, the less food they have for each child. It is a serious thing that surveys of milk consumption in working-class households have shown how rapidly the consumption of milk per head falls in the larger families; in other words, how rapidly it falls just where the need of it is greatest. The whole burden of poverty falls hardest upon those children who come into existence in large families and is itself a cause of the creation of poverty.'

Amery quoted from a statement made by the medical officer of a large industrial concern. It was a moving document about the relation of food to the physique of the young industrial worker and the doctor had concluded: 'Working-class parents have come to the unhappy pitch where they can have only one or two children if they are to afford an adequate diet for them. That is a major catastrophe.'

'It is,' was Amery's comment, 'and it is a catastrophe that is perhaps much nearer to us than we generally realize.'

This was catastrophe on the front at home, not in foreign affairs. This was what Britain was facing at home a year before plunging into the Second World War.

The whole debate that day is worth reading for the picture it presented of unemployment and its social implications to the country in the year before the war.

Harold Macmillan spoke later in the debate and it was undoubtedly one of his best speeches in the pre-war Parliament.

What had been said about conditions in industrial Lancashire was equally applicable to the industrial North-East of England and to Stockton-on-Tees which he represented. He said:

'The speech which set the tone of the debate was that of my Right Hon. Friend, the Member for Sparkbrook (Mr Amery), who gave a diagnosis with which everyone would agree. His was a formidable scrutiny, if not an indictment of present conditions, and I hope he will not think me discourteous if I say that I wish those revolutionary views were developed by Hon. and Right. Hon. Gentlemen not only when they are on the benches below the gangway but when they occupy the Front Bench. When he was speaking—and I agreed with almost everything he said—an Hon. Member on this side remarked that some of the facts were denied by the Government Front Bench. I observed to him *sotto voce* that any Front Bench will deny any proposition and also believe any proposition. As the White Queen advised Alice to practise believing and denying things for an hour each day, so they exhibit an extraordinary degree of scepticism and credulity.

'I wish to bring the Committee back to the facts in the hope of assisting to make this debate a useful and memorable service to the study of these problems. I was very much struck by a passage in the speech of the Prime Minister on Thursday evening, relating to a

[*Barratts*]

OPTIMISM

[*Barratts*]

DOUBTS?

[Barratts]

AT THE RHODESIA AND NYASALAND CONFERENCE, 1960

[Barratts]

WITH DR ADENAUER, 1957

wholly different topic, namely that of foreign affairs. Speaking of the terrible conditions in certain parts of the world, he used these words:

' "Indeed if it were not that China is so far away, and the scenes which are taking place there are so remote from our everyday consciousness, I think the sentiments of pity, horror and indignation which would be aroused by a full appreciation of these events might drive the people to courses which perhaps they have never yet contemplated."

'Distant events far removed from our eyes cannot move us with the same force as those which are near to us, and yet, in these home problems, it is not a mere question of geographical distance, but of the wide chasm made by the lack of imagination on the part of a portion of the people who have never been able really to have brought home to them (as we have in this House) the problems that confront large masses of our fellow countrymen. Those of us who attended church last Sunday will have read in the Gospel for the day the wonderful words of the parable of Dinas and Lazarus—terrifying words—and besides all this

"Between us and you there is a great gulf fixed".

'That great imaginative gulf, that incapacity to bring home to people the true realities of what is going on in this country in the twentieth century, is the problem which confronts the Government, who cannot solve our problem without methods which would seem revolutionary to many people, and for which, they fear, they could not get adequate support. To paraphrase the words of the Prime Minister, if it were not that the circumstances in which one half of the population of this country live are so foreign to the average experience of the other more comfortable and influential half, and so remote from their everyday consciousness, such pity and horror and indignation might be aroused as to drive us to a course of action sufficiently effective to solve these problems.

'This remarkable Report (of the Unemployment Assistance Board) is full of individual and detailed cases, and I will not burden the Committee with great numbers of figures, but if any Hon. Member will turn to page 170 he will find the record of a family living in a three-roomed house.

'It is as follows:

' "Room 1. Applicant (householder, wife and two applicant sons, nephew (applicant), wife and six children. (Total in room 12.)

Room 2. Sublet to—man (applicant), wife and five children.

Room 3. Sublet to—man (applicant), wife and five children. Total for three rooms = 26."

'The House of Commons is pressing the Government day by day to a solution of the problems of rearmament and the dangers that may face us from foreign invasion.

'I wish the House of Commons would show the same enthusiasm

D

to solve the problems of protecting the people against the insecurities of peace.'

This was a fair point for the House used to fill up at times of international crisis and empty again when such matters as the treatment of the unemployed on public assistance came to be discussed. The men who were living with their families a dozen or so to the room were being urged upon to join the army to protect their homes against the foreign invader and Macmillan rightly thought there was a certain amount of irony and incongruity in this situation.

As he continued his speech he revealed that he had studied the statistics and economics of unemployment a great deal more than most of the Members on the Government benches. He had carefully studied Lord Rushcliffe's Report on the question, had broken down the figures and revealed that there were 500,000 people — heads of families, workers — who were normally in receipt of fifty shillings a week. Mr Colin Clark, the statistician, had estimated that twenty-three per cent of the total male workers of this country received wages of forty-five shillings a week or less and forty-five per cent received fifty-five shillings a week or less. The evidence which could be piled up on the income side showed that we had not yet achieved anything like a wage structure sufficient to keep a proper standard of nutrition and health for at least one-third of the working population.

He begged the House and the Government to set up a committee of inquiry into the position.

He went on to consider the retail distributive system with its 750,000 retail shops which created a levy of the order of £650,000,000 a year. The whole trade of the mines and the railways together was only £150,000,000 and the whole trade of the cotton industry only £41,000,000.

He believed we could cheapen the distribution of vital commodities to the people and he believed this should be an essential corollary to the policy of the Government.

It was a searching criticism of capitalist society and a die-hard Conservative indicated he realized this by his interruptions.

Macmillan concluded:

'It is the stock-in-trade of all of us, of whatever party, to end with the same peroration about the superiority of democracy over any other form of government. But democracy will not, in the long run, be protected by speeches but by action. In the long run, the peoples now subject to the pagan dictatorships of the world will be dissuaded or converted if they can see that now, in this Christian country, by universal effort of men of all parties, it is decided, if not to build today, to make at least some attempt to lay the foundations of the Commonwealth of God.'

His speech was frequently cheered from the Labour benches. George Buchanan, the Clydesider, paid him the compliment of saying it was 'a powerful speech', and Buchanan was not in the habit of paying compliments to Tories.

What Macmillan had said about the plight of the unemployed people being overcrowded in one room Buchanan had often said himself.

Earlier in the year, on March 23rd, Macmillan had made a speech in the same vein. He had become rather cynical about the House of Commons:

'Is not the House,' he asked, 'sometimes remote from what the people are thinking nowadays?

'What do they care, if I may say so with equal respect to both sets of Hon. and Right Hon. Gentlemen who sit on that bench and who sit on this. It matters very little to them. Their names have for a few years, hardly for more than a decade, passed rapidly in and out—they are far less known than film stars. You will never get such fame from the Cabinet as you get from Hollywood today. They go after a few years to a Chamber where, disguised under some remote and unknown name, they finally disappear into political limbo. Who cares? Not the democracy. We are here to serve the public which is really rather bored with our political conventions but is interested in the presentation of any mechanism that may seem to give them what they want.

'They are bored with the old terms of Private Enterprise and Socialism, Protection or Free Trade, but they are interested in any movement that can give them what they believe can, by energy and enterprise and effort and intellectual and mental power, be done with the vast resources, technical and scientific, that we have at our command.

'And sooner or later either this democracy will die, either it will pass away and seek vainly enough, perhaps its instrument in some other form of government hostile to all our notions, and to most of us horrible to contemplate; or sooner or later, whether it is Hon. Gentlemen on that side of the House or as I hope and believe the party to which I belong, we shall be able to lead this country steadily, not by revolutionary but still by progressive and ambitious means, into the realization of the new society, which is open—there for us to take it if we have the courage to seize the opportunities that are ready for us today.'

He asked the questions which usually came from the Socialist benches:

'The problem of unemployment is only half the problem in this country today. If unemployment were the whole problem I should feel happier about it. But what about the problem of under-employment and poverty? Can anyone read the objective statements made by those who have studied these questions, Sir John Orr and all he has done, Mr Rowntree and all his work, and not realize that, in addition to the problem of unemployment, there is the problem of millions of men who are not living on the standard of life which ought to be provided by a modern society.'

He added ironically, 'Unemployment is not in itself a harmful thing. When it is unemployment of the upper classes it is called leisure.'

He thought that 'for the purpose of obtaining stability, order and co-operation in the new society, we shall have to place the organization of the great basic industries and great basic utility services under some form of public control'.

He thought that finance should operate as the servant and not the master of industry. He said:

'You should have a policy which is not based on vested interests, which is prepared to take quite new standards of distribution and new methods. You charge for water not on the amount of water you consume but on the rateable value. Should you not distribute milk in the same way?

'Why are we to say that because a thing has once been done it is respectable, but to extend it is revolutionary?'

These arguments were dangerously near being Socialist arguments. If you are prepared to distribute milk like water where did the argument stop?

If you were prepared to nationalize or municipalize milk why not beer? If he had gone on like that he would certainly have risked expulsion from the Conservative Party.

In October 1938 there was an important and historic by-election in Oxford City. Dr A. D. Lindsay, afterwards Lord Lindsay, stood as an Independent Socialist and as an opponent of Chamberlain's Munich policy. Quintin Hogg, afterwards Lord Hailsham, was the official Tory candidate. *The Times* of October 24th reported:

'Mr Harold Macmillan, Unionist M.P. for Stockton-on-Tees, in a letter states that if he were a voter at Oxford he should unhesitatingly vote and work for the return of Mr Lindsay to Parliament.

' "The times are too vital," he adds, "and the issue is too vital for progressive Conservative opinion to allow itself to be influenced by party loyalties or to tolerate the present uncertainty regarding the principles governing our foreign policy.

' "We are faced with the urgent need for a vital effort to ensure that safety of our country and Empire and to preserve our conception of freedom and civilization. I hope therefore that progressive opinion in Oxford, whether Liberal, Labour or Conservative, will seize the opportunity of returning you to Parliament next Tuesday." '

After the election Quintin Hogg said it was not his victory but Mr Chamberlain's, a victory for democracy, for peace by negotiation, and it was a victory for a united Britain, 'a victory above all for the ordinary man and woman who have shown again the traditional common sense and judgment of the British electorate'.

Macmillan's action in publicly saying he would work and vote against the official Tory candidate was certainly an act of open mutiny but there is no record of any action having been taken against him by Tory headquarters or by the Tory Party in the House of Commons.

He was luckier than Sir Stafford Cripps, who was expelled from the Labour Party but who had certainly not been guilty of any such defiant action as this.

Of course any attempt to expel Macmillan at this time would only have caused trouble for Churchill and his group of followers were in opposition to Chamberlain too. The Tory Party was either too easy going or did not want to create further trouble by expelling Macmillan.

At the Tory headquarters it was certainly regarded as a stab in the back for Quintin Hogg who was regarded as one of the bright young Tory hopes at the beginning of his political career. The Tory majority at Oxford, a Tory stronghold, had gone down by half.

Macmillan certainly did not show a great deal of the admiration for Chamberlain shown by Hogg in those days or in more recent times by Iain Macleod, who wrote Chamberlain's biography.

Had Quintin Hogg been defeated at this election the Tory Party in Parliament would have been deprived of one of its more colourful personalities and he might never have risen to be chief bell ringer at a Tory Party Conference.

Macmillan and he were to be members of the same Cabinet in later years and when Lord Salisbury departed Macmillan made him the Leader of the Tory Party in the House of Lords and Minister for Science. But he certainly did his best to keep him out of Parliament in 1938 and to end a promising political career before it had been begun.

In later years, during the time of the Labour Government and afterwards, the theme of innumerable speeches by Macmillan was the differences of opinion among the leaders of the Labour Party. When he was in an awkward corner he always fell back on this, as if the Labour Party had a monopoly of differences which as the history of the Tory and Liberal Parties show, are inevitable in political parties.

Actually Macmillan should have been the last to do this, for as this incident and many others in later years showed he was often in the centre of similar controversies in the Tory Party. True Bevan differed from Morrison and Gaitskell. But he had in his time differed with Hailsham and Chamberlain and many others as well.

If he had very little time for Chamberlain it does not seem that Chamberlain had much time for him either. In the extracts from Chamberlain's letters quoted in Macleod's biography there are short, brusque references to Macmillan, whom Chamberlain obviously resented interfering in questions which he thought were his own preserve.

Chamberlain regarded him as the spokesman in the House of the nuisance group who had ideas about a New Deal for Britain similar to those that Roosevelt was campaigning for in America. And he had obviously been annoyed when Macmillan had arrived on some deputation with unsolicited advice on how to run the Exchequer.

Certainly Macmillan did not go out of his way to curry favour with Chamberlain. He retained his intellectual independence and thought the pledges he had given to the people who had elected him to Parliament were more important than the party loyalties demanded from him by the Party Whips at Westminster.

CHAPTER VI

THE MIDDLE WAY

IN 1938 Macmillan wrote another larger book which he called *The Middle Way*. It was an elaboration of his other books and of the views that he had expressed in his speeches on social and economic questions in the House of Commons. It was a serious, argumentative, not very lively book, but interesting in so far as it had been written by a young back bench Conservative M.P. He had obviously read a lot about unemployment and had devoted a great deal of study to Blue books, White Papers and Government reports. The problems of mass unemployment and poverty in the Britain of the 'thirties had obviously impressed him and he was familiar with the books of Seebohm Rowntree, J. K. Keynes and Boyd Orr. The arguments were the same as he had advanced before but were presented in greater detail, and there were large masses of statistics.

He was attempting to outline new proposals for dealing with poverty and unemployment which were not Fascist, not Communist, not Socialist and not *laissez-faire* Capitalism.

It was obviously a well-meaning book. He had no compulsion to write it. It certainly could not advance his promotion in the Conservative Party of the day, it was the work of one who had acquired a social conscience and was interested in ideas.

There were certainly passages in it which would have made the average Conservative M.P., if he had the patience to read it, wonder whether Harold Macmillan was drifting towards Lloyd Georgian Radicalism or to Fabian Socialism. Socialists who had the patience to read it, on the other hand, wondered if he realized the implication of his arguments and how holding these views he could possibly remain in the Conservative Party, which was the political instrument of predatory private enterprise.

There were passages in it which showed he was completely out of sympathy with the conventional outlook of the ruling class. For example, in discussing income and education he wrote:

'In so far as snobbery and class alienation exists in this country it is largely a product of class differences in education. The public mind is probably not yet ready for the obvious remedy. It would do nothing but good to the children of every class if the early years of life were spent in the same school. Even when some children went to higher education and others directly into manual or clerical employment, the early association would not be forgotten. The class differences which now tend to go according to incomes might in future be replaced by the natural functional and intellectual differences, but these would be superimposed upon a common training upon which mutual understanding could be preserved.'

He was in favour of the drastic re-planning of our industrial society. He was against piecemeal planning and was in favour of large-scale planning.

'The object of economic effort,' he wrote, 'must be to increase the production of wealth and, as a result of rising prosperity, to enable society to increase the leisure and cultural opportunities of *all* the people. In so far as the criticisms discuss whether this result will in fact be achieved they are legitimate and helpful. The weakness of partial planning seems to me to arise from the incomplete and limited application of the principles of planning. The lesson of these errors, which I regard as errors of limitation, is not that we should retreat. On the contrary we must advance, more rapidly and still further, upon the road of conscious regulation.'

Whole passages from the book could be taken and be incorporated without any incongruity in any Labour Party programme published in the post-war years.

He concluded a chapter on 'Public Enterprise and Private Combination' with the sentence:

'The whole trend of development is in the direction of greater integration, and the supersession of unrestrained competition by methods of co-operation.'

His arguments led him to propose the large scale organization and distribution of the basic foods.

He outlined a scheme of Public Utility Distribution in which the distribution of milk, for example, was to be reorganized:

'It appears to be technically possible by the elimination of competitive redundancy and by the creation of a single national organization concerned only with *delivery* by the shortest and most economical route, to reduce the costs of bringing these standardized commodities from the producer to the consumer. But the case for action on these lines does not rest entirely upon the argument that savings would be effected. There is a strong case for placing in the hands of the community an instrument of distribution that would provide a direct contact with the nutritional requirements of every household. The organization for supplying these elementary human needs should be non-profit-making and above any suggestion of reproach in the matter of prices.'

He went on to suggest ways in which this national distributive organization might be utilized to provide cheap and guaranteed supplies of milk and certain other foodstuffs to all families 'whether the breadwinner is employed or unemployed'.

'Milk, butter and margarine, cheese, eggs, bread and flour, potatoes and sugar' he mentioned 'as commodities which might for reasons that have already been explained, lend themselves to highly organized distribution.'

He knew that these ideas would not be popular to vested interests. He wrote:

'I am under no delusion that it will be an easy matter to overcome the resistance of vested interests in the undertakings now engaged in the retail distribution of these commodities. To launch such a scheme will require courage of the first order. But a Government that engages in the task of creating the means by which we may begin to eradicate malnutrition in this country may be confident that it will be supported, not only by the people to be benefited but by every person with a sense of society's moral duty to its citizens. There may be room for doubt as to whether this is the best means of achieving the desired end, but there can be no doubt that the end itself is desirable and must be achieved whatever opposition has to be overcome in the process. In a matter so vitally important to the life of the people as nutrition every theoretical prejudice must be forced to give way to practical necessity.'

Much as the author denied that his proposals were Socialism, Conservative critics could justifiably argue that he was going a long way towards it.

Even Karl Marx would certainly have approved of the assertion:

'The important thing is that society should be organized in such a way as to bring the economic system under conscious direction and control, and that the increased production should be directed towards raising the standard of comfort and security of all the people.'

Anybody who carefully read *The Middle Way* when it appeared in 1938 might easily have come to the conclusion that Harold Macmillan might well end up as a Socialist Prime Minister.

It was not that he was emotionally attracted towards the Labour Party. At Stockton, of course, he had inevitably come up against the problem of unemployment in all its grimness. Men out of work through no fault of their own, with wives and children living on bare subsistence level in shabby back streets, used to turn up at his meetings and ask what he was going to do to get jobs for them.

He had never been hungry and unemployed himself but the people he was supposed to represent in Parliament were.

He had tended to look upon unemployment rather as an abstract problem of economics, an exercise in statistics, which was unescapable and had to be solved somehow in a calculated, constructive way.

This mood was reflected in his books, which dealt in tables and figures and were mathematically logical and austere.

He certainly, while repudiating Socialism as a philosophy, was not violently, emotionally anti-Socialist, as the propagandists of the Anti-Socialist Union were. In fact his arguments led exactly in the opposite way. As long as Socialism was called public ownership or nationalized industries were labelled public utilities, he appeared to have no objections but was prepared to welcome an extension of the principle.

He knew the weaknesses of the capitalist society as well as the Fabians, for he had carefully studied the works of Seebohm Rowntree who had examined family incomes in York, and Boyd Orr who had studied the problems of undernourishment in Scotland.

Tom Jones had compared him 'to a professor of economics'. Professors in economics in the late 'thirties were very different from what they had been a generation before. They were no longer afraid of the word Socialism, although the word Communism, due to its Russian associations, still terrified them. Many of these found their way into the Labour Party as the logical conclusion to their thinking.

Before the war Macmillan was certainly not scared of Socialism.

But the next year came war and that put an end to this kind of theorizing.

CHAPTER VII

THE WAR—AND AFTER

DURING the short Russo-Finnish War he went to Finland and on his return delivered a lengthy speech in the House describing what he had seen. He did not blame the Government for its failure to rescue Finland from her fate. At its best it was a difficult and hazardous enterprise. Serious geographic and diplomatic obstacles presented themselves, and many of the most astute observers predicted that it would be impossible to overcome them.

He might have added that we were fortunate in not being able to send the contemplated expeditionary force to Finland. Otherwise we might have been engaged in fighting the Russians and the Germans at the same time and the whole course of the war might have been changed. A little over a year afterwards our whole attitude to Russia had changed and we were fighting side by side.

He criticized the Government for not having sent more war material to Finland in the early phase of hostilities.

From Helsinki he had sent a telegram to the Government, urging them to send guns. He criticized the Government for its slowness in sending military material to Finland. 'It is not fair to say,' he said, 'that the Finnish Army fell for any reason except that of exhaustion coupled with the fact that in many parts of the sector there was nothing with which to fire back at the advancing army.'

Macmillan wasn't sure what would have been the best strategy in Finland. An expeditionary force might have succeeded brilliantly or it might have failed disastrously.

The Finnish episode, however, 'did throw a piercing light on the present machinery and the method of government. The delay, the vacillation, changes of front, standing on one foot one day and on the other the next before a decision is given—these are patently clear to anybody. The moral of the history of these three months to be drawn for the future is, to use a phrase of

Burke's, "a proof of the irresistible operation of feeble council".'

This was no doubt meant to be a direct attack on Neville Chamberlain, who had sat listening and had interrupted him.

There was another clash with Neville Chamberlain when the Prime Minister came to wind up the debate. Chamberlain accused him of having given 'an altogether false picture of what happened'.

Chamberlain's days as Prime Minister were, however, numbered. When the fateful division on the adjournment took place late in the year Macmillan was one of the Tory Members who voted with the Opposition against him.

Churchill followed Neville Chamberlain as Prime Minister. Churchill did not forget the younger Tories who had supported him in his struggle. He gave Macmillan his first ministerial appointment. He became the Parliamentary Secretary to the Ministry of Supply. Two years later he moved to the Colonial Office as Under-Secretary of State. When the Allied forces landed in Algeria a new ministerial post, that of British Resident Minister at Allied Headquarters in North-West Africa, was created and Harold Macmillan went out in that capacity at the end of 1942. He held this post for three years and was closely associated with General Eisenhower during the Italian campaign and during this period he and Eisenhower became close personal friends.

In North Africa Macmillan met General de Gaulle. Macmillan had been instructed to unite the rival French factions under General Giraud, as had Murphy, the representative of the USA.

De Gaulle noted in his diary on March 17, 1943:

'Macmillan in anger, wanting every side to get united around Giraud. Macmillan violently irritated, crying "If General de Gaulle refuses the hand which is stretched out to him you must know that America and Great Britain will abandon him altogether and that he will not be anything any more".'

But when Macmillan departed to Italy, De Gaulle wrote in his diary for December 1943:

'Mr Macmillan was the representative of Great Britain in Algiers. Chosen by Churchill to associate himself, although reservedly, to the Allied political action in North Africa, he had understood gradually that there was something better to do. His lofty soul, his clear mind had found themselves in agreement with the French team who wanted France without fetters. I myself felt, as we met, that he was less and less prejudiced. In return, he had all my esteem.'

He was present at the signing of the Italian Armistice and he accompanied the Allied Headquarters to Italy and became Acting President of the Allied Commission in Italy.

Later he was sent to Greece on a difficult mission—to mediate between the parties in the Greek Civil War.

When the Labour Ministers left the Churchill Government he was appointed Secretary of State for Air in the 'Caretaker Government', a month before the General Election. A month later he was out of office. The Churchill Government had been defeated at the 1945 Election and Macmillan was defeated too.

At Stockton-on-Tees the result was:

Capt. G. R. Chetwynd (Lab.)	...	27,128
Capt. Macmillan (Con.)	... ...	18,464
G. P. Evans ...	... ...	3,718

He had been defeated by 8,664 votes by a young Labour candidate of twenty-eight.

Macmillan did not have to wait long for a seat. He was now in the good books of the Conservative Head Office and he was no longer suspect as a potential Parliamentary rebel.

He had finished with Stockton-on-Tees and the industrial North.

He was adopted as the Conservative candidate for Bromley in October.

In an election message Winston Churchill, now Leader of the Tory Party, sent him a message which read:

'The work which you did as British Resident Minister in the United Mediterranean, and afterwards, as acting president of the Allied Commission for Italy during the war was important, difficult and delicate. It required qualities of an exceptional order, and it must have given you an acquaintance with the affairs of the Mediterranean States and the Middle East which few can rival.'

After this tribute he went on to deal with the work of the Conservative Opposition 'on which great responsibilities devolved':

'Already in the short time the Socialist Government has been in office it has displayed a greater readiness to arm itself with autocratic powers than to grapple with matters vital to the nation's existence. It dilates upon its grandiose plans for a visionary future, while fumbling ineffectively with the practical problems that demand immediate action such as demobilization, the building of houses, the re-conversion of industry and the recovery of trade. The Opposition will spare no effort to awaken the Government to a proper sense of urgency. It will support all measures which are truly in the public interest. It will criticize with a view to improvement or to prevent, as far as possible, disastrous blunders. These are our tasks, and we shall discharge them all the more successfully if we can display our full strength in council and debate.'

Harold Macmillan, he thought, would be an asset in all this. He would strengthen the Opposition.

'Moreover, in the social field at home you are distinguished for your constructive and progressive outlook. We need you very much on the Opposition Front Bench in the Commons.'

Churchill had a high regard for Macmillan's abilities and was grateful to him for his support when he was unpopular with the Tories in pre-war days.

And in turn Macmillan was grateful to Churchill who had first given him office and had sent him to North Africa and Italy where he had been entrusted with missions which had given him influence and power.

What Macmillan had said about pre-war Tory Governments did not worry Churchill. He had said much worse things about the Tories, in his early days, himself. Macmillan was just the type of politician that Churchill needed now, in his role of truculent Leader of a Tory Opposition to a Socialist Government. Churchill could do the spectacular stuff in Parliament and Macmillan could be relied upon to help in the day-to-day detail work.

Bromley was a safe Conservative seat. At the Election the figures were:

Harold Macmillan (Con.) ...	...	26,367
Alexander Bain (Lab.)	...	...	20,810
J. C. Sayer (Lib.) ...	...	...	5,990

He took his seat on November 20th and immediately went on to the Tory Front Bench.

He made his first speech on December 5th and began by saying that he had left England in 1942 and felt rather like a political Rip Van Winkle. He saw on the benches opposite some of the colleagues with whom and under he had served in the great Coalition administration. What a transformation! Ebbw Vale (Aneurin Bevan) and Limehouse (Attlee) together. Wandsworth (Bevin) and Seaham (Shinwell) side by side. The lion lying down with the lamb! 'How long it will last or what will be the end of it, I do not know.'

He did not seem to know either where he stood in this new political situation. 'The fundamental divergence between us comes to this: Socialists—and that part of the Labour Party which is really Socialist—trust to find every possible reason for applying their nostrums in season and out of season. The rest of us would bring an open mind to each problem as it arises.'

Did he really believe this? Did he really think that the Tories behind him would bring an open mind to bear upon whether the coal mines or the railways were to be nationalized? Was he a simpleton or a cynic? Were the Tories, led by Churchill, Oliver Lyttelton, Sir John Anderson and the rest of the spokesmen of big business really open-minded men in the Middle of the Road or were they not men of the Right opposed to nationalization and everything else that the City of London and the Stock Exchange thought against their interests?

'The larger questions of the ultimate adjustment of the next period of the rights and functions of the State need careful study and solution in an atmosphere of reasonableness and normality. There are many new issues to be faced and dangers to be avoided in achieving this balance. Even to determine the most desirable system of management for any service or enterprise in the public domain requires careful and objective experiment.' The unorthodox back bencher who in the pre-war years had urged Parliament not to be afraid of revolutionary changes was obviously trying to reply in advance to those who had remembered what he had said before. Indeed he might have been trying to reply to himself.

For what the Labour Government was embarking on was a programme of transferring to public ownership the basic industries which he himself was prepared to see public utilities in his pre-war days.

But he was no longer an independent-minded back bencher. He was now on the Tory Front Bench which had determined to oppose by every means in its power Labour's plans for nationalizing coal, gas, electricity and transport, and its plans for reorganizing unemployment and health insurance and establishing the Welfare State.

He ended by declaring that 'we will offer nothing but constructive help and assistance towards the fulfilment of this high national purpose'.

There indeed had been a transformation in the House of Commons since he had last addressed it. Members who had been there with him before the war thought there was a transformation in Macmillan too. They recalled what he had said when he was a back bencher not so many years before.

Then he was a crusader for a new society. Now his crusading days were over. He had deserted the crusaders to join the mercenaries.

Later on, as the Tory Opposition obstructed and misrepresented everything that the Labour Government was trying to do, we understood what 'this constructive help' meant.

On August 27th he was sent to the Bridgeton By-Election, which followed the death of James Maxton, to support the Tory candidate, and *The Times* reported his speech. Bridgeton was a conglomeration of slums and a housing problem which had been accumulating under Tory Governments for over a hundred years. He complained that under the Labour Government there was no national planning. 'The housing programme faltered. Disappointed and indignant, the "squatters" were taking the law into their own hands.' Labour had not been in office for a year and the Tories had been there for a century. 'Mr Attlee and his followers were just drifting, amiably, hopefully, with a new plan each day and plenty of well-meaning suggestions from the crew but no very clear idea of their position or their course. The ship of state drifted on. We had dropped the old pilot. We had never needed him more than now.'

He was fast becoming the typical conventional Tory political hack.

He wrote a letter to *The Times* on December 19th attacking Ernest Bevin, who had said:

'We are nationalizing certain industries. They ought to have been nationalized long ago. The industries are incompetent. I speak as one who knows a good deal about it.'

Macmillan commented:

'The case for and against the national ownership and control of certain industries and services can be argued from different aspects. I cannot help thinking that the Foreign Secretary, on reflection, will regret so sweeping an accusation against those responsible for the running of these industries and the large number of workers in them. Had these industries been guilty of such inefficiency, we could scarcely have won a war in which they played so vital a part.'

When the Coal Industry Nationalization Bill came up for Second Reading Debate, Harold Macmillan was put up by the Tories to make the concluding speech against it.

The Tories were against nationalization. They wanted the industry left in the hands of the coal owners. They were in favour of compulsory amalgamations with the financing of the re-equipment of the industry itself, through machinery provided by the State if necessary, a charter for the miners, the restoration of managerial responsibilities, a safeguard for the consumer through competition between the reorganized but proportionately much smaller groups in the industry, but the industry was to be left with the coalowners who had proved themselves incompetent to manage it.

Macmillan's speech was long and tortuous with many cheap debating quips and taunts, a defence of the coal owners whom he argued should not be dispossessed, a too clever by half speech in which he claimed to be speaking both on behalf of the owners and the consumers, putting up rhetorical Aunt Sallies and knocking them down again.

The House was to get accustomed to these speeches during the Labour Government. The Tories divided against the Mines Nationalization Bill and against the Financial Resolution that accompanied it. They employed every obstructive tactic they could. At one point in the debate the Deputy Chairman called Macmillan's attention to the rule against continuous repetition.

The coal owners, the big business men, the gentlemen of the Stock Exchange, reading the papers next day, could not complain that the Tories had let them down.

On April 28, 1947, Macmillan spoke in the Committee stage of the Transport Bill. He argued in favour of the claims of the private road haulier interests and undertakings. He said that the Tory Party was concerned about protecting the interests of 'the small man'. The Minister, he said, was 'guilty of blackmail of the worst and most filthy kind'.

During the Committee stage and the Report stage the Tories obstructed the proposals for the nationalization of the railways. If the railways were to be nationalized the best possible compensation should be paid to the railway shareholders and directors.

Macmillan made several speeches and on April 28th said that if the nation took over anything he thought 'that an even higher

E

standard of probity and equity ought to be maintained by the nation, the highest possible example of absolute fairness'. There ought to be outside arbitration 'to ensure that the railway share-holders and directors received justice'.

Considering the way the big railway companies had swallowed up smaller concerns this consideration for the small men was rather touching. It was understandable too that the Tory Party in the House of Commons should fight to the last ditch for the shareholders of the railway companies to whom the Labour Government terms of compensation were not ungenerous. Every one of the big railway companies had Tory lords or M.P.s on their boards of directors. On the Board of Directors of the Great Western Railway was Harold Macmillan himself. When the Transport Bill reached the statute he and his fellow directors would be displaced and redundant.

They were not treated unjustly or ungenerously. They were well compensated. When Macmillan came to Scotland when he was Prime Minister in 1961 a conscientious ticket collector asked him for his ticket. He did not require one. The press explained that as an ex-railway director he was entitled to free travel.

Macmillan soon became the Tory Front Bench speaker who could most easily raise the temperature of the House. He culti-vated an oratorical style of the Gladstonian period. He would put his hands on the lapels of his coat and turn to the back benches behind him for approval and support. He would raise and lower his voice and speak as if he were on the stage. One would not have been surprised to hear that he had rehearsed this the night before in front of a mirror. His polished phrases reeked of midnight oil. He delighted in jibes at the benches opposite and the taunts that invited retort.

To those opposite he seemed the political actor and poseur, the cynic, the knock-about artiste of the Parliamentary stage, whose sincerity they began to doubt. He was too glib. Did he know when he was acting and when he was not himself? He could put on a synthetic smile which didn't look the genuine thing. A Parliamentary sketch writer described him as 'switching on a smile'. A few seconds later he switched it off. He exaggerated and improved on what Labour Ministers had said in order to sneer at them.

A passage from his speech in the Debate on the Address to

the King's Speech in October 1947 can be taken as a sample of his Parliamentary style. He was referring to the Labour Front Bench.

'There was one fatal worm in the bud, one lurking disease which, like a poison began to eat into them from the very start. This Government ever since they took office have been haunted by their promises. Of course I know that the Leader of the House, astute politician as he is, has been able—as he did last night—to quote a few saving phrases, a few warning sentences which were put into the pronunciamentos of his party and which he was able to call to his aid. Of course that is why he put them there. It is an operation which, if I have been properly informed, is known in another connection as "hedging"—£50 each way on Utopia and £5 on that likely outsider Austerity. Let each Hon. Member opposite remember and honestly search his heart and mind. Let him ask himself this question: is it not a fact that the general impression created on the public mind two years ago was that a Labour Government would bring into being—I do not say a universal millenium in a fortnight —I think it was housing that was to be done in a fortnight—but at least a good long step towards it. Abroad, a Socialist Foreign Minister would automatically achieve a deep and sympathetic friendship with the rulers of the Soviet Union. At home after all the sufferings of the war, conditions of clothing, transport, housing, food and leisure —in a word, all general comfort—would rise to standards hitherto undreamed of . . . How far away it all seems now. These dreams have melted like the snows of yesteryear and now comes the veritable judgment upon them.'

Old Parliamentary journalists wondered whether he was trying to imitate the rhetorical insolence of Churchill in his younger days or perhaps F. E. Smith.

Sometimes he got more than he bargained for. There was the occasion on January 28, 1949, when Mr Pritt punctured his eloquence. He was indulging in his usual taunt that Labour had tried to bribe the electorate by false promises and added in a burst of self-righteousness:

'Let us get therefore one thing quite clear in our minds. Any party or group of men which tries to tempt the electorate by bribes, or by holding out some agreeable picture of an automatically realizable Utopia, will incur more than ordinary guilt. [Hon. Members: 'Hear, hear.'] Hon. Members opposite have done it once; they must not do it again.'

Mr Pritt (Hammersmith, North): The Right Hon. Gentleman and his friends have done it a hundred times, and lied every time.

Mr Macmillan: The Hon. and learned Gentleman says that we

have done it a hundred times and lied every time. I do not think his language is worthy of himself, and his historical background must be even weaker than the arguments from him usually are.

Mr Pritt: I can remember occasions in this House when I gave details of instances of the Tory Party, in fact, going to the country on false pretences, and when not one Member of the party got up to deny it.

Mr Macmillan: Even the insults of the Hon. and learned Gentleman will not induce me to vote in his Lobby this afternoon.

Mr Pritt: Thank God for that.

Aneurin Bevan was Minister of Health and one of Labour's most popular speakers in the country, and he was a frequent target for Macmillan's attacks on the Government from the Front Opposition Bench.

Bevan had not been to Eton or Oxford but had acquired his political education in the hard school of experience. He was quick-witted and his mind moved like lightning. He was a dangerous opponent to bait, especially if the baiter was not sure of his ground.

Macmillan in his speech on the Address went out of his way to attack Bevan over a speech he had made about the steel industry.

He said, according to the Hansard report:

'The Government know that to nationalize steel would be an act of criminal folly. It would be too much even for them—except of course for the Minister of Health, who differs from his colleagues, and accuses the managers of the steel industry of having betrayed the nation's interests.'

Bevan was on his feet instantly to demand: 'When?'

Macmillan replied: 'At Hull. "Betrayed the nation's need." I have the quotation.'

The interchanges continued.

Mr Bevan: The Right Hon. Gentleman is as inaccurate as usual. Will he quote the words in which I said 'the managers of the steel industry'?

Mr Macmillan: Of course, if the Right Hon. Gentleman withdraws them——

Hon. Members: No.

Mr Bevan: It is altogether too disingenuous. Will the Right Hon. Gentleman quote the words in which I said 'managers of the steel industry'?

Mr Macmillan: I understand that is a quotation from a speech [Hon. Members: 'Withdraw.'] the Right Hon. Gentleman was

reported in the Press [Hon. Members: 'Ah!']—I regret I have not
the cutting—as having said that the people who have been running
the steel industry had betrayed the nation's needs. Is that right? 'The
people who have been running the industry have betrayed the needs
of the nation.'

Mr Bevan: The Right Hon Gentleman, in a few minutes, has
already changed the original quotation. His first statement was that
I said——

Churchill, who was always ready to join in a row, chipped
in:

'What did the Minister of Health say?'

Mr Bevan: I know the Right Hon. Gentleman wants me to make
his speech for him.

Mr Quintin Hogg (Oxford): Why does not the Minister of Health
tell us?

The House was in an uproar and the Speaker rose to appeal
for order.

'There is so much noise on both sides of the House that I do not know
what anybody is trying to say.'

Mr Bevan: I merely wish the Right Hon. Gentleman—which is
customary in this House—to quote his authority. Why should I
make the Right Hon. Gentleman's speech for him? Let the Right
Hon. Gentleman give the quotation.

Mr Macmillan: Both the Right Hon. Gentleman and myself have
some experience of this House. Since he challenges me I must frankly
admit I am not armed with the precise words. I therefore withdraw
the remark. But I shall look up carefully the quotation from which
I had drawn only a few phrases—I have not the whole thing with
me now—and in a proper way I shall certainly publish again what
he did say—and I do not think there will be very much difference in
the broad meaning.

Before he concluded his speech somebody handed him up a
press cutting and he returned to the subject:

Mr Macmillan: I have just obtained his exact words as quoted in the
Yorkshire Post, on October 18th, in a report of a speech he made at
Hull. He said:

'We will not leave the industry in the hands of those who have
betrayed the nation's interest and cannot be trusted to develop the
industry to the extent required by the necessities.'

Mr Bevan: That is not the managers.

Mr Churchill: In view of the disturbance which arose in the
House just now, will the Right Hon. Gentleman say whether that is
an accurate quotation or not?

Mr Bevan: Certainly, but it is the owners, not the managers.

Mr Macmillan: I cannot allow the Right Hon. Gentleman to ride out on that. If he says the words 'the hands of those' does not include management as well as ownership, then I do not know what it does mean.

The two were obviously talking at cross purposes. Aneurin Bevan had worked at the coal face and the managers to him were the men who were directly in contact with the work of the mine. It was the same in the steel works. He was attacking the policy of the owners not the work of the managers. To Bevan the managers and the owners were different people. Macmillan could see no difference. He had neither worked in a coal mine nor a steel works. Bevan was talking of the policy of the men in the boardrooms, not the work of the managers at the steel works.

Macmillan had slipped up in not having the exact quotation. He had yet to learn the lesson of what Churchill once told the House were the last words of the dying historian to his son: 'Verify your quotations'.

Of course there was the clash of personalities of men who came from entirely different backgrounds. When Bevan thought of steel he thought of the men working in the furnaces of Ebbw Vale. When Macmillan talked of steel he was thinking of the directors in the board room.

The Tory back benchers did not see Macmillan in the same way as the Labour M.P.s opposite. They thought that when Macmillan was baiting Bevan and the Socialists on the Government Front Bench he was doing well. His stock in the Tory Party went up.

It depended largely on what side you were on.

When the Socialists thought that Macmillan was flippant, superficial, supercilious and arrogant, the Tories thought he was clever, hard hitting, forceful, convincing, eloquent, one who knew all the tricks of the Parliamentary game. He encouraged those behind him—just what a Tory Front Bencher should do, although few of them in those days thought of him as a likely future Prime Minister.

CHAPTER VIII

FOR THE COLD WAR

MACMILLAN was frequently absent from the House of Commons in these years. He paid many visits to Europe in connection with the proposals that were made to establish the Council of Europe. He helped Sir Winston Churchill to organize his United Europe Movement and was a delegate to the Congress of Europe at the Hague in May 1948. Until he took office in 1951 he was a member of the European Movement's International Council and chairman of its Central and Eastern Europe Commission. In 1949, 1950 and in its first 1951 session he was one of Britain's representatives to the Consultative Assembly of the Council of Europe.

He was early interested in the moves and trends of the thinking about the future of Europe which eventually culminated in the Treaty of Rome and the establishment of the Common Market.

He took a pessimistic view of the situation in Europe. He told Hugh Dalton: 'I think Europe is finished . . . If I were a younger man I should emigrate from Europe to the United States.'

In a debate on the European situation on March 23, 1949, Macmillan opened the debate as spokesman of the Tory Opposition and came out strongly in favour of continuing the Cold War with Russia. He argued against increasing trade with the East European countries. He did not believe that we could 'cajole or wheedle the present Governments of these satellite countries by economic benefits'. He added:

'With Communists, we cannot say it with flowers . . . I say be careful. Do not give away guns in order to get butter. Go elsewhere. Go to the Dominions. Go to the Empire. Go to the Colonies. Go to Western Europe. Make the world on our side of the Iron Curtain a demonstrably better place to live in and then ultimately the news of this success will filter through.'

He concluded:

'The cold war must be fought with as much energy and single-

mindedness as the shooting war . . . Step by step the cold war must
be won. If the way be long and weary, let us have courage and faith.
For this is no ordinary journey that we must travel together.

'It is, perhaps, the last Crusade.'

This of course was House of Commons rhetoric.

Earlier in his speech he had argued that stronger action than
the air lift should have been taken over Berlin.

'The air lift,' he said, 'was essentially an act of political appeasement . . . It is true that we got over this by hopping over the top,
but have we solved the problem? I often wonder what history will
say of that decision in June last year. Were we right or wrong?
Would we have done better to face the issue squarely then.'

An Hon. Member: 'War'.

'I do not think there would have been war. I think there would have
been a Russian retirement.

'At any rate, if we had decided not to enforce our rights could we
not have taken some stronger counter-measures such as the economic
boycott of the Eastern zone? That has been very slow in getting
under way.'

He thought we should have used military force over Berlin or
resorted to economic boycott.

In his reply Ernest Bevin pointed out the dangers of the policy
that Macmillan had advocated. 'That means sanctions,' he said,
'and sanctions mean war'. Neither did Bevin agree with Macmillan's suggestion for an economic boycott and asked, 'How far
can we go in punishing the ordinary folk? That is an anxiety to
me. Do we make converts of people in another country, however
much they hate their regime, if we join in starving them?'

Bevin thought that Butler, who later had said that he did not
agree that all trade should be stopped, was more sensible than
Macmillan.

Macmillan had sounded more belligerent than Butler. It
seemed as if Butler had thought that Macmillan had gone rather
far.

What grounds Macmillan had for believing that if the West
had been prepared to use military force to get to Berlin and that
the Russians would have retired nobody knew.

It was probably just wishful thinking to fit in with his line
of argument, an impromptu retort to an interruption that had
presented him with the dilemma. Would that have been the
policy of a Tory Government if Macmillan had been Foreign

Secretary? What support would there have been in the country to start the war all over again about Berlin?

He had obviously a lot to learn about the facts of life in Berlin and Eastern Europe in those post-war years. He was to learn them later.

This early enthusiasm for the Cold War was of course based on ignorance and quite baseless assumptions, and a totally wrong assessment of Russia's position in Europe.

It was quite as easy as it was irresponsible to accuse the Labour Government of weakness because it was not prepared to go into an impossible war over Berlin.

Ten years later he was in Moscow himself, not as a representative of a country that had gained anything from the Cold War but as one who had been forced to realize that the West had not won it and that it was time it was ended.

On various occasions he was one of the Front Bench spokesmen of the Tory Party and in these speeches followed the line which had been proclaimed by Churchill in his famous speech at Fulton in the U.S.A. in 1946 which the Russians had denounced as being the declaration of the Cold War.

In a speech in the House on November 17th, 1949, Macmillan said that at Fulton Churchill had spoken 'in a prophetic mood'.

'He was bitterly attacked by what are called prophetic circles. Some Hon. Members wanted him repudiated; some almost wanted to have him impeached. One hundred Members put down a motion in the House of Commons that he should be publicly repudiated. The Government showed no particular enthusiasm. But they had to follow his advice. They did not like it. In fact they started quite a different policy. They toyed with the same idea at the time that they should act as a kind of arbiter or umpire between the United States and Russia. But, of course, "the third force" policy was based on an illusion. The logic of events proved inexorable, and three years after the Fulton speech came the Atlantic Pact.'

When he became Prime Minister, ten years later, Macmillan came to the conclusion that it would be wise policy if he were to try 'to be an arbiter or an umpire between the United States and Russia' too, for the Fulton policy and the Atlantic Pact and the arms race were leading the world towards the cataclysm of a third world war.

But in 1949 Macmillan was as anti-Russian as Churchill. In this speech, too, he came out strongly in favour of the European

Movement and passages in it are interesting in view of Macmillan's attitude to the Common Market in later years. He argued in favour of joining up with Europe and keeping in the Commonwealth at the same time. In the 'halcyon days of the mid-Victorian era', he said, there was a movement against colonialism.

'I think the fashionable expression in those days was that the colonies would drop like ripe fruit from the parent tree. In those days the only imperialists were exotic imperialists like Mr Disraeli or pushing young men from the provinces like Mr Chamberlain, but as usual the clever people were wrong, they usually are.'

He was all for the Commonwealth:

'We are in the Commonwealth; in the same family. We know and trust each other. Nevertheless I think we shall have to strengthen rather than weaken the links of Empire, both in the economic and strategic field, if the British people are to do their job. We ought to build and use in peace at least as close a machinery of Imperial co-operation as we create in war. The stronger and better the British Empire, the greater will be our contribution to the recovery and security of Europe.'

At the same time he was in favour of joining up with Europe. But, he added, 'I do not believe that we can play our part in Europe alone as the people or as the Government of the United Kingdom. We are the centre of the Commonwealth and Empire. In this truly British conception we do not need perhaps the kind of formal and constitutional matters which some Europeans like.'

The only conclusion that could be drawn from this speech was that if it were a choice between Europe and the Commonwealth we should choose the Commonwealth.

On February 14, 1951, Macmillan led the attack on the Labour Government on its Defence policy. The Government had decided to embark on a big rearmament programme and this was a historical and fateful debate. Shinwell, as Defence Minister, had introduced a motion calling upon the House to approve of an estimated expenditure on Defence amounting to approximately £1,500,000,000 for three years.

The Tories, of course, approved of the rearmament programme. Their only criticism of it was that it should have been begun before and should have been more.

Macmillan was chosen to lead the Tory attack. It was a typical Macmillan speech of those days with a good many sneers and taunts at Shinwell and the Labour Front Bench.

He was completely convinced of the 'very heavy burden' on the nation and we should not ask them to carry it if we were not completely convinced of its necessity.

Shinwell, speaking before him, had said:

'Nearly every aspect of this great new Defence programme will involve additional works services. Airfields, storage accommodation, factory space—these are just examples of what will be needed. This will make big demands on our already overtaxed building industry and special measures may have to be taken.'

Macmillan approved wholeheartedly of the expenditure that was to be incurred, not raising the slightest objection. He attacked the Government for what he called 'its obstructive, not to say even contemptuous attitude towards the one effort that certain European nations are trying to make, which they call the European Army'. The call-up of the Class Z reservists had his full support. It should have been done earlier and for a longer period. He was for a bigger and a better bombing force. And 'it might be desirable that the production of the new British bomber should be placed, either in part or whole, in the Commonwealth or in the United States'. The bombers should be built as far away from the danger zone even if the British civilian population had to stay at home.

It was 'very important to make a really efficient Civil Defence available in the shortest possible time'.

Macmillan's speech indicated that the Tories wanted a still bigger Army, Navy and Air Force, and even a heavier expenditure than Shinwell had outlined in his speech. There was a row when he talked about the numbers of Russian submarines.

'Russia has not 300 but between 300 and 400 submarines. It is said by some authorities that they are likely to have 1,000 within two years.'

Commander Pursey had said that he was exaggerating. In any case where were they? Surely some of them must be in the Pacific where the responsibility for dealing with them would be America's. Were these facts being taken into account or were these figures being given to justify further large expenditure on the Navy?

When he mentioned the figure of 1,000 Russian submarines, Mr Woodrow Wyatt improved on it.

Mr Wyatt (Birmingham, Aston): Probably one million!

Commander Pursey: And snow on their boots.

Mr Shinwell: How does the Right Hon. Gentleman know all this?

Mr Macmillan: I challenge the Right Hon. Gentleman, when he replies, to deny the figure of 400.

Mr Shinwell: The Right Hon. Gentleman is telling us.

Mr Macmillan: Can the Right Hon. Gentleman deny it?

Mr Shinwell: The Right Hon. Gentleman is making a positive statement. He is saying that the Russians have 400 submarines and I am asking him how he knows.

Mr Churchill (Woodford): What is the Minister's estimate?

Mr Shinwell: Never mind my estimate.

Mr Macmillan: Everybody must recognize that those of us who have to speak on this side of the House have responsibilities, which we try to fulfil. We are not given the information which, of course, only Ministers have, but if the Right Hon. Gentleman says that my estimate of 300 or 400 is absurd, I ask him, when he replies, to make his estimate.

Mr Shinwell: I have offered no estimate to the House. [Hon. Members: 'Why not?'] I have not offered any estimate to the House. I am asking the Right Hon. Member for Bromley (Mr H. Macmillan), who himself has made an estimate, a simple question: How does he know? Or is it simply guesswork?

Mr Macmillan: The Right Hon. Gentleman cannot get away with it like that. He has the responsibility. He says that he has given no estimate to the House. I ask this further question: Has he been given an estimate by his Secret Service?

Mr Shinwell: I am surprised at the Right Hon. Gentleman—as though, when I was given information by the Secret Service, I should convey it to the public.

Mr Macmillan: I am now becoming more and more lost in the tortuous nature of the Right Hon. Gentleman's replies. He now tells us how dangerous it would be if we were to tell the Russians how many submarines they have. In any event, I think it will be admitted that the preponderance and danger is far greater than it was at the outbreak of the war and, therefore, that nothing should be left undone to increase the readiness of the Fleet and of the Reserve Fleet in respect of destroyers, light frigates and similar craft.

The Tories wanted nothing undone 'to increase the readiness of the Fleet and of the Reserve Fleet in respect to destroyers, light frigates and similar craft'. Costs did not seem to enter into it.

Later one of the General Staff said, 'We were given a blank cheque and we filled it up'.

The Labour Government had embarked on the big rearmament programme that did so much to destroy it. Together with the Korean War, the new rearmament programme added vast sums to the expenditure on the Army, Navy and the Air Force and there was a steep rise in prices which before the end of the summer had culminated in a financial crisis.

This the Tory press attributed to Socialist bungling and inefficiency and to nationalisation. At the Election in 1950 they cashed in on it. The fact that the Tories had strongly supported the Korean War and the expenditure incurred on it and had been in favour of even heavier defence expenditure was forgotten. For years afterwards in nearly every political speech that he made Macmillan spoke of the way the Socialists had brought the country to ruin.

As far as the rearmament programme was concerned he certainly did his best to help them.

The rearmament programme had its political as well as its economic consequences. It brought the Labour Government down. Churchill again became Prime Minister. He made Macmillan Minister of Health in the new Government.

CHAPTER IX

HOUSING MINISTER

IN HIS biography of Neville Chamberlain, Iain Macleod compares the task of Harold Macmillan at the Ministry of Health and Local Government between 1951 and 1954 with that of the work done by Neville Chamberlain at the Ministry of Health before the war.

Chamberlain had been given charge of Housing in the Baldwin Government between 1925 and 1928.

'Chamberlain,' says Macleod, 'had lost nothing, and perhaps politically had gained much, as did Macmillan in 1951 by taking on the endless tough challenging work of Housing.'

Undoubtedly the work that Macmillan did during the time that he was in charge of Housing was the most useful work that he undertook in his political career and he deserves every credit for it. But he was not in charge of Housing for very long and to see it in perspective one must recall what happened before, and what happened after he left office.

The work that Chamberlain carried out would of course have been impossible if it had not been for the task that John Wheatley had accomplished before him in the shortlived Labour Government of 1924.

Chamberlain succeeded Wheatley and inherited his plans for a drive to build more houses. The Tories had shown precious little enthusiasm before that. Had the Labour Government which came into office in 1924 remained there for the normal life of a Parliament and Wheatley had continued as Minister of Health there would have been far more houses built than under Chamberlain. Wheatley was in office for less than twelve months and although his work was taken over the Tories reduced the rate of progress that might have been achieved by reducing the housing subsidy.

Macleod throws a light on how the Tory Government of those years looked upon housing when he remarks:

'Actually in December 1928, a few months before the Election,

Parliamentary authority was obtained for reducing from October 1929 the subsidy on "Wheatley" houses and abolishing it on "Chamberlain" houses. No one could accuse this Government of being adroit in their political timing of events.'

That last remark is not without a tinge of cynicism. Macleod evidently thinks that it would have been cleverer and more politically astute to have waited until after the Election. At any rate the housing problem had become so acute in 1929 that it contributed to the Tory defeat at the General Election of that year.

After the war Macmillan was among the first to realize the importance of housing as a political issue. Indeed he had shown more interest in it in the years before the war than most Tory M.P.s.

One of his earliest political attacks on the Attlee Government was in a speech at the Bridgeton by-election before the Labour Government had been a year in office. It was easy enough to criticize for slow progress then. There had been an enormous amount of damage during the war and this had to be repaired. During the war little building had been done and building labour had been depleted. It was impossible for house building to get into its stride immediately the Labour Government had taken office. Had Labour not been defeated in 1951 and had Bevan still been Minister of Health the work of house building would have continued at an increased rate because by that time the building and building materials industries were getting into their stride.

Without depreciating Macmillan's energies and capacities as an administrator in any way it is a mistake to look back upon his work as Minister of Housing as if he had showed extraordinary capacity for building houses where his predecessors had failed. Like Chamberlain, he inherited the work and organization that had been carried out by the Labour Government between 1945 and 1951.

By a decision of the Conservative Party Conference a programme of 300,000 houses a year had been put into the party election programme and Churchill thought that Macmillan was the best man he had to carry it out.

Undoubtedly at this Ministry Macmillan did well. But it is necessary to look at it in perspective. Having won the Election of 1951 and achieved their target, the Tories had something to boast about. But what happened afterwards?

Was Macmillan's drive for 300,000 houses during his period of office part of a long-term programme to solve the housing problem of the country on imaginative lines or was it a temporary effort to do something spectacular in order to attract votes for the Tory Party?

What Macmillan inherited from his predecessor was indicated in *The Times* review of the building industry:

'At the end of the year (1951) Mr Macmillan had inherited 226,000 unfinished houses started under his Labour predecessors. Thus regardless of the Government's completions, only some very singular bungle could prevent the completion of 230,000 during 1952.'

The rate of building was on the up grade before Macmillan began.

There was an interesting debate on housing in the Queen's Speech in November 1953 when Macmillan stressed the importance of making the housing drive 'a real national crusade'. He said:

'As a result of this effort I am fairly confident about the programme of new houses but I want to sound a warning. There must be no relaxation, no feeling that the target is reached or passed, and no let up. The present drive must continue towards maximum production, and above all towards the use of modern methods, to bring about the much desired reduction in costs.'

The relaxation was to come later and as Chancellor of the Exchequer Macmillan was to help it by increasing the interest rates to local authorities, which was to continue during the years of his Government.

The crusade was to be slowed down later, long before its objectives had been achieved.

In the debate Aneurin Bevan examined Macmillan's record on housing critically. He pointed out how much had to be done by the Labour Government in repairing war damage. Approximately two and a half million houses had been repaired and building materials and labour had to be diverted to this work. This was all forgotten when the Tories criticized the number of houses built and compared the number of houses built under the Labour Government and the Tory Government which came into power after this had been done.

Bevan accused Macmillan of transferring building labour to new house building and neglecting repairs in order to get spectacular results. After giving the figures for the previous years he said:

'Let me go to 1951 when the Right Hon. Gentleman began his depradations. In May 1951 there were 234,000 on new houses; 219,000 on repairs. In May 1952, 261,000 on new housing; 188,000 on other building work. In May 1953, 314,000 on new housing, 174,000 on other building work. In other words the Right Hon. Gentleman has thrown the building force completely out of balance and now we are engaged in trying to bring it into balance again.'

Bevan went on:

'We have always said—and I give this to Hon. Members opposite— that it was always possible to build 300,000 houses a year. Any fool could do it and I have said so. All what one needs to say is what one is not going to do, and what the Right Hon. Gentleman said he was not going to do was to repair the houses occupied by the tenants over whom he has been shedding crocodile tears this afternoon. There was more humbug in that speech than I have read in most speeches for a very long time.'

Bevan's solution was the Socialist solution:

'If the old laws of supply and demand could operate the problem would be solved. But long before it becomes profitable for builders to build houses to let at rents which soar upwards, the people are unable to afford the rents and they crowd into other houses and so the new houses are not built. The fact of the matter is that as a means of ordinary capitalist enterprise, the provision of rented houses for the vast mass of our population has now miserably failed. We have indeed to take the provision of low rented houses out of the whole area of private enterprise if the problem is to be solved at all.'

Macmillan of course rejected this proposal. Anything like long-term planning of house building on Socialist lines was unacceptable to the Tory Party.

His road was the road of no building controls, high interest rates, high rents, the encouragement of the property owner, the private builder, the speculator in land.

At the Conservative Party Conference held at Blackpool, October 10, 1952, Macmillan delivered a long speech on the question of housing.

He said he had tried to make housing 'a great national crusade'. He was always talking about crusades. Everything that he was enthusiastic about for the time being was a crusade. Even the cold war was a crusade. He said:

F

'Housing is the greatest of all social needs. It is the first priority among the social services. Even the best of schools, clinics, hospitals, playing fields and libraries are something of a mockery to those thousands of families who have no home of their own. For the home is the basis of the family, just as the family is the basis of the nation. A nation—at any rate a Christian nation—is not just a jungle of warring individuals; it is a community of families.

'I have therefore tried to make housing a great national crusade . . .

'Well we have made a start of course. It is only a start but it is quite encouraging. The buildings are going up, and so are the figures: houses completed, houses building, houses started—all are going up.'

He concluded on a sentimental note which brought tears to the eyes of the delegates to the Conference, including the considerable number of property owners and slum landlords who were present.

'Often it is the case in our country that the popular tunes and ditties of the day reflect more of the true feelings and moods of the people than more solemn and elaborate compositions. This has been true throughout the ages, from Lillibullero to Tipperary. There is a song which has a refrain something like this: 'Ours is a nice house, ours is'. Compared, I think, with the large and majestic themes we were discussing yesterday [they had been discussing foreign affairs and the economic situation] that is by no means an ignoble aim.'

It was by speeches like this that Macmillan endeared himself to Conservative Party Conferences and increased his popularity among the rank and file. He had set out to give the Conservative canvasser on the working class doorstep something by which they could convince the slum dwellers and the overcrowded and those on the housing waiting list that the Conservative Government was their greatest friend.

No demagogue could have improved on this speech. It had everything, the crusading spirit, the moral and family appeal, the high note mixed up with a popular sentimental appeal with a music hall touch about it. 'Ours is a nice house, ours is' was certainly an inspiration.

No cheapjack on the market place could have improved on it. It revealed the undiscovered talent that was later to be used so effectively on the television screen. If Macmillan had not become a successful politician he certainly would have made a living as an advertizing agent or an auctioneer.

The crusader, however, must not only crusade for something. He must be prepared to encounter difficulties and make enemies.

He, himself, had realized that in his earlier days when he warned his readers that vested interests would be against his proposals for reorganizing industry.

Nobody can hope to crusade for a bold new housing policy for Britain without coming into conflict with the powerful landed interests, with property owners, and building speculators of all kinds.

A real housing crusade must inevitably be a threat and a challenge to them. While they were quite prepared to allow Macmillan to get votes for the Tory Party at Election time they wanted something more. The landlords and property owners had not just subscribed to the funds of the Tory Party to join in a housing crusade.

They were a powerful pressure group in the Tory Party to get rid of Rent Control. They wanted the legislation which would enable them to increase rents.

Macmillan had no intention of carrying his housing crusade to the extent of offending them. While they cheered his speeches at the Conservative Party Conference they wanted the opportunities to charge higher rents. The private builders, too, wanted a chance to build houses themselves from which they could get bigger profits than from municipal housing schemes. Then the money lending vested interests wanted to see interest rates charged to local authorities go up.

In the housing legislation that Macmillan introduced, every possible consideration and concession was given to the private vested interests. In every possible way he assisted them and appeased them. While he was always making speeches against appeasement in foreign policy he was the greatest appeaser on the home front.

The Rent Act was the greatest act of appeasement to the property owning classes that could have been devised.

It inflicted hardship and untold misery on innumerable people living in the back streets. It reduced their standard of living because it sent up their rents. It led to demands for increased wages which helped to bring about inflation and financial crises later on.

But it was not only the lower paid working class that suffered as a result of the Tory policy to increase rents. The people who bought their houses through the building societies saw their monthly payments go up too as the result of increased interest rates on their mortgages.

Macmillan had no hesitation in criticizing the Labour Government on its housing record in 1946, even when it had only been a year in office, and it is quite pertinent in the light of this to ask to what extent Macmillan's great housing crusade had solved the housing problem ten years afterwards.

The rate of building slowed down after Macmillan's initial efforts and a decade afterwards two and a half million people in Britain lived in houses officially condemned as 'unfit for human habitation'.

Ten years after Macmillan had called for a great national housing crusade the official reports told of four million houses in Britain which had no bath and two million with no internal w.c.

In 1955 the Government announced a five-year target for clearing the slums—378,000 slums to be cleared by the end of 1960.

This first five-year programme proved a dismal failure. It involved clearing away 75,500 slums a year. The average was 52,000. By the end of 1960 the total actually cleared was only 255,000, 123,000 short of the target.

Over a three-year period from 1958 to 1960, according to the report on housing trends issued by the Economic Commission for Europe, France built 20·6 dwellings per 1,000 inhabitants. The Netherlands built 22·9 per 1,000, Norway 22·5, Sweden 26·8 and West Germany 30·5 per 1,000 inhabitants. In this period the United Kingdom built 16·8 per 1,000 inhabitants.

It is in the light of these facts that we must judge Macmillan's crusade for housing.

He remained in charge of housing until October 1954, when Lord Alexander resigned from the Ministry of Defence. Churchill chose Macmillan to succeed him. Their views on defence and foreign policy were the same.

CHAPTER X

SHADOW OF THE BOMB

'OVERSHADOWING all else in the year 1954 has been the emergence of the thermo-nuclear bomb.'

This was the first sentence in the White Paper on Defence which Macmillan presented to the House of Commons in his capacity of Minister of Defence in March 1955.

It was the most frightening and sinister sentence contained in the White Paper, probably the most important sentence that he had ever written. It certainly was true. It went on: 'New and revolutionary problems are posed requiring courage and imagination for their solution.'

There followed a long paragraph on nuclear weapons. We were given a short history of the development and testing of thermo-nuclear weapons by the United States Government. It had announced that it was proceeding with full-scale production. The Soviet Government was clearly following the same policy, 'though we cannot tell when they will have thermo-nuclear weapons available for operational purposes'. The paragraph concluded:

'The United Kingdom also has the ability to produce such weapons. After fully considering all the implications of this step the Government have thought it their duty to proceed with their development and production.'

The Government had committed us to the strategy of the H-bomb.

We were told of the destructive power of the new super-bomb. It was many times more powerful than the atomic bombs which were used at Nagasaki and Hiroshima in 1945. There were no technical or scientific limitations on the production of nuclear weapons still more devastating.

The facts about the terrible nature of the new weapons were outlined in great detail.

'If such weapons were used in war, they would cause destruction, both human and material, on an unprecedented scale. If exploded in the air, a hydrogen bomb would devastate a wide area by blast and thermal radiation. If exploded on the ground, the damage and blast would be somewhat less; but there would be additional extremely serious indirect effects. A great mass of atomized particles would be sucked into the air. Much of it would descend round the point of explosion; but the rest would be carried away and descend as radio-active "fall out". The effect on those immediately exposed to it without shelter would certainly be fatal within the areas of greatest concentration of the "fall out"; it would become progressively less serious towards the outer parts of the affected region. Large tracts would be devastated and many more would be rendered uninhabit-able. Essential services and communications would suffer widespread interruption. In the largest areas, central and local government would be put out of action partially or wholly, Industrial production, even where the plant and buildings remained, would be gravely affected by the disruption of power and water supplies and by the interruption of the normal complex inter-flow of materials and components. There would be serious problems of control, feeding and shelter. Public morale would be most severely tested. It would be a struggle for survival of the grimmest kind.'

The White Paper went on to say that it was essential that these facts should be widely known 'not only to our own people but to the whole world'. All should realize the magnitude of the disaster war would bring.

These were the facts about the H-bomb. They were not only the themes which ran throughout the strategic thinking of the 1955 Statement on Defence, the concepts and arguments of this White Paper were to form the basis of British Governments for the years that were to follow. We were now committed to what came to be known as the Policy of the Nuclear Deterrent.

The House of Commons debated the White Paper for two days and it was a historic debate.

It was opened by Sir Winston Churchill in one of his last long speeches as Prime Minister and concluded by Harold Macmillan as Minister of Defence.

On such occasions Churchill's opening speech attracted a crowded house. He was still far and away the best orator of the old school in Parliament. In range of language, in the richness of his vocabulary, in his capacity to outline ideas and state argu-ments in historic perspective and background he still had no equal. Bevan could come nearest him, but even he on such sub-jects came a long way behind.

He began by an introductory survey of the developments in

nuclear science. 'The atomic bomb with all its terrors,' he said, 'does not carry us outside the scope of human control or manageable events in thought or action in peace and war. But when Mr Sterling Cole, the Chairman of the United States Congressional Committee, gave out a year ago—February 17, 1954—the first comprehensive review of the hydrogen bomb, the entire foundation of human affairs was revolutionized and mankind placed in a situation both measureless and laden with doom. It is now the fact,' he said, pointing to the Dispatch Box in front of him, 'that a quantity of plutonium, probably less than would fill the Box on the Table, would suffice to produce weapons which would give indisputable domination to any great Power, which was the only one to have it. There is no absolute defence against the hydrogen bomb nor is any method in sight by which any nation, or any country, can be completely guaranteed against the devastating injury which even a score of them might inflict in wide regions.

'What ought we to do? Which way shall we turn to save our lives and the future of the world? It does not matter so much to old people; they are going soon anyway, but I find it poignant to look at youth in all its activity and ardour and, most of all, to watch little children playing their merry games, and wonder what could lie before them if God wearied of mankind.'

What ought we to do? Churchill had posed the question but we waited in vain during his long speech for him to supply any adequate answer. The answer was certainly not to be found in the Government White Paper with its platitudes and its clichés, its statistics about the armed forces: the ships, the guns, the tank formations and bombers. In the light of what Churchill had said most of this was already obsolete.

In addition to the vast sums we had spent on rearmament since the Labour Government had begun it, we were now to spend more money on the hydrogen bomb and all the paraphernalia of nuclear war.

The Labour Government in its White Paper had proposed spending £1,500,000,000 for three years and, after that, we had been told, we would be able to sit down with the Russians and negotiate from a position of strength. But there were no signs that we were getting stronger than the Russians. On the contrary all the arguments now were that we must spend still more to prevent them catching up with us. The Government did not talk now about a programme which meant spending £1,500,000,000 a year for three years. The £1,500,000,000 a year had now become an annual sum, to figure every year in the Budget as the established and correct sum that was necessary for our defence.

But against the hydrogen bomb, Churchill had told us there was 'no absolute defence'. There was not the slightest sign that the Russians were on their knees begging to negotiate; on the contrary they were more difficult than ever. Our rearmament programme had not made them slow down theirs, it had caused them to speed up their defence plans. There was nothing for it, according to Churchill, but to go on with the arms race.

'I am anxious to repeat and to emphasize the one word which is the theme of my remarks, namely "Deterrent",' said Churchill. 'That is the main theme.' He added, 'The hydrogen bomb has made an astounding incursion into our lives and thoughts.'

He had made a typically Churchillian peroration. He was still good at perorations.

'To conclude, mercifully, there is time and hope if we combine patience and courage. All deterrents will improve and gain authority during the next ten years. By that time, the deterrent may well reach its acme and reap its final reward. The day may dawn when fair play, love for one's fellow men, respect for justice and freedom, will enable tormented generations to march forth serene and triumphant from the hideous epoch in which we have to dwell. Meanwhile, never flinch, never weary, never despair.'

This was good, sound, sonorous rhetoric, but nobody could have been left with any delusions. It was not a Defence Policy. Indeed, had he not told us that there wasn't one?

Shinwell, who had been Minister of Defence in the Labour Government, followed Churchill and asked some questions which dispelled the rhetoric. Churchill had made an impressive oration but he had said nothing original. It had all been said before.

Churchill had said we could counter-attack on Russia's wide open spaces. Churchill had talked about our power 'to increase the deterrent upon Soviet Russia by putting her enormous spaces and scattered population on an equality or near-equality of vulnerability with our small, densely-populated island and with Western Europe'. Shinwell replied:

'If the Russians should attack us and we respond on their wide open spaces, in spite of what the Right Honourable Gentleman said, there is one vulnerable target beyond all others. That is in London and in our ports. Does anyone really believe that we could withstand an attack of that kind? If so, for how long? Chaos, confusion, disloca- tion, everything disorganized—that is the prospect. "Prospect" is not the right term to use; but that is what lies before us. Of course we could retaliate. But the Right Hon. Gentleman said that millions of people will be killed. There is no particular satisfaction derived from the fact that when you are killed someone else will be killed after you——'

Churchill retorted: 'It may prevent it'.

This was always Macmillan's argument in later years.

Shinwell followed up the argument:

'Where we part company is when the Right Hon. Gentleman wishes to pursue the deterrent objective, at the same time knowing what the consequences will be if an attack is launched and we retaliate, or if an attack meets attack simultaneously. What we want to know is, why does the Right Hon. Gentleman cling to all the paraphernalia of the organization, which might have served our purpose in bygone wars but is not relevant to the situation which the Right Hon. Gentleman describes.'

Churchill had said very little in defence of the heavy expendi- ture outlined in the White Paper and after all this was what the debate was about.

Shinwell took the expenditure on the Army, Navy and the Air Force in turn. This was what his critics had done when he was Minister for Defence. How could it all be justified in the light of what Churchill had said?

He turned to the amount allocated to Civil Defence. Out of the huge total it only amounted to £70 million.

'Is this the way to handle the protection of the civil population?' he asked. 'If, on the other hand, the Government say there is no protection the public should be informed. They ought to know where they are. I believe that the Government feel that because there is no adequate protection possible, they must rely exclusively on the deterrent.'

What were the Government's plans?

'What was in last year's White Paper? There was a reference to the dangers of atomic attack and broken-back warfare resulting. There is no talk about broken-back warfare now. That has gone by the board. How can there be broken-back warfare when millions of people are destroyed as the result of the launching of a hydrogen bomb, when ports are destroyed, when shipping and movements and transport are dislocated?'

Shinwell was asking the questions which were to be asked by many more people as time went on. It was the beginning of a great debate which was to go on and in which millions of people were to ask the same things. The only answer they could get was that if the H-bomb could not be called defence it was a deterrent. Every kind of expenditure by the Army, Navy or Air Force, however irrelevant and wasteful and futile it might be, could always be defended on the ground that it formed part of 'the Deterrent'. In time we began to spell it with a capital D. We wrote Deterrent as we wrote Deity.

It fell to Harold Macmillan, as Minister of Defence, to wind up the debate, but before that he had to listen to the attack by Aneurin Bevan.

On this occasion Bevan did not speak from the Front Opposition Bench but from the corner seat of the First Bench below the gangway. He had resigned from the Shadow Cabinet and after this speech he was to be expelled from the Parliamentary Labour Party, be deprived of the Whip and come within an ace of being expelled by the National Executive of the Labour Party.

But this was one of his best speeches on the issue of the H-bomb and some of his more searching questions were directed to his own Front Bench.

Referring to Churchill's speech he declared, 'The mediocrity of his thinking is concealed by the majesty of his language'. There was certainly truth in this because while Churchill had gone into a great deal of vivid description of the position created in the world by the invention of the H-bomb he had certainly not said very much about what the Government could do about it.

Bevan recalled the vote of censure debate in 1951 when Churchill and Macmillan had so strongly attacked the Defence Programme of the Labour Government. Now Churchill and Macmillan were responsible and what was their policy! Who were Churchill and Macmillan to accuse the Labour Opposition of playing politics after the line they had taken when Labour was in office. Churchill had an 'extraordinary capacity for presentation' but what had he presented? Bevan went back to refer to the historic and controversial decision of the Labour Government in 1951. He said:

'The fact is—and it is now being increasingly recognized—that the decisions of 1950 and 1951 were, to some extent, based on wrong political assumptions. Those assumptions were very soon revealed to be invalid. They were based upon advice, presented to Ministers and to Right Hon. Gentlemen, by the heads of the Armed Services in America and Britain, that in three years at most, the Soviet Union would reach the summit of its power and that a threat of invasion of the West of Europe would mature and that we had to do everything we could to meet that eventuality. That is to say, that the peril would reach its summit at the end of 1953.

'It is now 1955, and if the peril had eventuated in 1953 we should have nothing to meet it. We have not very much now but we would have had nothing then.'

He recalled that in 1951 he had used the same argument as Churchill, even if the language had not been 'so scintillating'. The atom bomb with its creation of the feeling of mutual fear among the nations had created a situation when Governments could not go to war without risking mutual suicide.

'What we want to know,' asked Bevan, 'is when negotiations are going to start? We have had campaigns of hate and hysteria and we have now a war machine which is almost out of control.

'The Right Hon. Gentleman yesterday made a speech which astonished me, because, fundamentally it had no sense in it at all. I admit it was well garbed—but let us look at what the Right Hon. Gentleman told the House. He said he believed that the principle of deterrents intrinsic in the existence of the hydrogen bomb would make negotiations possible and might even result in peace because the use of it would mean mutual suicide. If that be the case, why wait for three years until the Russians have the bomb to deliver?

'We have been told that we wanted to talk out of strength. That has been the argument all the while. "The stronger we become," said the Right Hon. Gentleman, "the more willing the Russians will be to be conciliatory." In the next breath he went on to say that today the Russians have not got the hydrogen bomb and the bombers to deliver it, and that the power to do so rested with the West. So we have the power to negotiate. In those circumstances one would have thought that we would be sending Notes to the Kremlin asking Soviet leaders to meet us, because we can talk out of strength.

'But the contrary is the position. The Notes to negotiate are coming from the Soviet Union all the time. [Hon. Members: 'Why?'] I tell them — and this applies not only to the Conservative and Socialist Parties but to the country as well—that the ordinary man and woman is beginning spiritually to contract out of the quarrel. We are all displaying the posture of little men before big events and the ordinary man in the street is beginning to sense it. He is beginning to realize that we have not got the stature for the occasion.

'If what the Right Hon. Gentleman said yesterday is true—as I think it is—will he tell the House why it is that he does not insist upon meetings with the Russian leaders? It may be that they are not sincere in what they say, but there is only one way of finding out—and that is to meet them. It may be that the Right Hon. Gentleman would like to do it but that the United States will not permit him. This is a sombre thing to say, and a wicked thing to believe—that we have now reached the situation where Britain can, in a few short years, run the risk of extinction of its civilization, and we cannot reach the potential enemy in an attempt to arrive at an accommodation with him because we are now at the mercy of the United States.'

Bevan in that last sentence had stated a truth which was to become more apparent as the years went by. Britain had become for all practical purposes a satellite of the United States. Our policy towards Russia was being directed from Washington and the Pentagon. Britain could be destroyed as a result of decisions taken in the United States. It was the inevitable result of the policy begun by the Labour Government when it had agreed to the North Atlantic Treaty and continued under the Churchill administration. When Macmillan was to become Prime Minister it was to become more obvious still.

Attlee wound up for the Opposition and had a few criticisms for the policy which had been outlined in the Defence White Paper. He agreed there was now no real defence. He said:

'I have lived with this sombre topic for some time; indeed it is present in my mind every day. We all recognize there is no defence of this country in the ordinary and accepted sense of the word. That is naturally a great shock to older Members of this House, who remember the time when we used to sit secure behind the guns of the British Fleet. We have to recognize that. The hope of averting the catastrophe of another war which would not only mean catastrophe to ourselves but to civilization, is the realization that there will be no victor in another war.

'We have to get right away from the idea of victory in war. We may continue to read of victories in the past but there will be no victor in another war.'

That had now become a platitude, even in the Parliament that was annually voting about £1,500,000,000 (most of it for weapons and ships and planes which were obsolete) for what were still politely called Defence Estimates.

Attlee recalled Ernest Bevin saying to him how he always felt a dislike in even meeting the people who ruled Russia because he thought of the millions of innocent people, the Kulaks, who had been killed.

Had Bevin felt like that towards the rulers of Europe he would have disliked meeting anybody and have had to operate the Foreign Ministry from a monastery. But Attlee did think that 'somehow or other there has to be a meeting of the great Powers to persuade the rulers of Russia that, in their own interests, peace must be preserved . . . Putting it on the lowest level that is the materialistic conception.'

Attlee had little faith in the Civil Defence proposals that Macmillan had outlined in the White Paper.

Evacuation would mean 'widely dispersed depots of food, and so on, because it is not much use evacuating people to perhaps the only unbombed area in Caithness and Sutherland and having nothing to eat when they get there'.

He asked: 'Where are the people to go to? Where is the safe area? It depends which way the wind is blowing. It depends on where the bombs are dropped—and no one knows.'

Certainly Macmillan did not know when he came to reply.

It was no doubt a difficult debate to which to reply. Nobody had challenged what Churchill had said about the destructive power of a hydrogen bomb. Most of the other speakers in the debate had just underlined it.

There was indeed very little to be said. Churchill and Bevan in their own way were masters of debate and to go again over the ground would be very much anti-climax. Macmillan was new to the Ministry of Defence. He could hardly have learned much of the detailed work of the job and his speech was composed mainly of generalities.

It was not exactly an inspiring speech and hardly one of his notable Parliamentary performances. He had only just come to the Ministry of Defence—and he was soon to go. And it was not the occasion for a winding-up knock-about performance or the kind of party speech that the House had come to expect from him. He had to spin out the time and he did by putting up a few rhetorical Aunt Sallies and knocking them down again. There was a long dissertation in which he dealt with the horrors of two world wars. In the First World War there was the slaughter on the Somme and Passchendaele where there had been 360,000 casualties. In the Second World War there were 'the terrible losses by land, sea and air and the first great mass attacks upon the civil populations'.

'Is this,' he asked rhetorically, 'such a tolerable experience that it can be looked at, even in retrospect, without horror? If "Ban the Bomb" means going on with war without nuclear weapons I am against it.'

In 1955 the 'Ban the Bomb' movement had not been born and Macmillan seemed to be anticipating it in advance. The arguments he used became more familiar in the 'sixties.

He went on:

'Apart from that argument let us suppose there could be such a ban. If such an agreement were scrupulously observed on both sides, how could the conventional forces that we could recruit and maintain bear any comparison with the huge manpower of the vast Communist countries? Such a result would be fatal to Europe and the whole world.'

He ruled out the idea that we could have a war with conventional weapons. We must have the H-bomb, was his argument, in order to counteract the manpower superiority of the Communist countries? He seemed to assume that we should always be superior to the Communist countries in nuclear weapons. It was not long before he was proved wrong.

He went on:

'Is it not obvious that if such a degree of international agreement between the two great rival factions could be reached so as to give confidence in the scrupulous observance of any plan for ruling out nuclear warfare, that would itself involve a complete system of inspection and control of almost every detail of industrial production and scientific research.

'If we could reach agreement on that, surely we could reach such a degree of understanding that it ought not be difficult to reach agreement on the rest. If we can go some of the way, we ought to go the whole way. What I say we cannot afford to do is to go halfway and leave ourselves exposed.'

This was an argument not for nuclear disarmament but for total disarmament. These were, later, the arguments which the Russians were to use in their case for total disarmament.

'Genuine disarmament,' he said, 'must be based on two simple but vital principles. It must be comprehensive and it must provide a proper system of control. It must be comprehensive, by which I mean it must include all weapons, new and old, conventional and unconventional. The control must provide effective international, or if we like supernational authority invested with real power. Hon. Members may say that this is elevating the United Nations, or whatever may be the authority, into something like world government. Be it so, it is none the worse for that. In the long run this is the only way out for mankind.'

The least convincing part of his speech were the passages in which he endeavoured to reply to the criticisms that had been made in the debate of the Government's plans for Civil Defence. It was certainly a rather large claim to make that the Government had 'a clear and coherent scheme' for the Civil Defence Service. It was 'a plan upon which we can build up and develop as our knowledge grows'. But the more our knowledge grew about the area which would be devastated in the event of an explosion of a hydrogen bomb over Britain, the more the scepticism of what could be done by the Civil Defence plans grew. 'It may not be a complete defence,' he said, 'but it is a mitigation. Surely to say that there is no mitigation, that there is nothing we ought to do except to lie down, is to make an assumption that we have no right to make. It would be simply taking a defeatist or a disinterested attitude.'

He tried to make up for the obvious futility of the Civil Defence plans in the White Paper by a burst of rhetoric. 'We must make these preparations for home defence,' he said, 'proudly and boldly, to let the aggressor know what is the mood of a people who have been often bent but never yet broken. This is an essential part of the deterrent itself.' Remembering what Attlee had said, that one hydrogen bomb could make an area the size of Wales unsafe for human beings, and that any potential enemy would know this too, one did not feel that he would be impressed by the nature of our Civil Defence.

He ended with a quotation from John Bunyan in which Bunyan had seen

' . . . the country beyond the Valley of the Shadow of Death, and also out of the reach of Giant Despair; neither will they from this place so much as see Doubting Castle.'

No doubt it was as good a peroration as could be found in the Book of Quotations. But then Bunyan lived before the discovery of the hydrogen bomb.

CHAPTER XI

DUET WITH MOLOTOV

EDEN'S first task on becoming Prime Minister in April 1955 was to find someone who would succeed him at the Foreign Office. His first thought was of Lord Salisbury, who was 'exceptionally experienced and qualified for the post'. He had the 'greatest admiration' for his mind and character.

But Lord Salisbury sat in the House of Lords and (unlike Macmillan, who later appointed Lord Home as his Foreign Secretary) came to the conclusion that a Foreign Secretary must be in the House of Commons.

Eden explained in his memoirs that he could not make Lord Salisbury his Foreign Secretary because there was a 'danger of misunderstanding if foreign policy statements, or an important part of them, were made in the Upper House and if the main debates were held there'. He felt it 'impossible to ask a member of the House of Lords to be Foreign Secretary'.

He then offered it to Macmillan whose 'active and fertile mind would work well with the high quality of Foreign Office leadership under Sir Ivone Kirkpatrick which he was to inherit'.

He thought that Macmillan had 'brilliantly fulfilled the housing programme' which he himself considered over-ambitious but had not been so happy at the Ministry of Defence under Churchill, 'who had never accepted in his heart the position of a Minister of Defence divorced from his own authority'. In impatient moments Churchill would sometimes murmur that 'the post did not exist'.

With Lord Salisbury ruled out, Harold Macmillan was an obvious second choice. He had been Minister in North Africa during the war and was experienced in diplomatic negotiations. In that capacity he had met Americans, Russians and French and spoke French, it was said, like a native.

Then he had presence, deportment, and looked like a Foreign Secretary. He did not look rather out of place at the Foreign Office like Ernest Bevin and Morrison sometimes did. He was

Eton, Oxford and the Guards, exactly the kind of 'old school tie' idea of what a Foreign Secretary ought to be.

He harmonized with the place like any of the old Victorian furniture that was there. Even if he were to make blunders he could at least pronounce the place names properly. He would be able to entertain the representatives of foreign governments with decorum and dignity.

Perhaps Eden thought that it would be the same in the Foreign Office as it had been at the Ministry of Defence and that he as Prime Minister would remain supreme overlord in the realm of foreign affairs which he knew so well.

Macmillan was not destined to remain at the Foreign Office long and when he changed places again the following year people wondered why.

Eden may have discovered that Selwyn Lloyd had 'a more active and fertile mind' still.

Certainly Eden remained very much in the picture as far as foreign affairs were concerned.

Macmillan did however arrive in the Foreign Office in time to be present at what was an important and significant international event, the signing of the Austrian Treaty which took place in Vienna on May 15, 1955.

It was indeed a historic occasion.

The Foreign Ministers of Britain, France, the United States, Russia and Austria signed the Treaty in the Belvedere Palace and afterwards went out on the balcony and received an enthusiastic ovation from a crowd of many thousands assembled in the gardens of the Palace.

The cheering went on for nearly an hour. The Austrian people were overjoyed that a Treaty had been concluded which guaranteed their neutrality. They would henceforth be as neutral as Sweden and Switzerland. They would be outside both NATO and the Warsaw Pact. They would not have to bear the cost of maintaining big armies nor burdened with a big armaments bill. Their joy was due to the fact that the people who had known the horrors of two world wars and had been in the middle of the maelstrom of the fighting in Europe believed that they had finished with wars and armies of occupation for ever.

They cheered the Ministers of the different countries over and over again. Molotov, who had signed for Russia, shook his

G

clasped hands above his head in the manner of a champion boxer. It was not because Molotov regarded it a victory for Russia over the West. It was a victory for peace and the Russians, like everyone else, had every reason for rejoicing that the problem of Austria had been solved by both sides agreeing to regard Austria as neutral. Macmillan, so *The Times* Correspondent reported, 'imitated the motions of a windmill' and Foster Dulles from America waved his handkerchief.

The Treaty when ratified would bring to an end ten years of armed occupation and would re-establish Austria as an independent and sovereign state. As a final gesture of conciliation Molotov conceded the Austrian request that the war guilt clause in the preamble should be dropped.

The signing ceremony was held in a setting of baroque splendour recalling the past glories of the Hapsburg Empire but about which the Austrian people no longer cared.

Molotov in a short speech paid tribute to Austria's struggle for freedom and said that the signing of the Treaty marked the beginning of a new development in international relationships. 'The Soviet Union,' he said, 'is anxious that the solution of the Geneva question should not be postponed but circumstances had proved this impossible. New obstacles had arisen seriously complicating the situation and the danger of the revival of an aggressive German militarism had forced the peace-loving European states to new measures for safeguarding their security.'

Molotov said that the signing of the Austrian Treaty was 'an event of the utmost world importance'.

He continued: 'This proves the existence of possibilities for the solution of other acute international problems.' He especially welcomed Austria's decision to become a neutral country, adding: 'There will now be a neutral Austria besides Switzerland in the heart of Europe'. He was convinced, he said, that other states should also follow this path.

Macmillan, who followed, said that a great honour had fallen to him, 'the honour of signing this long-awaited Treaty in the name of the Queen, my gracious Sovereign'. He added:

'It is a great honour, and a great fortune, for me to have been able to take some small part in the closing weeks of its ten-year history. But it is only right that I should pay tribute to the patient work in connection with the Treaty of the eminent men who preceded me at the Foreign Office—the late Mr Ernest Bevin, Mr Morrison and the present Prime Minister, Sir Anthony Eden.

'Over the last ten difficult years the Austrian people have shown their constancy and courage. Under their Coalition Government they have achieved great progress. Today's ceremony marks the beginning of a new epoch for Austria. It is a happy day for all of us. But for Austria itself it is also a day of challenge. In meeting that challenge she will know that she can always rely on the warm and steady friendship of the British people.'

Macmillan said this amid loud applause from all the delegates.

After the ceremony the Foreign Secretaries drove through the beflagged streets, cheered by enthusiastic crowds, to a luncheon given by the President of the Austrian Republic at the former Imperial Palace and attended a dinner later, given by the Austrian Chancellor.

The same night the Austrian Government published the text of a resolution which was to be placed before the Lower House of the Austrian Parliament as the first stage in implementing Austria's neutrality.

The most significant passages read:

'(1) Austria declares, with the object of the lasting and perpetual maintenance of her independence from without and the inviolability of her territory, as well as in the interest of maintaining internal law and order, of her own free will, her perpetual neutrality, and is resolved to maintain and defend it with all means at her disposal.

'(2) Austria, in order to secure these objectives, will in future join no military alliances and will not permit the establishment of military bases of foreign states on her territory. In this connection, she declares her desire to observe at all times in her relations with other states, the principles laid down in the United Nations Charter, and once again voices her willingness and ability to accede to and observe the obligations contained in the Charter.'

On his return to London Macmillan said at the airport:

'In the last eight or nine days a great deal has been done. The actual phrases do not fully describe the immense amount of work and effort which has gone to produce these results—the forming of a West European Union, the admission of Germany to NATO, and now the signature of the Austrian Treaty by the four powers. All these are a tribute to the steady efforts of long years. They are in fact the justification of the policy which Sir Anthony Eden has pursued—the policy of peace through strength. The fruits are beginning now to ripen. That is not to say there are not anxious and difficult times ahead. The breaking of the ice itself opens new problems of navigation. They will require the same combination of firmness and patience.'

Macmillan was entirely justified at this date in thinking that the signing of the Austrian Peace Treaty was 'the breaking of the ice jam' between East and West. Molotov was no longer saying 'Nyet' and the Russians were prepared to negotiate further.

They were asking why, if the Western Powers were prepared to agree to a neutral Austria, shouldn't they agree to a neutral Germany too. There was no fundamental difference of principle. Germany and Austria had fought against the Allies in two world wars and would not the setting up of a neutral Germany as well as a neutral Austria be a further and more important and final step towards a permanent peace settlement in Europe. There was logic in it. Austria had been occupied at the same time as Germany and through Austria as well as Germany had come the armies that had marched on Russia and which the Allies of the Second World War had united to destroy.

But whenever anyone had mentioned the proposal for a neutral Germany the old objection was raised: 'We could not have a vacuum in Central Europe'. The West was, however, quite prepared to take the risks as far as Austria was concerned. They were willing for Austria to become neutral and for a vacuum there. Although why a recognized neutral state, whose neutrality would be guaranteed by either side, should be regarded as a vacuum is not clear.

There were those who thought that it was quite impossible for Austria to become a neutral state and that the Soviet armies would immediately march in to fill the vacuum created by Austrian neutrality. That, however, did not happen. Six years later Kennedy and Khrushchev met in Vienna because Austria was neutral and had remained so after the Treaty of 1955 had been signed. Both sides had come to accept and recognize the neutrality of Austria as a fact. There was no trouble in Vienna as there was in Berlin.

In Vienna, Molotov and Macmillan and Foster Dulles had been able to appear side by side, to be greeted and cheered by an enthusiastic populace.

But immediately the Russians started talking about the neutrality of Germany the ice froze again.

The West had accepted the solution of a practically disarmed and neutral Austria. What they thought was good for Austria they held would be a calamity for Germany.

There were no signs that Macmillan, at the Foreign Office, was in this respect any more ready to pursue a new line of policy than any of his predecessors.

On June 22, 1955, Macmillan went to San Francisco to a celebration of the tenth anniversary of the United Nations. In a speech to the Assembly he said:

'Whatever the immediate future might bring, the United Nations must be preserved and cherished. Britain would continue to use and perfect "this unique instrument for international co-operation"—the only place in the world where all the world's problems could be considered as a whole. As it stood today, it probably represented the highest common factor of agreement among the powers; and it was still evolving. Such an organization of universal character matched the needs of the twentieth century, and if they were to avoid a third and far more terrible world war and build up the strength of the free peoples they would need the United Nations. After a long review of the United Nations record Mr Macmillan referred specifically to the imaginative proposal to create an international agency which would open the way to the use of atomic energy for the benefits and not for the destruction of mankind. This endeavour, he said, could be accurately described as spectacular and it was in the United Nations itself that President Eisenhower had announced it.'

Macmillan was enthusiastic about the United Nations as long as what happened there did not conflict with British policy.

The wholehearted enthusiasm he had shown about the United Nations, when he went to San Francisco, had evaporated when the United Nations opposed British and French aggression in Suez.

In July 1955 Macmillan, as Foreign Secretary, accompanied Eden to the Summit Conference at Geneva, but there is no evidence to show that he was the dominant personality or played a leading role there.

From Eden's memoirs one gathers that the Summit at Geneva was definitely a heads of Governments affair with Macmillan playing a secondary role behind the scenes, evidently being concerned with the U.S.A.-Chinese differences overseas, about which Eden noted:

'By the end of the Conference the Foreign Secretary and I were convinced that all present would have been sincerely happy to see the Off-Shore Islands sunk under the sea.'

But even though Macmillan had become something of an expert on the geography of South-East Asia, that did not convince Eden that he had become indispensable at the Foreign Office.

At Geneva, however, Macmillan had the opportunity of meeting an international personality of whom he was to see a great deal more later. His opposite number was Mr Molotov, who was on the eve of his way out. Bulganin and Khrushchev were there, the former as the figurehead and the latter as the authoritative figure in the Russian Delegation. Macmillan had the opportunity of conversations which must have shown him the fear of Germany which was even then dominant in the Russian mind.

It was one of the first opportunities he had of meeting Khrushchev, of whom he was tosee so much a few years later. It gave him the chance to study the new personalities who emerged in the Soviet Union and who were to direct its foreign policy in the following years. If he only acted in the role of a listener he must have learned a great deal of the problems that a British Foreign Secretary would have to face.

Eden and Macmillan had got on so well with the Russians that an invitation was extended to Bulganin and Khrushchev to visit London.

CHAPTER XII

PREMIUM BONDS AND A PIPE DREAM

ONE OF the first communications that Macmillan received
when he became Chancellor of the Exchequer was a memorandum from Eden on the economic situation.

Eden's views on economic questions were always rather naïve.
His memorandum ended:

'I am still troubled about building. Our two heavy import bills are
for coal and for steel. I presume that building is responsible for some
of the latter. I do not mean houses. I think the action we have taken
there is just right. Factory buildings will be affected by the credit
squeeze, but office building still seems to leap ahead. This last cannot
be so urgent. If we could find some way of checking office building
without re-imposing control this would help us to reduce our
imports.'

The reason given by Eden for transferring Macmillan to the
Treasury was that Butler had been there for four strenuous years
and needed a change. This time it lay between Macmillan and
Heathcoat Amory. The latter was, however, doing 'very well in
agriculture' and being only a new member of the Cabinet
'hardly possessed the authority for so senior an office'.

So on December 22, 1955, Harold Macmillan found himself
next door to 10 Downing Street, as Chancellor of the Exchequer.

Eden had certainly given Macmillan a rather difficult task.
How was it possible for anyone to check office building without
re-imposing control? If this was so vital a matter which was
seriously affecting our economy, why was Eden so frightened of
re-imposing control?

The obvious reason was that many of the Tory M.P.s behind
him were building the offices. Had the Government come out
with a curb on office building with control of the activities of
this form of private enterprise there would have been a Tory
revolt within twenty-four hours and Eden and Macmillan
instead of interchanging memoranda in Downing Street would
soon be writing their memoirs.

It is quite clear that Eden had realized the fact that big

business had run amok on office building, but he had no idea of how to stop it except by re-imposing building controls which the Tories had so strongly denounced when Labour was in office.

Eden went on:

As to this question of imports, I should be most reluctant to contemplate any return to licensing and Government control, as I am sure you would be. Is it not, however, possible to get something of the same results by other methods. Cannot the banks, for instance, be given some indication from time to time that such and such materials are those for the import of which we should be most reluctant to see money advanced. If something of this kind were practicable I should much prefer it to import control.'

But surely this meant some Government control over the bankers? What use would 'some indication' be if there was no power behind it?

Eden turned to the question of the cost of living. He went on:

'The most disturbing feature of our economy is that the Americans' cost of living and that of many other countries has remained about stable over the last four years while ours has climbed steadily, and of late sharply.

'I do not believe we can persuade the people of this country that the Government is tackling the cost of living by putting on more taxes, e.g. purchase tax, which would raise the cost of living and cause a scramble for the goods before they are taxed. Is there not some other way in which we could make a more evident frontal attack which would enlist their sympathy and support? That is what I had in mind when I suggested a reduction in the beer duty this autumn. I accepted that it was not appropriate then but I think it would be appropriate in the future and it would take (is it two points?) off the cost of living index. There are other measures of this kind that could be taken in the Budget to reduce the cost of living.'

This proposal for reducing the cost of living by a reduction of the beer duty was certainly a constructive suggestion which Eden could only have come to after a great deal of concentrated thinking on economic matters. It was not, however, highly original. It would hardly reduce the cost of living for those who did not drink beer. Then the Chancellor, having to find the money for defence, had to get it from somewhere. But it certainly would have been welcomed by the Tory Party's traditional friends, the brewers.

He then turned to the trade unions and the demand for increased wages:

'Now the trade unions do understand that if our costs go on rising we shall eventually price out of world markets and they will be the first to suffer. Therefore they will always lend a sympathetic ear to any doctrine aimed at avoiding this danger.

'If in addition to the measures I have suggested we could call for restraint in dividends and expenditure generally and produce an attractive savings programme, we should have a fair chance of enlisting their help in trying to keep wages steady over the next few years. We have simply got to do this somehow.'

Eden was certainly an optimist if he imagined that a call for restraint in dividends would be either welcome in the city or bring the trade unions over to the side of the Government.

One can only surmise what Macmillan thought when he received this naïve communication.

Of course Anthony couldn't expect to know as much about British economic and financial problems as he did about foreign matters like the 'Off Shore Islands' near the Chinese coast. But he was trying to be helpful.

One of the first events of Macmillan's term as Chancellor of the Exchequer was the raising of the bank rate on February 16th to what Gaitskell described as the 'unprecedented rate of five and a half per cent', which indicated that Britain was again facing a financial crisis, and this was followed on February 17th by a statement on the economic situation.

He announced that further measures were needed to deal with the strain on our balance of payments.

The Defence expenditure had gone up from £1,494 million to £1,499 million due to increases in Service pay, and the Civil Estimates for the year to £2,481 million.

As the Tories had been elected at the General Election on a programme for reducing Government expenditure only a few months before, this news was greeted with ironic cheers.

Macmillan announced that the measures to reduce this expenditure would include a reduction of the bread subsidy by a penny on the 7½d loaf and would mean an economy of £18 million a year. The retail price of milk would be put up by a halfpenny a pint from July 1st and this would save the Exchequer some £20 million a year.

The Liberal leader, Mr Clement Davies, asked the pertinent question that as the Government had known about 'the weak economic position of the country for some considerable time' why the statement had been so long delayed?

This was certainly not the picture of prosperity that had been presented to the country at the General Election.

There was a two days' debate the following week ending in a vote of censure motion on the Government.

Macmillan had the task of opening the debate.

Eden had expressed concern about the rate of office building but Macmillan brushed the idea of building controls aside and also any proposals for import controls. There were, however, to be restrictions on hire purchase, the Government had no fundamental objections to controlling that.

Macmillan said:

'The extension of the control of capital goods is a new feature. The reason is that the excess of investment demand is now plain for all to see and the nation cannot afford to let it be inflated yet further by credit from this source.'

We were evidently not able to afford the prosperity of which Macmillan had boasted at the General Election.

We were face to face with the economic consequences of the unplanned economy.

Harold Wilson described Macmillan's statement as profoundly disappointing and developed a long, devastating attack on the Government's lack of any real economic policy to deal with the situation. He dealt in detail with building. There had been an enormous increase in petrol stations, 1,100 new ones at an additional cost of £11,000,000 a year on unessential building while the Government were cutting down on the school building programme and council houses.

Wilson concluded with a warning about production:

'This country is lagging behind in production. We reject the Soviet methods, we reject the American methods. But this country is lagging behind; our production increase is limping year by year and, while those two nations are expanding their industrial base we are confining our increases in the main to some of the frivolities and inessentials which this country cannot at present afford.

'Without economic strength the voice of the nation will be muted, nor shall we have the means of helping nations less fortunate than ourselves.'

The Government had a comfortable majority but the economic problems of the unplanned and 'free for all' society remained.

It was a bad curtain raiser for Macmillan's year as Chancellor of the Exchequer.

Macmillan was to be Chancellor of the Exchequer for about a year and to introduce one Budget. One of his first tasks was to make a statement about the ending of the bread and milk subsidies. This was bound to lead to a rise in the cost of living, about which Eden had written in his letters and to inevitable demands from the trade unions which would add to the problem of inflation, and Macmillan had to defend the Government early in the year.

The Budget, however, was his great occasion. He began by recalling that the first Budget speech he had listened to in the House of Commons as a new Member was that of Winston Churchill in 1925. He remembered the scene vividly, 'how the dullest and most prosaic of topics leaped into life under his magic touch'.

It was during the debate on Churchill's Budget that Macmillan had made his maiden speech.

Since Churchill's day he had listened to many Budget speeches but he had often thought of Budget day as rather like a school speech day—a bit of a bore 'and he would try not to prolong the agony'. He certainly did not think 'it necessary to start with the usual long review of the events of the last financial year'. Probably this was a tilt at Sir Stafford Cripps who had thought that a Budget could only be understood against the economic background of the country. Cripps had felt it his duty to do this rather thoroughly and one had the impression that Macmillan was rather slurring over it and as he proceeded with his speech it was not as lively as Churchill's nor as learned as that of Cripps.

Next day Harold Wilson described it as a shambling, fumbling, largely irrelevant and at one point degrading speech'. 'The Chancellor told us that the Budget was prepared under the piercing eye of Mr Gladstone. There was one passage that was quite obviously written under a portrait of Horatio Bottomley. With few exceptions, the Chancellor's proposals were imprecise, not fully worked out and half-baked. They were the sort of thing we might have expected him to jot on the back of an envelope the day after he arrived at the Treasury.'

Macmillan's speech was certainly rather off-hand and hardly worthy of a great occasion. He had not even treated the House with the respect and courtesy of his predecessor, R. A. Butler.

One wondered whether it had been by accident or design that Macmillan had not dealt with the 'Economic Survey'.

Perhaps he was considerate of the House and did not wish to bore, but after all the House of Commons is not quite the same as a school prize day and should be capable of assimilating some economic facts, especially on a day on which it is supposed to be giving special consideration to the way Parliament is being called upon to decide on how the Government proposes to spend the nation's money.

And the Economic Statement had by no means been a reassuring document and had drawn attention to some disquieting facts. It had revealed that every other country in Europe had a better rate of industrial production than we had. While every other industrial country was increasing its production ours was falling. The economic barometers were showing disquieting signs not only that Britain was not forging ahead but lagging behind.

We were at least entitled to some explanation to the questions that were in the minds of M.P.s who had read the 'Economic Survey'.

But what Macmillan was serving up was the same old mixture that Butler had served up for the past four years, with the difference that as it was not Election year there was no £150,000,000 in tax concessions. It was the same mixture only being served up by a new and rather insolent-looking waiter, who gave the impression that he was not really concerned whether it was cold and unappetizing or not. There have been some strange Tory Budgets and strange Tory Chancellors during the last hundred years. When Lord Randolph Churchill had to stop in his Budget speech because he was puzzled 'by the damned dots' he could at least plead ignorance because he genuinely didn't know what decimals were doing in the Budget. Macmillan, however, could not plead ignorance about financial matters, for he had written quite a lot about them. Indeed he had made quite a reputation in the pre-war years by his books dealing with finance and industrial problems. One had expected to hear something new, some attempt at original thinking, some adequate attempt to outline Britain's economic future.

Yet there was only one thing that was new in his Budget; there were to be Premium Bonds !

He had hardly mentioned them to a surprised House of Commons than he was on the defensive, as if anticipating criticism.

'I have something completely new for the saver in Britain; that is a Premium Bond. Let me say that this is not a pool or a lottery, where you spend your money. The investor in the bond which I propose is saving his money. He will get it back when he wants it. But as long as he holds it saved, his reward, instead of interest, is the chance of winning a tax-free prize. The idea of course is not novel. Various forms of it have been advocated in the Press recently and schemes of this kind are being operated by the State in more than one country overseas. But hitherto the State in this country has fought shy of using chance as an incentive to save.'

There was the moral objection and the cost of the organization. He was obviously uneasy about this. He went on:

'Let me deal with the moral objection. This is not gambling, for the subscriber cannot lose. Let me put it this way. This is an encouragement to the practice of saving and thrift by those members of the community who are not attracted by the reward of interest, but do respond to the incentive of fortune. My object is to invite the people to save for interest—in which case they buy the new Defence Bonds —or save for the chance of a prize, according to their preference.

'There is a great deal of organization to do, but this is an outline of the essential features.'

The House was listening fascinated now, like a crowd in the market place listening to a tipster.

'It will be a £1 bond. There will be a limit on individual holdings— at any rate at first—for we want the savings of ordinary people. The limit might be 250 to start with, or a little more, I am not quite certain. A holder will get his pound back on giving due notice. Each £1 bond that has been held for a fixed period will qualify for a draw to take place every three months. As for the prizes, I have in mind, to begin with, an annual prize fund equal in amount to four per cent of the bonds drawn, divided into prizes ranging from a few top prizes of £1,000 to a larger number of prizes of similar amount.'

Horatio Bottomley certainly could not have explained it more persuasively, although he might not have discussed the morality of it in such detail.

It certainly got the headlines next day. The Budget of 1956 would go down into history as the Budget of Premium Bonds. Deny it as he might, what was it but a State Lottery? The people who bought the bonds, said somebody, would of course not be gambling with the principal but with the interest. It was fair comment. If the Chancellor had decided to go in for this sort of thing why need he have been so mealy mouthed about it? Didn't they gamble on the Stock Exchange? There was one thing to be said for Premium Bonds from the Government point of view: it distracted public attention from the rest of the Budget, from the fact that the withdrawal of the bread subsidy would mean a rise in the price of bread, from the fact that the tax on tobacco would be an injustice to the old age pensioner, whose special concession was to be withdrawn, and from the fact that there was to be no taxation on capital gains.

As for the failure of the Budget to face up to the bigger issues of the rise in prices and the threat of inflation and the whole future of the economy, when did the British public understand the things that result in economic crisis until it is upon them?

There was an interesting debate on the whole question of Premium Bonds at a later stage in committee on the Finance Bill. The Chancellor again spoke eloquently on the morality of his proposals. The debate on morality and taxation ranged rather wider. Someone asked him where he was going to draw the morality line. Would he be prepared to take increased taxation under Schedule D for an immoral house?

He replied indignantly, 'I know of no basis for that distinction. I think it is absolutely wrong and vile. The Right Hon. Gentleman says I should take the profit of a bawdy house. Never when I am Chancellor of the Exchequer—no!'

He made a generous concession to those who were doubtful about the ethics and morality of his Premium Bonds. They would definitely not be allowed to be sold to children under sixteen!

He was evidently concerned about the morality argument and embarked upon a dissertation about the attitude of the Church to gambling:

'As I say, I have a deep respect for those who believe a prize to be wrong. Among them I specially include, of course, the leaders of my own Church, some of whom expressed that view. However, I am fortified by very strong opinions of leading theologians on the other side. The Bishop of Exeter, for example, came out very strongly the other way only a few days ago.

'As a matter of pure theory I wonder why a prize is thought to be disreputable when interest has become respectable. Of course there was a long period in the history of the Church when exactly the opposite view was widely held. During the early years of the Christian era, interest was regarded as something wrong, being identified with usury; rent from real estate was all right but not interest upon money. I seem to remember, though it is many years ago now, reading a very interesting book by Mr Tawney on this very subject. However, times have changed and, with them, interest has become as it were sanctified. Under cross examination, that appeared to be the view of the Honourable Member from Wrexham. I do not know of any authoritative opposition to a prize based upon Scripture, or upon later theological authority. In any case I think it is an arguable point and I will not accept the accusation of heresy for putting forward a view that a prize is not in itself something which it is wrong to receive.

The theme evidently appealed to the argumentative Scot in him for he defended his plan at great length.

There was a more materialistic line of argument to which he had no convincing answer.

Would not the money invested in Premium Bonds come from money which would have been invested in savings anyway and the money diverted from other Government Bonds?

The Banker pooh poohed the idea that Premium Bonds would bring in extra savings. It said:

'Only a small proportion of the expected additional net flow into National Savings media is likely to be provided by a genuine net addition to real saving, and the bigger the flow, the smaller the proportion will be. Most of the demand, and almost the whole of the initial demand, will come from switches, direct or indirect, from existing bank balances—balances in the banks, the building societies and even the hire purchase finance companies.'

On the whole it hardly seemed likely that a new way of greatly increasing savings which would help the financial crisis had been discovered in the Chancellor's plans for Premium Bonds.

Macmillan's Budget had a bad hammering in the House and his defence at the end of the debate was unconvincing and he seemed to realize it.

He fell back on his favourite debating point—the record of the Labour Government in 1951—abusing his opponents was always his line in times of difficulty. He turned on Gaitskell, who had spoken before him, and said:

'Let us take a quick look at his Budget in loving retrospect—a "flash back" I think it is called. There was sixpence on Income Tax, on all rates, standard or reduced. Purchase tax was doubled on cars, wireless sets and refrigerators. Petrol tax was up. Initial allowances were suppressed completely. Entertainments tax was up on cinemas and racing. The National Health Service charges were introduced for the first time. [Hon. Members: 'Why?'] Why? Because the Labour Government had made such a mess of it.

It was his usual getaway. In 1951 he had been one of the supporters of the rearmament programme and the Korean War which had been the main causes of Gaitskell's Budget. Then he had no complaint. Had he objected to the raising of the Health Charges? Not at all. If the Labour Government had made a mess of it in 1951, Macmillan had been up to the eyes in the mess too. It was a typically Macmillan speech. It delighted his supporters—but the economic problems with which his Budget had failed to deal remained.

He was not Chancellor of the Exchequer for the next Budget. He bequeathed the problems to his successor. Nobody could claim that his period at the Treasury was one of the great achievements of his career. In the words of the jockey in *The Arcadians*, it had been 'a short life and a gay one'.

In the summer he had to face another vote of censure on the decision of the Treasury to approve of the financial arrangements involved in the acquirement of control of the Trinidad Oil Company by the Texas Oil Company, under which British interests in the company and the industry were acquired by America.

Not only was the Texas Company acquiring control over the life of a British colony but over a part of petrol distribution in this country too. But it had been a good thing for the speculators and the Stock Exchange was in favour of it.

Macmillan yielded to the Stock Exchange. It was one of the big financial sell-outs. British interests were completely sacrificed to an American oil company and to the City.

The most notable speech that he made during his term as Chancellor of the Exchequer was the one he delivered to the Foreign Press Association at a lunch on May 6, 1956.

He devoted a part of his speech to showing how much Britain was spending on defence compared with other countries.

He said:

'Organization for European Economic Co-operation have recently begun to publish national income figures of member countries, made as far as possible internationally comparable. Their latest figures are for 1954: but the 1955 picture is unlikely to have been much different.

'In 1954, we in Britain devoted nine per cent of our national income—or, to be technically precise, our gross national product at market prices—to defence.

'The figure for all other OEEC countries put together was five per cent. France, with seven per cent, was above that average; so was the Netherlands, with six per cent.

'At the other end, Denmark was three per cent; Western Germany and Norway four per cent.

'I know the precise percentages may vary a little, with different definitions of defence. But I don't think there's much doubt that, broadly speaking, it is true to say this: compared with the rest of Western Europe, we are devoting nearly twice as large a share of our resources to defence.

'Suppose our figure, too, was five per cent, not nine per cent.

'I think this particular piece of speculative arithmetic is illuminating—indeed, tantalizing. Our defence programme would be, not over £1,500 million a year, but about £800 million, giving £700 million worth of spare resources.

'If we got only half of that £700 million shifted into exports, it would completely transform our foreign balance.

'And if we got the other half shifted into fixed investment, there would be a good deal less critical comment about our low investment percentage. Seven hundred million pounds worth of extra resources devoted to defence can make a lot of difference to an economy.

'That extra £700 million is the more tantalizing because it would not only be a freeing of resources: it would mean a cut in Government expenditure.

'That would be a most welcome relief.

'At present the central Government's expenditure in Britain is a higher percentage of the national product than it is in any other country in Europe. Reduce defence spending by £700 million and it would resolve one of the Treasury's main dilemmas—that it is dangerous to reduce taxation until we get more savings: and it is dreadfully difficult to get more savings until we reduce taxation.

'With £700 million off Government expenditure, I would certainly be able to make considerable reductions in taxes. This would be one way of encouraging more savings and of financing more investment. Big reductions in taxation might have other far-reaching effects too.

He went on to discuss how Britain's heavy defence expenditure handicapped us in other ways.

'So—to any who may have commented in recent years that we were not making the economic running in the European race—let me just comment: it does slow up a person's running pace a bit, if he has to carry two rifles, not one.

'It is not only that our defence programme is so much heavier in total. It also catches us at a number of particularly weak spots.

'Our two-year conscription period, with no exemptions for skilled

H

technicians, makes it very difficult to find the manpower we need—and we are short of labour in Britain.

'Then the fact that we have heavy military expenditure overseas, and that it has risen very fast in the last five years, catches us in our balance of payments—always a tender spot.

'In 1950, overseas military expenditure was about £100 million. Last year it was just on £160 million. One hundred and sixty million pounds, to give you an order of magnitude, equals all the exports of our tractor industry, and of our agricultural machinery industry, plus all our exports of aircraft, plus, for good measure, our total exports of whisky and of cocoa preparations—all gone down the drain, as it were, to pay for our military expenditure abroad.

'So it is not surprising, I think, that we are not very keen to make the figures even bigger.

'So much for the extra burden of defence.'

Macmillan must have given a great deal of thought to preparing this speech and it was all the more interesting because he already had been in the Foreign Office.

As Chancellor of the Exchequer he had now to find the money for defence which amounted to £1,500,000,000 a year. He would certainly be a popular Chancellor of the Exchequer if he could get national expenditure by reducing this. He certainly was correct in pointing out that conscription was costly and a drain on our manpower, and that overseas military expenditure was a heavy handicap on the British economy—'all gone down the drain as it were'—from the point of view of increasing production.

He had produced sound arguments for reducing defence expenditure. But what was he going to do about it? Was he embarking on another of his crusades? He was always announcing some new crusade and then retreating from it. He was the Grand Old Duke of York of politics, marching his crusaders to the top of the hill and then marching them down again. He retreated from this one almost as soon as he had announced it—in the same speech.

But having stated the problem, he proceeded hastily to say:

'Of course, these calculations about a spare £700 million are a pipe dream; we know we can't have it. We are not going to behave in an irresponsible way. It is true that we are looking for a cut of £100 million in Government expenditure, and defence may well have to find part of that; but it won't find it all. By and large, we shall go on carrying our second rifle.'

A lunch of the Foreign Press Association was a curious place to have a pipe dream of this kind. Having stated the problem he gave no indication that he was prepared to agree to a really drastic cut in this heavy expenditure on the Army, Navy and Air Force.

Perhaps he remembered what had happened to Lord Randolph Churchill, who had been Chancellor of the Exchequer over half a century before.

Lord Randolph Churchill had not only said that in those days the War Office was getting too much money. He fought the War Office and lost and resigned. Macmillan was evidently not prepared to do anything so drastic as this.

One of the reasons Aneurin Bevan and Harold Wilson had resigned from the Labour Government was the cost of rearmament. Macmillan was not prepared to do this.

CHAPTER XIII

THE SUEZ ADVENTURE

WHEN Anthony Eden succeeded Winston Churchill as Prime Minister few people dreamt that he would be out of office two years afterwards broken, discredited and almost forgotten. For Eden had all the qualifications to be a popular, conventional Conservative Prime Minister. His background, like Macmillan's, had been Eton, Oxford and the Guards; he was good looking, he had long experience at the Foreign Office before and during the war and in Churchill's Government. He made a good impression on foreign governments, was not regarded as belligerently anti-Russian and if our relations with the Soviet Union could be improved through the channels of orthodox diplomacy he was as likely to achieve this as any other British politician. Indeed in the first eighteen months of office Eden had shown promise of becoming a successful Prime Minister, popular in the House of Commons and an asset to the Tory Party in the country.

And then like a bolt from the blue came Suez. How in his years of obscurity and retirement must he have hated that fatal word—Suez—and everything connected with it.

His autobiography throws very little light on how he came to decide on this fatal gamble, the collapse of which sent him crashing to his political downfall. One would have thought that Eden was intelligent and progressively minded enough to have realized beforehand that this sort of adventure was not for the twentieth century. The more one reads the history of the events that led up to Suez the more one wonders why any Cabinet of intelligent and reasonable men should have decided to take the clear and obvious risks involved in a military attack on Egypt, to say nothing of the way it was done.

However one looks at it in retrospect, Suez was a criminally stupid international adventure completely indefensible as an act of foreign policy. From a military point of view it was open to devastating criticism and from a financial and economic point of view it was an act of utter folly.

"Not guilty!"

1 June 1957—Although dismantling step by step the Suez Policy, the Prime Minister still claimed that it "has been right".

['Vicky'—Evening Standard]

When the Suez crisis burst Harold Macmillan was Chancellor of the Exchequer, the Minister in charge of British finances. From the point of view of the Chancellor of the Exchequer what was there to be gained from a war with Egypt over Suez?

One would have thought that if any Minister would have been compelled to urge restraint, caution and discretion on such as issue it would be the Chancellor of the Exchequer. After all Macmillan had written a couple of short books which indicated that at one time he had been thinking in terms of economics. He was not a Right-wing imperialist like Amery nor regarded as a crusted old diehard like Captain Waterhouse. They were the natural leaders of the irresponsibles of the Suez Group. There is still a veil of mystery hanging over what happened in the Cabinet over Suez, which, Macmillan, by his refusal to appoint a Select Committee of Inquiry, has not helped to lift.

When the plans for military intervention were being worked out, did any warnings or objections come from Macmillan? Certainly there was alarm in certain quarters at the Treasury. That was shown by the courageous resignation of Sir Edward Boyle, the Parliamentary Secretary to the Treasury.

Sir Edward Boyle was not regarded as one of the impetuous or impulsive members of the Government. He was a young man at the beginning of his political career and would hardly have resigned if he had not felt strongly on the matter. It would be interesting to know what advice Macmillan received from the more experienced civil servants at the Treasury about Government policy in Suez.

The Government, we were repeatedly told, was anxious to reduce expenditure. Macmillan had said so in his Budget speech. To embark on a costly invasion of Suez was a curious way of going about it. There would have to be additional expenditure on all the armed forces, there were the possibilities of our being involved with other countries. True a spectacular victory over Nasser might add to the Government's prestige, but even if the attack succeeded and Nasser were overthrown that would mean re-occupying the Canal Zone and perhaps the greater part of Egypt, which would be a very costly affair indeed.

Whether we won or lost in a war with Nasser it would certainly mean finding extra millions in taxation.

One wonders whether Macmillan as Chancellor of the

Exchequer, and responsible for the financial affairs of the nation, seriously considered the possible economic consequences of Suez.

On the contrary was it not his plain duty to warn Eden and the Cabinet that this was likely to be a disastrous adventure?

One hint from Macmillan that he would resign from his post as Chancellor of the Exchequer if the Government went ahead with an armed attack on Egypt and that would have been the end of it.

What economic advantages could possibly come out of an attack on the Suez Canal Zone? It was true that a large supply of our oil came from the Middle East via the Suez Canal and some of the supporters of the venture argued that military action would be justified because it would safeguard our oil supplies and keep the Canal open to British shipping. Did the Cabinet look ahead at all? Did they realize that there was a possibility of sabotage in the Canal and that it could be blocked by the sinking of a few ships? Did they realize that the cutting of the oil pipes would effectively stop the supply of the precious oil?

One could understand the War Office or the Admiralty or the Air Force thinking that there were chances of a glorious victory in Suez. But the Chancellor of the Exchequer! Surely he would see both the short term and the long term stupidity of it and especially when it became clear that America was against military intervention in Egypt and that Russia was preparing for action.

Policy was being decided by an inner Cabinet of which Macmillan was a member. And instead of being against Suez he was in favour of it.

Our finances were in such a serious condition that one of the first actions of Eden, when he had appointed Macmillan to be Chancellor of the Exchequer, was to ask him to reduce Government expenditure. He had written to him when he had taken over: 'We are right to expand but now we have done it we are bursting at the seams'. He had drawn his attention to the 'continuing fall in the value of money'. He had stressed the importance of saving 'which by reducing demand on goods would directly help against inflation', referred 'to our excessive spending as a nation' and added 'that the trade unions do understand that if our costs go on rising we shall inevitably price ourselves out of world markets and they will be the first to suffer'.

FAMILY GROUP

['Low' in *The Guardian*]

'Will the gentleman in the hat please smile'

Eden had called 'for restraint in expenditure generally'. He had again written to Macmillan in a minute in April, expressing concern about the economic situation and urging the need for economy: 'We should do all we can to discourage wage demands both by explaining that the true interest of the community lies in price stability and also by doing what we can to keep prices stable when they are in our control . . . I am sure that it would be dangerous to do nothing about the inevitability of price increases over the rest of the year.'

Eden had apparently forgotten all about the economic situation of the country in his determination to inflict humiliation on Nasser.

Had the Chancellor of the Exchequer done his duty he would have reminded him of these warnings and told Eden that we could not afford any foreign adventures!

Instead of this he backed him up in the inner Cabinet. The only person whom rumour said to be urging caution and common sense was Butler.

In his memoirs Eden tells us that Macmillan, after a visit to America, said 'that he found Washington confident that six months of economic pressure upon Nasser would accomplish all he wanted. On this point I was less sanguine, especially as nearly two months had passed since the Canal had been seized and user nations were still as far as ever from applying any effective pressure, economic or otherwise'. Eden went into the Suez business, he says, with his Cabinet behind him.

'There were, of course, shades of opinion, but these did not obtrude. The points of view ranged from that of the Minister who fervently informed Mr Dulles at the United States Embassy that we would go through with the business, even if it meant "pawning the pictures in the National Gallery", through those who were quietly determined, to the more cautious characters who, whether from conviction or loyalty, were there all the same.'

It is a pity that Sir Anthony Eden was not more precise. Posterity surely deserves to know who the Minister was who was prepared to pawn the pictures in the National Gallery to pay for Suez.

Marshal Bulganin had sent a note which Eden declares was 'threatening'. But there were also intimations from USA.

A run on the pound, at a speed which threatened disaster to

our whole economic position, had developed in the world's financial markets.

Had the Treasury or the Chancellor of the Exchequer not thought that this was likely to happen?

Eden says that two months earlier the Cabinet had considered the financial consequences of taking action at Suez. 'The cost of the military precautions had been some £12 million. Holding our proposed operation in readiness from mid-September onwards had been costing us about £2,000,000 a month. The operation itself was estimated to cost about £100,000,000, equivalent to one-sixteenth of the annual cost of the defence programme. The Treasury had felt satisfied that these outlays could be borne without undue stress, though if the canal were blocked and the pipeline were cut indefinitely our balance of payments would be endangered.'

But Macmillan should have foreseen them and warned his colleagues of the risks they were running. There was increasing speculation against sterling, largely in America. Later on Macmillan gave the House the figures.

The pressure against sterling increased at the beginning of November. Our reserves fell by fifty-seven million dollars in September, eighty-four million in October and 279 million in November (this represented about fifteen per cent of our total gold and dollar reserves).

Macmillan should have been warning the Cabinet about the risks to the pound which would be inevitable if it went on with the military adventure in Suez.

If the Treasury had been so satisfied about the prospects why had Sir Edward Boyle resigned?

There was always a curious naïveté about Eden's references to financial problems and this was one of them. From this, however, it seems that the Government had been warned by the Treasury about the danger of running into a financial crisis.

But the financial consequences of going on with the Suez operation had not quite been foreseen.

There was growing alarm in the Treasury and on Tuesday, November 6th, Macmillan was told that the expected run on the pound had increased to such an extent that it was down to its maximal level of 2·78 dollars. The holders of sterling were afraid of what might happen to their money in the event of war. Any Chancellor of the Exchequer should have realized this.

In New York the Bank of England had been compelled to

support the market by buying blocks of sterling at £1,000,000, a much higher rate than the usual.

The Treasury also made it clear that if the Bank of England did not step in through the exchange equalization account it would be impossible to maintain the level of the pound that day.

The Americans were determined to exert every possible financial pressure on the British Government. Macmillan had to phone to Washington to appeal for an immediate loan of 1,000,000,000 dollars to save the pound. Washington replied that night that the money would only be forthcoming if Britain accepted the cease-fire by midnight. That settled the matter. The Cabinet had to yield. The Suez adventure was over. The cease-fire came into operation at midnight.

There must have been many dramatic scenes in the Cabinet Room at 10 Downing Street during these days.

If ever Macmillan's life story is filmed for television in the way that Churchill's was, some producer should have an opportunity for exciting shots of the Cabinet meetings during the Suez crisis. There could be one very dramatic one of Macmillan on the phone to Washington begging the Americans to lend the money to save the pound.

Ultimately the pound was saved but it would never have been in danger had the Chancellor stood firm to stop the policy that had resulted in the run on it in New York.

It was left to another Chancellor of the Exchequer to try to explain exactly what Suez had cost the British Exchequer. On February 3, 1959, Mr Amory was asked by Mr Arthur Lewis to give the total estimated cost to Great Britain of the recent Suez war, taking into account the actual cost of the military operations, the loss of arms and equipment at the Suez base, the loss of the Suez Canal; and using as the basis the total revenue received by Great Britain in the year preceding the Suez war, as a result of imports and exports between Great Britain and Egypt what has been the loss to British trade to date due to the severance of trade with Egypt?

Amory replied: 'The net extra expenditure incurred by the Service Departments on special measures taken in connection with the Suez emergency was estimated in their appropriate accounts at some £25 million. The value of the Suez base installations and the stores contained in it was estimated at some £60 million, though this was in no sense a realistic value in conditions of a forced sale. It is not possible to draw up any balance sheet of the cost of Suez operations to the United Kingdom in the absence of knowledge of what otherwise might have happened.'

Later on, when he was Prime Minister, Macmillan was asked if he would appoint an official historian of the Suez war. He gave the expected reply: 'No, Sir'.

John Strachey then asked him: 'While fully understanding the Prime Minister's reluctance to appoint an official historian, may I ask him whether he would agree that all the said historian would discover would be that the Government adopted in these matters a wrong policy and mounted a wrong military operation directed at the wrong objectives, which they then failed to take?'

Macmillan replied that the matter was discussed after the publication of General Keightley's dispatches.

He refused, too, to appoint a Select Committee of Inquiry into the Suez operations. Aneurin Bevan asked him: 'Why is the Prime Minister so coy about it? Is he afraid of what might be revealed about himself?' He replied: 'No Sir, and I shall welcome when the time comes [interruption]—it may come sooner than Hon. Members think—the opportunity to put these matters to the inquest of the nation'.

Colonel Wigg, speaking in a later debate, argued that there were many precedents for a Select Committee of Inquiry into unsuccessful military operations. He pointed out that Select Committees had inquired into the campaigns of the Dardanelles and Mesopotamia.

He said: 'It is very relevant for the British people to know whether the people running the country are still proud of Suez. The Prime Minister has said that the people will decide. They will, but in a democracy the people cannot decide until they are given the facts on which to decide. Democracy does not function when only one version of the facts and one selection of the secret papers are given out. . . . Here is a Government that claims to be proud of themselves, confident of their Suez record. If the Prime Minister and the Foreign Secretary are confident of their record they have one simple way of proving it—they can submit themselves to cross-examination by a Select Committee of the House. Why should they be afraid of a Select Committee if they are confident that the secret documents are on their side?'

Aneurin Bevan wound up the debate for the Opposition. He said: 'The Opposition are not basing their request for a Select Committee upon newspaper articles. They are basing it on new facts, one of which has emerged this evening from the speech of the ex-Secretary for War (Brigadier Head) in which he accused his ex-colleagues of having deliberately planned what they knew to be almost a suicidal operation and then ran away from its consummation.'

Head had said in his speech that the Suez operation was placed so to speak in a strait-jacket. 'From the day we got out of Egypt the nearest deep water port in the Eastern Mediterranean was Malta. Hon. Members may ask, "Why not make one in Cyprus?" But from a financial and engineering point of view it was impracticable and on that day the nearest deep-water port to Port Said was Malta . . . Whatever Hon. Members may think of this operation, therefore, its form was dictated by geography and ports——' At this point Aneurin Bevan intervened to ask, 'Was not that known at the time?'

Head replied: 'Of course it was well known. Nobody could have planned any operation to take place without being aware of that fact. It should have been apparent to anybody who either studied or thought about the operation. As far as I know nobody has made any attempt to conceal that this was so.'

John Strachey rose to ask the inevitable and obvious question: 'Does the Right Hon. Gentleman not see that what he is proving by dilating on "the military strait-jacket", as he called it, of this operation is that the conditions were such that it was bound to produce the terrible disaster which it did produce and that he is just proving up to the hilt our case against the folly of the Government?'

Clearly Macmillan shared the responsibility for Suez. But whatever the military, economic and financial consequences of Suez were, the political consequences were that Sir Anthony Eden ceased to be Prime Minister. When Anthony Eden resigned in January 1957 the choice was between Butler and Macmillan. Back bench Tories were under the impression that Butler had been hostile or lukewarm over Suez. Macmillan had been pro-Suez. It spoiled Butler's chances. They preferred Macmillan as Prime Minister.

CHAPTER XIV

BUTLER OR MACMILLAN?

VERY few people could have imagined in 1956 that in 1957 Harold Macmillan would have been called to Buckingham Palace and invited to form a Ministry.

Before Suez very few people at Westminster thought about Macmillan as the next Prime Minister. The betting would have been ten to one on Butler.

Francis Boyd, the well-informed correspondent of *The Guardian*, wrote in a short biography of Butler published a year before:

'I have no doubt myself that if a vacancy were to occur in the leadership of the Conservative Party within the near future, Mr Butler would not only be chosen to fill it, but would be better qualified than any other member of his Party to do so.'

That indeed was the prevailing view of Tory M.P.s at the time. Many of them were as surprised as the public outside when they heard the news that Macmillan had been chosen to be Prime Minister. He was not the Leader of the Conservative Party. He had not been elected by any democratic process. The rank and file of the Tory Party in Parliament had not voted on it. Had there been a ballot vote, similar to the one held when a Leader of the Labour Party is elected, Butler might have won.

It was all decided behind the scenes by the Establishment. Butler may have been 'better qualified than any other member of the Party'. The Tory M.P.s were not placed in any dilemma. The choice was made for them.

The sudden collapse of Eden was quite unforeseen and many people had assumed that Butler was the next in succession. Probably Butler thought so himself because during Eden's absence abroad he had presided over the meetings of the Cabinet. He was also Leader of the House of Commons as well as Home Secretary. Why then was Butler not called to Buckingham Palace instead of Macmillan?

In his book *The Modern British Monarchy*, Sir Charles Petrie tells us that the change from Eden to Macmillan 'presented no special difficulty' to the monarch, 'though in some quarters there was a tendency to make a quite unnecessary mystery about it?' He adds: 'The Queen consulted Lord Salisbury and Winston Churchill, and she also asked the advice of the outgoing Premier, Eden, who is generally believed to have been in favour of Macmillan; what is above dispute is that she acted constitutionally, and that she chose the man who carried the greatest weight with the Government's supporters. This has only served

[*Daily Mirror*]

to prove the correctness of her choice.' In his memoirs, however, Eden does not say whom he recommended and if he had recommended Macmillan one wonders why Lord Salisbury and Churchill were brought in afterwards. Surely there was no necessity. It was explained at the time that Lord Salisbury was invited to Buckingham Palace because he was Leader of the House of Lords. Churchill was of course an ex-Prime Minister but ex-Prime Ministers are not usually consulted on such occasions.

But if it was necessary to consult the Leader of the House of Lords why was it not equally necessary to consult the Leader of the House of Commons?

The Leader of the House of Commons was, of course, R. A. Butler. If he had been called in what would he have said? He would have been perfectly entitled to say that he could form a Ministry himself, for the Conservative Party in the House does not appear to have met and Butler had filled Eden's place in his absence.

Commenting on Eden's resignation, the Political Correspondent of *The Times* (10.1.57) said:

'Although no information on this point was available last night it seems probable that the Queen may have sought his advice as to his successor. It is the Queen's prerogative to choose whom she wishes to form a Government, but in making her decision she may take advice from any experienced counsellor, including the Prime Minister.

'It has generally been assumed that the natural successor to Sir Anthony Eden would be either Mr R. A. Butler, who is Lord Privy Seal and Leader of the House of Commons, or Mr Harold Macmillan, the Chancellor of the Exchequer. Mr Butler was, in effect, the acting Prime Minister during Sir Anthony Eden's recent absence in Jamaica and he has won for himself a commanding position in the party. But recent events have suggested that he may not be acceptable as Leader to the strong Right-wing element of Conservative M.P.s and Mr Macmillan might prove a more acceptable choice.

'On such advice as may be tendered to her the Queen will probably decide today or tomorrow to whom she should entrust the task of forming a new Government. In the circumstances of the case this decision may take a little longer than usual.'

In a leading article *The Times* speculated on the Queen's choice. It said:

'The choice who shall lead the Government rests with the Queen. The position is not unprecedented but it is unusual and not without difficulty. Constitutionally and theoretically the Queen can ask whoever she wishes to form an administration. Practically the choice must be primarily between Mr Butler and Mr Macmillan. It is not very likely that the leadership of the party would at the present time go outside these two. The balancing of what each has to offer the nation as Prime Minister is a matter of many different considerations. Mr Macmillan's gifts are obvious. He has shown a wise and firm hand at the Exchequer. He commands much support within the Conservative Party. Mr Butler, on the other hand, has for long been the hope and the leader of the young Conservatives. It is with the younger Conservatives and what they stand for that the future of the party must rest. Mr Butler, moreover, has acted on occasions when Sir Anthony Eden has been absent. Provided Mr Butler has fully recovered his health, vigour and grasp, he would seem the more likely to lead successfully the nation in its present strains and the

party at the next General Election. (There is no point in the idea of
Mr Macmillan as a stop gap Prime Minister with Mr Butler taking
over later. The Conservative Party cannot afford to have four leaders
within five years.) The nation has now to devise a new strategy in
world affairs and to engender a new dynamism and stimulus at
home. If ever there was a time for leadership it is now. We cannot
afford to improvise or compromise.'

The Political Correspondent of the *Manchester Guardian*
(10.1.57) expressed the view that Conservative M.P.s differed as
to who should become Prime Minister. He wrote:

'There is a strong element among Conservative M.P.s who blame Mr
Butler for having stayed Sir Anthony's hand in the Suez invasion.
As far as Suez is to be the test this element would prefer to serve
under Macmillan.

'Moreover the temper of the Conservative Party Conference at
Llandudno in October was hotly in favour of a militant Suez policy.

'On the other hand the cost of Suez is only too apparent and those
Tories who know that this country could not have afforded a long
campaign, who resent the breach in Anglo-American relations and
are sensitive about the damage to Commonwealth relations are on
the whole Butler men.

'Mr Butler also had a great personal success.

'Suez apart it would be astounding if in present circumstances
Mr Butler were not given the first invitation to form a Government.'

But there were elements strongly entrenched in the core of
the Tory Establishment who were determined that Butler should
not get this invitation. They were not afraid that he would fail
to form a government. What they feared was that he might have
been successful.

Next day it was announced that the Queen had sent for
Macmillan. Butler, who must have been keenly disappointed,
made the best of it and wished Macmillan the greatest possible
success. Commenting on the position the Political Correspondent
of *The Times* said:

'Mr Butler has never found too much favour with the Right-wing
element of the party and opposition to him as a potential Prime
Minister increased in recent weeks when the Suez crisis sharpened
and embittered party dissensions. It became clear that the active
Right-wing "Suez Group" of Conservatives and those sharing their
views would resist his selection as successor to Sir Anthony Eden—
although they had been clamouring for a new Prime Minister.

'There is powerful backing for Mr Butler in the party but the
impression has grown that those opposed to him were more likely to
make trouble in the event of his becoming Prime Minister than were

I

the smaller number of the Conservatives who may have been opposed to the selection of Mr Macmillan. Now that Mr Macmillan has been chosen the belief is that opposition to him in the party will be negligible and that he will command almost unanimous support from Conservatives. The Left wing and "middle of the road" Conservatives who would have preferred Mr Butler as Prime Minister have let it be known that their main concern is to restore unity in the party and they will undoubtedly exert all their efforts to this end by giving the new Prime Minister their full support.

The Times went on to recall Macmillan's housing achievements and continued:

'While Mr Butler is probably more in tune with the younger generation of Conservatives in the country, Mr Macmillan also enjoys a high reputation in the party—not least because of his great success when he was Minister of Housing and Local Government, in building the 300,000 houses a year—and more—which the Conservatives promised.'

Then it recalled that Macmillan had, in the now rather distant future, been a bit of a Left winger himself.

'Conservatives also remember Mr Macmillan as a leader of new thought in the party between the wars, whose ideas about social reform and industrial planning to relieve the misery of unemployment often startled the party leaders of those days. At that time, what were then regarded as his Left-wing notions about a better organization of society did not endear him to traditional Conservatives.

'In 1936 he voted against the National Government's decision to abandon the policy of sanctions against Italy, and afterwards refused the party whip and sat in the House for more than a year as an Independent Conservative. His keenest supporters in the party are confident that he will prove an imaginative and able Prime Minister.'

The editor of *The Times* in a leading article pointed out that 'many circumstances made this occasion when the Royal prerogative to choose a Prime Minister was no empty formality. After formal consultations with Lord Salisbury and Sir Winston Churchill she immediately summoned Mr Macmillan, who accepted her invitation to become Prime Minister.'

The editorial continued:

'Such consultations are among the most private proceedings of the Crown, and rightly so. Speculation would be irresponsible and comment has no basis to work upon. The Queen's Government having to be carried on by a working majority of the House of Commons, the essence of the inquiry must be to find out as definitely as possible who is most likely to command that majority and retain it. Generally the choice is obvious. Situations such as that which faced the Queen yesterday are not likely to recur often. If they did the modern difficulties of the position and the procedure would need to be examined more closely. For clearly it is almost an impossibility for the younger members of the dominant party to be consulted. With whom could a beginning be made? Where should it stop? Yet if an inquiry has to be confined to the elder statesmen is it not possible that where the balance is delicately poised and difficult to perceive instinct will most conscientiously be likely to point one way more than another.

'The ultimate responsibility, however, is the Queen's alone. It is a hard and heavy duty to discharge. She has discharged it. Time and events will show how wisely she has judged. Her House's record in these matters is a good one of sure instinct.'

The matter had evidently been decided by the Queen's instinct.

This view is hardly fair to the Queen. Constitutionally and theoretically the final choice lay with her. But what the Queen did was surely the culmination of a chain of events. It would be grossly unfair to blame the Queen for what ultimately happened to the country under Macmillan's Premiership or to place so much responsibility on her.

It could be argued, of course, that having consulted Lord Salisbury as Leader of the House of Lords that she should have consulted the Leader of the House of Commons. Was it really necessary for Sir Winston Churchill to be consulted? True he was an ex-Prime Minister. But so was Earl Attlee. Sir Winston Churchill, while being a distinguished personality in the House of Commons, was no longer in office but sat there as a Private Member. He held no office in the Government nor even in the Conservative Party. There was no precise precedent for calling in an ex-ex-Prime Minister to give his advice as to who should be chosen. Certainly Sir Winston knew far less of what was going on in the House of Commons in January 1957 than the Leader of the House, who was R. A. Butler. Sir Winston, it was hinted, preferred Macmillan to Butler because Macmillan had been one of his henchmen in pre-war days. But he had included Butler in his Cabinet and there was no logical reason why Churchill should have had the prerogative of picking potential Prime Ministers.

It has been argued that if Butler had been summoned to Buckingham Palace he would have had to say that he could not form a Ministry because his colleagues would not have served under him. There is no reason for believing this either. Had the news gone round that Butler had gone to Buckingham Palace and asked to form a Government it is hardly likely that all those who had been in Eden's Government would have been so unpatriotic as to go on strike. On the contrary they would have said 'The Queen's Government must be carried on' and accepted office. They would have been prepared to sacrifice themselves in the national interests and in twenty-four hours the Tory Party would have rallied round Butler as it rallied round Macmillan.

The Tory Party Establishment knew this quite well and so Butler was not given the chance to which he was entitled as the Leader of the House of Commons and as the one who had presided over the Cabinet in Eden's absence.

If Butler had become Prime Minister would Macmillan have served under him? Even to ask that question would be a reflection on Macmillan's patriotism too. He would not have deserted his country at its hour of crisis. It would have been a libel on Macmillan to argue that he would at such an emergency have gone on an unofficial strike.

There is little doubt that the main reason why Butler did not become Prime Minister was his attitude towards Suez whereas if the Tory Party had been really a party of patriots and statesmen that should have been in his favour.

One Tory M.P., at least, resented the way Butler had been treated.

Lord Lambton, writing in the *Evening Standard* two years later, said:

'There was no doubt at all that he was never enamoured of the Suez plan and that he openly and perhaps indiscreetly expressed these views.

'There is also little doubt that when the crisis was at its height he rather sank into the role of Cassandra and did not attempt to rally public support to the Government, but neither is there the slightest doubt that these are the only genuine criticisms which can be made of his conduct.

'Throughout the crisis, and once the operation was under way, he loyally stood by Sir Anthony Eden in the Cabinet. Nor should it be forgotten that the arguments which were finally to decide the operation were not put forward by him. Nevertheless there is no doubt at all that at the time of Suez nine Conservatives out of ten were privately convinced that Mr Butler had been the nigger in the wood pile. So great was his unpopularity that the Conservative Party regard him with such distrust that it would literally not have accepted him as Prime Minister.

'All along he had been against the Suez plan and now that he was proved right, the obvious thing was to make the most of it, and so it was whispered here, repeated there, ever gaining and magnifying, that Mr Butler had split the Cabinet against Sir Anthony Eden and so on, all without foundation, serving convenience not facts.

'This campaign against Mr Butler was singularly effective. It was also the most squalid political manoeuvre that I have ever been aware of and one which went to an inch of shocking me out of politics.'

When Macmillan was appointed Prime Minister *The Times* said:

'Mr Macmillan is essentially a man of good will and he has a capacity to engender it. He is a man of warm emotions and generous humanity. These can be great national assets at the top in politics. He is a man of energy. What he has done himself he should be able to inspire his subordinates to do. He is a man who at the Exchequer displayed a rather nice judgment and wisdom.'

One wondered whether this was a reference to Premium Bonds.

'His touch may not be absolutely sure in the House of Commons but he has shown he can strike exactly the right note. All these things should strengthen him in the great task he is about to undertake. At the same time Mr Macmillan is generally believed to be on the Right half of the party, as Mr Butler is acknowledged to stand on the Left. Right and Left are not happy descriptions. They have too many overtones and Mr Macmillan's rightness need not be overstated. In many ways he has been and is among the most progressive in the party. But it is fair to say that it is the older strain of Conservatism that is the more likely to welcome his appointment, just as it would have heartened more "the new Conservatism" if Mr Butler had been chosen.'

The Times went on to refer to Butler. 'After the defeat of 1945 it was largely Mr Butler and his young men who fashioned a new outlook and a new philosophy.' The existence of the old guard in the Tory Party could not be ignored.

'Their existence cannot be denied — their persistence cannot be ignored. They have not only to be endured but constantly rebuffed and rebutted. These things Mr Butler and the men who think like him have so far done. If he had become Prime Minister—leaving altogether on one side considerations which might be argued against that step—present forward positions would have been secure, the winning of new ground could confidently have been expected. The real measure of Mr Macmillan's success will be how far he can himself fulfil these hopes. There is only one road forward for Conservatism: there is no road back. However brilliant it may be in every other direction, the degree to which the Macmillan Government succeeds in the one will depend on the degree to which it is Butlerite.'

All this threw an interesting light on the way Macmillan had been selected. He had not been elected by the Conservative Party in the House of Commons. There had been no vote. If Eden had definitely recommended Macmillan as his successor undoubtedly the Queen would have immediately sent for him instead of waiting for the advice of Lord Salisbury and Churchill.

One can only sympathize with Her Majesty (she was not an expert on the good points of Butler and Macmillan—they were not Derby favourites) and she had to decide on 'instinct'. Neither Salisbury nor Churchill were at the Palace very long, so they must have known their choice before going in.

Macmillan had supported Churchill in the Munich days and Butler had been for Chamberlain. That could explain Churchill, who had a long political memory.

Lord Salisbury was to quarrel with Macmillan over Africa later. Salisbury could hardly have consulted Tory members of the House of Lords any more than anyone had consulted Tory members in the Commons.

Macmillan had evidently been the favourite of the Establishment. He was regarded (as The Times indicated) on the Right wing. He and Butler were on different wings from what they had been thirty years before.

Macmillan having been appointed Prime Minister, all that was left for the Conservative Party to do was to elect him the Leader. The motions of democracy were duly carried out on January 23rd, the eve of Parliament. In a feature article explaining how this was to be done The Times said: 'It all goes according to precedent—there will be no clash and no voting, not even a show of hands. Mr Macmillan will be certainly elected as the successor and will be suitably commended as the successor and will then be elected by acclamation as have been so many of his predecessors.'

Whether The Times was still feeling a little sore about it and whether there was a touch of irony in it one does not know, but this is exactly how it happened and on the motion of Lord

Salisbury and seconded by R. A. Butler (it would have been absolutely indecent to have invited other nominations), Macmillan was duly elected unanimously.

Macmillan made an appropriate speech in reply. He repudiated the suggestion that there were Rights and Lefts in the Tory Party. That was a lot of silly talk. He became eloquent. 'To the broad stream of our philosophy,' he said, 'there are many tributaries but they all flow to the great ocean.' The Tory Party, of course, was united, it was only the miserable Socialists who had differences about leaders.

Macmillan became more playful and a little reminiscent. 'We don't believe in expelling people; that is a good thing because I have no doubt I would have been a candidate for expulsion many years ago. It is this tolerance which makes us not only a national party but a party at the roots of whose philosophy lies the conviction that we are one nation and that we are all in the same boat, with common problems to solve and a common destiny before us. Our approach is not doctrinaire or dogmatic. To use Disraeli's phrase we must be "conservative to conserve all that is good and radical to uproot all that is bad". So it is that we have never been a party of any class or sectional interests.'

It was exactly the right thing to say. Even Lord Salisbury was convinced at the end of it that Macmillan was not to the Right of him. He need have no fears of being expelled for being too revolutionary either. Obviously *The Times* had got it all wrong.

On the front page (13.1.57) the *Manchester Guardian* reported under the headline:

STOCK EXCHANGE REJOICED
RIGHT WING CABINET BRINGS EXCELLENT BUSINESS
'Brokers on the London Stock Exchange yesterday had their best day for some time, with most of the interest in Government stocks. The reinforcement of the Government with Right-wing elements is regarded as responsible for the excellent line of business.'

Editorially, however, the *Guardian* was not so enthusiastic as the Stock Exchange.

It said of Macmillan:

'He has a flair and on occasions a fire which can stir people in a belief in his leadership. These are strong assets. But he comes in with one great disadvantage. It is that he represents the Right, the unprogressive, the backward-looking element in the Conservative Party.'

The *Manchester Guardian* said that 'Mr Butler's offence is

said to have been the undermining of Sir Anthony Eden's position'. If Butler had undermined Eden, Macmillan had certainly undermined Butler.

Lady Dorothy Macmillan, his wife, was present with him at the meeting. In this gathering a wife who was the daughter of a duke was a definite asset. She participated in his triumph. They had a son, three daughters and thirteen grandchildren, the gossip writers informed us next day.

Shortly after they had moved into 10 Downing Street, Lady Dorothy spoke to an audience of schoolgirls and gave them some advice on husbands: 'Be sure you know what your husband wants to do before you marry him. I married a publisher and at first led a normal life—and now look what I've got!'

Macmillan strode into the House of Commons, proud and confident, to the cheers of the Tories behind him. It must have been a difficult situation for Butler, who sat there pale and glum.

At the time Socialists thought that the Tories had chosen the wrong man. Butler was not such a good actor on the Parliamentary stage but he was a more dangerous opponent, cooler, more calculating, cautious, more expert in handling the House of Commons at awkward moments and understanding that if the Tory Party were to return to power it should seem enlightened and progressive.

They disliked Macmillan because of his supercilious, patronizing, winding-up speeches at the Dispatch Box.

Some of them prophesied that Macmillan would not last long as Prime Minister. Later on they were to revise their opinion. Macmillan was to be a more formidable opponent than they then thought.

CHAPTER XV

KING OF THE CASTLE

Macmillan's critics, who had prophesied that, after Suez, the Tory Government could not survive for long and that Macmillan would soon have to give way to Butler, were soon to be proved completely wrong.

Now that he had become Prime Minister Macmillan seemed to be developing a new attitude towards the House of Commons and a more conciliatory line towards his Opposition critics. He had obviously come to realize that a Prime Minister must at least appear to be something more than an adroit and provocative politician. He showed this at Question Time. He was courteous to his questioners, he stopped to think out what he was going to say and kept his temper, except when the old Adam of the pugnacious party politician came out when he snapped back with some gibe at the Front Bench opposite and taunted them about their internal differences.

The House of Commons soon realized that there was another side to Macmillan's character that he had not shown so much before. He appeared to be trying to be more thoughtful and was obviously anxious to be a success as Prime Minister. He tried to be cool and composed when tempers ran high and to behave with dignity and restraint. He had the appearance and deportment for this role and made an effort to appear as a Prime Minister who could command respect. He did this with such success that in a couple of months he had confounded his Parliamentary critics and had become a dominant personality to whom the House of Commons responded. He had followed Eden and Churchill and he was not like either of them. He had not Eden's polish and personal charm but he had a greater all-round knowledge of what was happening in the country. Eden was never really a Prime Minister. He was a glorified Foreign Secretary, a diplomat, and would have made a good ambassador somewhere. Anthony Eden was not long enough Prime Minister to create for himself a new reputation and he was completely out of his element in a debate which had little to do with foreign affairs. Churchill was, of course, in a class of his own, a past master of Parliamentary debate, with a mischievous sense of humour, thoroughly at home at the Dispatch Box, where he enjoyed himself immensely, always ready to take part in any row and good at repartee and the impromptu retort.

Macmillan was neither as suave as Eden nor as lively as Churchill, even in his last years as Prime Minister. But he knew a lot about politics and had an all-round knowledge of affairs equal to either of them.

If he was less polite than Butler he was more human and he had a pawky sense of humour which often helped him in difficult situations. He seemed more conscientious than brilliant and loyally stood by his Ministers when they made mistakes. It soon became clear that Macmillan had been underestimated and that he had qualities which had not been suspected. His popularity in the House of Commons grew immensely when it became known that he was in favour of an increase in M.P.s salaries. Old Parliamentary enemies were inclined to take a more benign view of him after that.

Then it was whispered that he did have the courage to take decisions, even if they were wrong ones.

So his reputation in Parliament grew and the Tory press and the Conservative Party Head Office cashed in on it for all they were worth.

Then it became known that one of the most experienced advertizing agencies in London had taken it in hand to build him up for the General Election. He made a good television appearance—he had always been the kind of actor who can come over on TV and he could talk to the British people over the screen like a father, speaking quietly, confidentially, friendly, disarmingly in a way that even appealed to the people who were suspecting that this was the dear old gentleman whose Government was aiming at doubling their rent.

Macmillan soon had trouble within his own Cabinet. The first sharp difference on policy occurred over the decision to release Archbishop Makarios from his exile in the Seychelles, as a prelude to opening negotiations over Cyprus. Cyprus had become a running sore, costing a considerable sum of money and causing a great deal of embitterment in our relations with

Greece. The Labour Opposition had opposed deporting the Arch-bishop and it had become obvious that if the military operations in Cyprus were to be ended Government policy must be reversed.

[Daily Mirror]

On March 20th, less than three months after he had played such a prominent part in making Macmillan Prime Minister, Lord Salisbury resigned his office as Lord President of the Council and Leader of the House of Lords, as a protest against the decision to release Makarios. 'I am afraid,' he wrote to Macmillan, 'I could not be a party to recommending to Parliament a course which I believe to be neither wise nor timely.' Macmillan dis-agreed and described the decision 'as an act of generous states-manship which will reap its reward'.

He realized that he was on strong ground here, for the British people were sick of the long drawn out struggle in Cyprus and glad of any move likely to end it. Macmillan turned out to be right and Salisbury wrong. But in antagonizing Salisbury he had made a powerful enemy who, later, was to return to the attack over Africa.

Salisbury, however influential he was behind the scenes in the House of Lords, was not popular in the country and Macmillan lost nothing in esteem of the public outside by his breach with this representative of the hereditary aristocracy.

The following year there was a more serious revolt.

In January 1958 Peter Thorneycroft, the Chancellor of the Exchequer, resigned and two junior Ministers at the Treasury, Enoch Powell and Nigel Birch, went with him.

Thorneycroft thought that there should be no increased Government expenditure during the year. He was not prepared to agree to a total higher expenditure than the previous year.

Macmillan thought the extra £50,000,000 expenditure was justified and that Thorneycroft should not have resigned over such a relatively small difference.

The Times backed Thorneycroft in an article headed 'Faltering' and wrote:

'So Mr Macmillan has not, in the long run, supported his courageous Chancellor of the Exchequer. All of those who have felt that the battle for Britain's economic security is still in the balance must have hoped that support would be forthcoming. But as it was not, Mr Thorneycroft had no choice but to resign.'

Macmillan was confident that the majority of Tory M.P.s could be rallied to his side. He let Thorneycroft go, expressing the view in a letter:

'You suggest that the Estimates for the next year must be the exact equivalent of the sum spent this year. The rigid application of this formula to be carried out immediately, and without regard to other considerations, would do more harm than good. For, as was made clear in our discussions, to apply it literally must involve cuts in vital services, including those especially affecting certain aspects of family life—and this without any regard to the effect upon the industrial front and on the task of those who have the responsibility of working for wage restraints. This is not a matter of popularity, we have never shrunk from unpopular decisions; it is a matter of good judgment.'

The controversy had been postponed; it was all to come up later, but Thorneycroft had overplayed his hand. Macmillan felt strong enough to let him and the others go. A much chastened Thorneycroft was to return to the Government as Minister for

Aviation a few years later and Enoch Powell came back also as Minister of Health.

Macmillan had won again.

The Prime Minister left on his Commonwealth tour on the day of Thorneycroft's resignation. At London Airport he read a statement to the press in which he spoke of 'some recent difficulties in our affairs at home' which had caused him 'a little anxiety' and continued:

'It is always a matter of regret from the personal point of view when divergencies arise between colleagues but it is the team that matters and not the individual, and I am quite happy about the strength and the power of the team, and so I thought the best thing to do was to settle up these little local difficulties and then turn to the wider vision of the Commonwealth.'

Many people thought that to refer to the disappearance from the Government of the Chancellor of the Exchequer and two other Ministers as 'these little local difficulties' was treating the matter rather lightly, but Macmillan was confident of his position.

At Delhi he was warmly received by Mr Nehru, who didn't see British Prime Ministers in India very often and in his turn he referred to Nehru as 'one of the great personalities of our day; it is always a rewarding and stimulating experience to meet with him'. 'My welcome,' he said, 'would touch every British heart'. This was a unique occasion. 'As the years go by let the ties between our two countries become closer and happier than ever before.'

At a banquet in Macmillan's honour Nehru said that they were welcoming the British Prime Minister at a time of deep crisis in human affairs. His 'suggestion in his broadcast speech for a non-aggression pact between the rival powers had been warmly received in India and he thought in every country in Asia. He earnestly hoped that it would be found possible in some form or other to give effect to it.'

In his reply Macmillan said it was a momentous event in history when India had chosen freely to be a partner in the British Commonwealth. It had paved the way for the Commonwealth 'to become the greatest practical working example of racial co-existence that the world knows'.

He was not, however, allowed to forget the political upset that he had left behind him at home.

At Karachi in Pakistan, the journalists asked him about it at his press conference. He replied jocularly, 'Party discipline at home will last for at least five weeks'. He was there 'as the representative of the British people, at least for the moment; I suppose how long depends upon the working of democracy but for the moment I represent them'. Asked about the prospects of a General Election and whether he had decided upon one, he smilingly dismissed the idea with 'We must always be ready, you know'. He knew he held the trump cards. The Election would be due the next year.

Did the Tory Party want to have a crisis in its ranks just before that? Did they want to change their leader again on the eve of a General Election?

Macmillan knew his Tory M.P.s. He was king of the castle; they knew it, and he knew it too.

So he went on his tour not unduly alarmed and making just the right speeches in all the capitals of the Commonwealth at which his plane touched down.

At Wellington, New Zealand, he was glad 'that the European Common Market had come into being because it strengthened Europe', but 'Britain could not join because it included agricultural products and the alternative was to try to build up an area around it'.

At Canberra in Australia, *The Times* correspondent said he met Dr Evatt, the Leader of the Opposition, who 'was quick to welcome his recent suggestion of a non-aggression pact'. He told a Press Conference at Sydney Airport that 'such a pact might be good if it gave to Russian leaders confidence'. He wanted a meeting with them but he wanted first an agenda in which the pact would perhaps be an item.

They debated Thorneycroft's resignation and the Economic Situation in his absence. The defeated counter-revolutionaries fought an unsuccessful rearguard action in a debate in the House of Commons in which Thorneycroft, from his point of view, made an effective and dignified defence of his resignation while recognizing that the forces were against him and that Macmillan had won. Some of the things, he said, however, constituted a grave indictment of the Government and indeed of the Chancellor who had preceded him—Macmillan. He had made his stand against increased expenditure which the country could not afford and which would lead inevitably to inflation. He said:

'The point I want to put is the quite simple one that for twelve years we have been attempting to do more than our resources could manage and in the process we have been gravely weakening ourselves. We have in a sense been trying to do two things at the same time. First we have sought to be a nuclear power, matching missile with missile and anti-missile with anti-missile—and with large—I am not suggesting economies have not been made—conventional forces in the Far East, the Middle East and in the Atlantic at the same time. That is one branch of endeavour which we have attempted. At the same time we have sought to maintain a Welfare State at as high a level as—sometimes at an even higher level than—that of the United States of America.'

In short the Government was trying to do an impossible thing, run an expensive Warfare State as well as a Welfare State at the same time. Thorneycroft continued:

'It has meant that over twelve years we have slithered from one crisis to another. Sometimes it has been a balance of payments crisis and sometimes it has been an exchange crisis, but always it has been a crisis. It has meant a pound sterling which has sunk from twenty shillings to twelve shillings. That is not a picture of the nation we would wish to see. It is a picture of a nation in full retreat from its responsibilities. That is not the path to greatness. It is the road to ruin.'

This was indeed a serious indictment of the Government. Macmillan was not there to reply but although Butler did his best he had not answered Thorneycroft. The crisis was to continue, the slithering was to go on. When the Macmillan Government was faced with a much bigger crisis three years later, Thorneycroft was back in the Government but not in a very strong position to say 'I told you so'.

Speaking for the Opposition, Harold Wilson crossed the t's and dotted the i's of the ex-Chancellor's speech and added some comments of his own.

He referred to the Tory Head Office propaganda that Macmillan had been protecting the social services from Thorneycroft and that the Prime Minister was the guardian of the social services.

'He is the man who, as Chancellor, imposed the meanest and most vicious of all the cuts there have been—the prescription charges for the old age pensioners and the chronic sick. That was done by the present Prime Minister. It was announced on October 25, 1956, only five days before the Suez invasion. That was for £5 million, not the £50 million which the Prime Minister now describes as "chicken feed". That was for £5 million and we all know, every one of us, that it has caused very great hardship.'

And although Thorneycroft had gone, the basic problem remained. It was not only a question of the heavy expenditure, it was one of the free-for-all economy, the lack of a plan which was to become more and more obvious as the Macmillan Government carried on its task of running Britain for the benefit of the big monopolies, the take-over bidders, the speculators who were making big profits out of capital gains, the vested interests of the City and the Stock Exchange.

Nigel Birch had some further relevant comments to make in the Defence and Budget Debates. Defence was proving 'a costly business' and the pace was not likely to slacken.

'People will invent counter measures; then there will be counter counter measures and again a counter-counter-counter measure, and each new thing that is invented always costs more than the previous invention. It is a costly business . . . Beyond that there is one other aspect of the cost which I think is of very great importance. That is the number of our very best scientists who are locked up in these prospects.

'My fear throughout all this has been that by indulging too much in our ambitions we shall lose the attainable. One of the greatest lessons of Suez was that after four days of tin-pot police action the pound was in danger. In our hand we still had the hydrogen atomic ace, unplayed and unplayable. Therefore, I believe that there is on grounds of economics and also on grounds of grand strategy some case for us to look critically at what we are doing in this matter.'

Nigel Birch was in a position to know. Like Macmillan he had not only been at the Treasury, he had been at the Ministry of Defence too.

All this, however, did not shake Macmillan's position as Prime Minister. He had become irreplaceable. The Tory back benchers were relying upon him to win the next Election for them.

[*Associated Press*]

AN AUDIENCE WITH THE POPE, DECEMBER 1960

[*Barratts*]

WITH MAJOR GAGARIN, JULY 1961

[*Barratts*]

1959 GENERAL ELECTION

CHAPTER XVI

THE STRATEGY OF THE NUCLEAR DETERRENT

IN CHOOSING Duncan Sandys to be his new Defence Minister, Macmillan knew what he was doing. Sandys was the Minister most likely to carry out ruthlessly any policies and any duties which had been entrusted to him and Macmillan had calculated that a tough political personality was essential to push through the defence policy which he had in mind.

A month after Macmillan had taken office the Opposition put down a motion of censure. It regretted that 'despite the expenditure since 1951 of more than £7,500 million, recent events had emphasized the wasteful and ineffective character of the present defence arrangements' and called 'upon Her Majesty's Government to prepare forthwith a revised defence plan which will ensure greater efficiency and lead to both a substantial cut in expenditure and the abolition of National Service'.

In moving it George Brown recalled the speech that Macmillan had made on May 16th the previous year at a lunch given by the Foreign Press Association when he was Chancellor of the Exchequer.

Macmillan had talked about the possibilities of substantial cuts in defence and indulged in what he had described as 'a particular piece of speculative arithmetic' which was 'illuminating—indeed tantalizing'.

Brown pointed out that between his first reference to £700,000,000 and his last reference he had mentioned £700,000,000 no fewer than five times in six lines and asked what was the point of doing this unless Macmillan had wanted the public to get the idea that £700,000,000 was possible.

Macmillan rose to say:

'The Right Hon. Gentleman has created a remarkable, not pipe dream, but phantasy out of my speech. What I was trying to say to the foreign correspondents was that this country was carrying so great a burden that it was unfair upon our economy. I was trying to show that this second rifle we carried—this high percentage greater than that of many other countries — showed the fundamental strength of our economy and that we were able to carry that burden. The Right Hon. Gentleman has misrepresented me and has done it on purpose.'

But Brown's question was quite pertinent. Macmillan's speech may have been a pipe dream but it was surely a strange place— the lunch of the Foreign Press Association—to have pipe dreams about finance. What exactly did he mean and how much did he estimate that defence expenditure could be reduced? What were his plans?

Sandys replied for the Government and gave a forecast of what was to come in a White Paper later.

He agreed that we had reached 'a turning point in defence when large decisions must be taken'.

'The basic responsibility of any government,' he said, 'is to protect the lives and independence of its people', and he proceeded to outline how it proposed to do this 'in a period in which there have been phenomenal advances in the development of weapons of mass destruction'. He hinted at cuts in expenditure but said that he had seen it suggested 'that defence expenditure is now going to be halved overnight' and that 'others have raised the hope that defence cuts are going to knock several shillings off the income tax in the Budget in a few weeks' time, but that was wishful thinking', but reductions were obviously coming.

In April, Sandys produced what has become a historic 'White Paper' and this contained the details of the large decisions which the Government had taken and which he had described as 'the turning point'. Its first paragraph was headed 'Need for a New Approach' and declared:

'The time has now come to revise not merely the size, but the whole character of the defence plan. The Communist threat remains, but its nature has changed; and it is now evident that, on both military and economic grounds, it is necessary to make a fresh appreciation of the problem and to adopt a new approach to it.'

He proceeded to discuss the demands that defence expenditure had made on Britain's economic resources and went on:

'Britain's influence in the world depends first and foremost on the health of her economy and the success of her export trade. Without these, military power cannot in the long run be supported. It is therefore in the true interests of defence that the claims of military expenditure should be considered in conjunction with the need to maintain the country's financial and economic strength.'

Some of us had been saying that for the previous six years.

The next paragraph was even more significant. It read:

'Over the last five years, defence has on an average absorbed ten per cent of Britain's gross national product. Some seven per cent of the working population are either in the Services or supporting them. One-eighth of the output of the metal-using industries, upon which the export trade so largely depends, is devoted to defence. An undue proportion of qualified scientists and engineers are engaged on military work. In addition, the retention of such large forces abroad gives rise to heavy charges which place a severe strain upon the balance of payments.'

This was as important a paragraph in its significance as had ever appeared in a Government White Paper. It stated precisely one of the main causes of Britain's economic difficulties and in implication was a condemnation of the defence policy of every Government since the war, but especially the Government which had been in power since 1951. It was also an indictment of the Ministers who had been responsible for it. Macmillan, for example, had been in the key Ministries for the previous years at the Ministry of Defence, at the Foreign Office and at the Exchequer.

He had advocated the defence expenditure in his speech as Minister of Defence in 1955, he had sanctioned it in 1956 when he was Chancellor of the Exchequer and he had been responsible for the foreign policy of which it was the expression when he was the Foreign Secretary.

Describing the nuclear deterrent he said:

'It must be frankly recognized that there is at present no means of providing adequate protection for the people of this country against the consequences of an attack with nuclear weapons. Though in the event of war the fighter aircraft of the Royal Air Force would unquestionably be able to take a heavy toll of enemy bombers, a proportion would inevitably get through. Even if it were only a dozen they could with megaton bombs inflict widespread destruction . . . The free world is today mainly dependent for its protection upon the nuclear power of the United States. While Britain cannot by comparison make more than a modest contribution, there is a wide measure of agreement that she must possess an appreciable element of nuclear deterrent power of her own. British atomic bombs are already in steady production and the Royal Air Force holds a substantial number of them. A British megaton weapon has now been developed. This will shortly be tested and thereafter a stock will be manufactured.'

There was a new kind of paragraph headed 'Defence of the Deterrent'. The defence of the bomber bases had now become a priority over the defence of the civilian population. The importance of Civil Defence in the general plan of things was getting less.

We were told that 'while available resources should as far as possible be concentrated on building up an active deterrent power it would be wrong not to take some precautions to minimize the effects of nuclear attack should the deterrent fail to prevent war. Civil Defence must accordingly play an essential part in the defence plan', but 'as in other fields the country's economic capacity limits the effort which can be devoted to this purpose'. As Minister of Defence he had been eloquent about Civil Defence. Now expenditure on it was to be reduced.

Parliament spent two days discussing the new Defence Policy. Sandys opened the debate and Macmillan concluded it.

Sandys explained that it was based on two basic facts. Firstly 'it is impossible effectively to defend this country against an attack by hydrogen bombs'. Secondly 'whether we like it or not, we cannot go on devoting such a large part of our resources—and particularly of manpower to defence'.

The Policy of the Nuclear Deterrent would mean that we would concentrate more on nuclear weapons and reduce expenditure on the Army and the Navy. These Services would be contracted and arrangements made for compensation for those discharged. Conscription would be ended and a much smaller Army was contemplated. About 300,000 men, said Sandys, would be released from the Forces as well as many civilians on defence work, among them a considerable number of much-needed scientists. The new policy had already saved the taxpayer 'quite a lot of money. I hope that we shall, over the next few years, be able to save a good bit more.'

The new policy came in for considerable criticism in the debate. It ranged from those who were against the H-bomb on principle to the military men who wanted more money spent on the army and less on nuclear weapons. R. H. Crossman expressed a view which was to become more common among military critics of the Sandys policy like George Wigg later and he summarized what Sandys had said as argument 'in favour of getting nuclear weapons on the cheap. We can get out of spending so much on defence by adopting nuclear weapons and getting rid of conscription and winding up overseas bases; we can have defence on the cheap if we concentrate on weapons which we cannot possibly use. [Interruption.] I know that we could use them, but we have to consider what happens to us if we do', which was a common sense conclusion enough considering that Sandys had told us that the basic responsibility of any government is to protect the lives and indeedence of its people.

There was always a tendency in these debates to forget exactly what defence was for.

In his reply Macmillan described the Sandys White Paper as 'an imaginative and constructive statement of military policy, perhaps the most imaginative and constructive that has been made by any great nation since the war'. He said:

'Whether we like it or not, the decision upon the weapons—and it is a terrible decision—governs the whole issue. Without the nuclear deterrent it is obvious that a reduction of forces of this kind is impossible. Indeed much larger forces would be required if we were to rely entirely upon conventional forces. In that case there would be no hope of raising the necessary men on a voluntary basis, and then it would be all over with any chance of abolishing conscription.'

The fundamental question was 'whether or not the nuclear deterrent is to form the basis of British defence planning'.

'If this is not faced no one, except a genuine pacifist, has a right to urge the ending of National Service. There can be no doubt at all about this. Short of general disarmament—which is the ideal we all seek—the end of conscription must depend upon the acceptance of nuclear weapons.'

The Labour Party amendment had called for 'an immediate initiative in putting forward effective proposals for the abolition of hydrogen bomb tests' and Macmillan turned to this in order to dwell on the differences in the Labour Party, a subject in which he inevitably sought refuge when he was in difficulties himself.

'Everyone in the House knows, and the whole of the party opposite know, that is why it is a triumph for those below the gangway—that if these tests are postponed they will never be held.'

Gaitskell rose to say that that was a great misrepresentation of the amendment and the point of view of the Labour Party.

'What the Labour Party is asking the Prime Minister and the Government to do is to postpone the tests until the proposals, which we hope they will still put forward, for all-round abandonment of the tests have been considered by the other Powers and until replies have been received. If the replies are unsatisfactory there is no reason on earth that we should not proceed to carry out the tests.'

Macmillan retorted:

'I will leave it at that. With a growing pressure from different quarters, all kinds of pressure brought upon us to abandon them, it is my view that if they are postponed, they will never be held. [Hon. Members: 'Why not?'] In my view they will never be held and I am bound to tell the House that this is a responsibility which I am not prepared to take.'

He went on to talk about conventional and unconventional weapons.

'The contrast, of course, between the new and the old is great, but let nobody think that if we could ban all nuclear weapons it would be all right to have a massive third world war with conventional weapons. That is why I believe we must strive for full disarmament covering unconventional and conventional weapons alike. Until we get that we have only two choices—we must rely on the power of the nuclear deterrent or we must throw up the sponge—this is a harsh choice to make.'

Mr George Chetwynd: 'Is there no middle way?'

The Prime Minister: 'I do not think there is. I believe that most of my fellow countrymen would prefer to stand boldly on the deterrent rather than to hazard all the traditions of our religious and civil freedom.'

That was the theme on which he was to make many speeches and it was to be the basis of his defence and foreign policies of the Government of which he was the Prime Minister.

It was indeed a fatal decision. How fatal it was to prove for Britain we do not yet know.

'There had been a serious deterioration in Anglo-American relations during Suez,' Macmillan admitted, and he as the new Prime Minister was invited by President Eisenhower to visit him in America. A three-day conference took place at Bermuda between March 21 and 24, 1957.

The communique said that Eisenhower and Macmillan were 'well satisfied with the results of the conference' and a debate on the lengthy document that was issued took place in Parliament later.

'It was not the purpose of the conference,' said Macmillan in

opening his account of the meeting, 'to cry over spilt milk
and certainly not of wallowing over it'. Who had spilt the milk,
he did not say. Questions about the reasons which, as Amery
had said, about why the American Fleet had threatened us over
Suez and about the American financial decisions which had
called a halt to the Suez adventure were discreetly avoided. It
was the future that mattered and what Eisenhower was mainly
concerned about was what was to happen about Britain as
America's principal bomber base in Europe. On that Macmillan
satisfied him completely. The Government was all for being
under the American 'umbrella', even if Britain was destroyed as
a result of it. They were agreed about the need for hydrogen
bomb tests and nuclear strategy. Macmillan admitted he had
been disturbed about the possibility of fall out (and there was a
great deal of interruption at this point) but the tests must continue. We were going ahead with our tests at Christmas Island
in the Pacific. He thought the 'apprehensions' that were being
expressed by the Japanese Government were not justified. 'They
are 4,000 miles away and I really think they have no ground for
them.'

'I think I am justified in saying that we should continue the tests,
that we should continue this careful watch upon what is happening
and that our addition to it, while it will make a great addition to our
strength that is the basis of any sensible defence, in the future makes
really an insignificant addition to the figures I have given.'

America was prepared to provide Britain with guided missiles
but the nuclear warhead would be in the control of Americans.

Macmillan's critics after Bermuda asserted that he had been
so anxious to appease America after Suez that he had leaned
over backwards in his approval of American policy.

Reginald Paget called it 'an intense humiliation that no major
country had ever accepted before'.

Within a few months of taking office the defence policy that
Macmillan intended to follow was quite clear. It was to be the
Nuclear Deterrent and complete subservience to America.

ST. MARY'S COLLEGE OF EDUCATION
FALLS ROAD. BELFAST. 12

CHAPTER XVII

DR JEKYLL AND MR HYDE

ON MARCH 12, 1958, Macmillan addressed the Conservative Political Centre and his speech was published as a pamphlet under the title *The Middle Way : Twenty Years After*. His book *The Middle Way* had long been out of print and certainly the Conservative Party was not enthusiastic about re-publishing it although a new edition with some footnotes, explaining why he thought the arguments were out of date or bringing them up to date, would have been widely read.

He began by saying that a perplexed gentleman in Scotland had written to the Conservative Party Research Department in 1950 asking to what extent the book reflected Conservative Party policy and had been told that 'what a Conservative Member of Parliament writes in his own book are his own opinions and not necessarily those of the Conservative and Unionist Party and what he thinks in the 'thirties he does not necessarily think in the 'fifties'. Then he went on:

'A remarkable degree of heresy is, of course, the prerogative of youth. It is always necessary, frequently stimulating and sometimes it is also sensible and turns into tomorrow's orthodoxy. It was said of Swift that he was once found in his old age seated in the chimney corner turning over the manuscript of a piece of juvenalia, muttering to himself with a sad pride, "My God, I was clever when I wrote that". Such retrospection and such self-admiration are not, of course, universal. On the other side it has been said that there is no fool like an old fool—except a young fool; but the young fool has first to grow up to be an old fool to realize what a damn fool he was when he was a young fool.'

And then he went off at a tangent to put up a lot of Aunt Sallies of what the Socialists stood for and proceeded to knock them down again, to the delight of his audience who seemed to think that this was what he did in *The Middle Way*, twenty years before.

Now nobody, whatever they had thought of him before, was inclined to dismiss Macmillan as 'a damn fool' in March 1958, and nobody knew this better than he did. He could indulge in a little self-depreciation, in order to liven up an otherwise rather dull speech, because he had already made good as a conventional Tory Prime Minister and even his previous detractors grudgingly admitted that he was as an astute and as adroit a politician as any that the Tories had discovered for half a century.

But he was a very different personality from the young rebel who had denounced his front bench leaders as a row of slag heaps, twenty years before. The old Tory hands who had sat at Westminster under Baldwin and Chamberlain and MacDonald and had sneered at him as the leader of the Y.M.C.A. had all become his enthusiastic supporters now.

Had they changed or had he?

Churchill, in his Liberal days had described the Tory Party not as a party but as 'a conspiracy'. He had called it 'a party of great vested interests banded together in a formidable confederation: corruption at home, aggression to cover it up abroad, the trickery of tariff juggles, the tyranny of a party machine, sentiment by the bucketful, patriotism by the imperial pint; the open hand at the public exchequer; the open door of the public house; dear food for the millions, cheap labour for the millionaire.'

Macmillan had never been such a demagogue or had the same command of colourful language that Churchill had, but, in his more restrained way, had said some harsh things against the Tories in his time too.

Having denounced the Tory Party 'as a party of great vested interests' Churchill ended by leading it, and Macmillan had also travelled the same road.

Stevenson, another Scot, had given the world an immortal study of dual personality in his *Dr Jekyll and Mr Hyde*. Macmillan was very much a political Dr Jekyll and Mr Hyde, the younger Macmillan, the political rebel against the Tory Government, always in the background to remind the Tory Prime Minister of what he had crusaded for in his youth.

The younger Macmillan had not been such 'a damn fool' in his day either. The Prime Minister had no need to apologize for him. He may have talked like a professor of economics and written some rather dry books but he had attempted a serious study of the social problems of his time and had come, for a Conservative M.P., to some radical conclusions. True the language was not so flowery as that of the more cynical elder politician but there was thought and a seriousness of purpose of a mind that had become deeply interested in the problems of poverty and unemployment and social injustice and was trying to find a remedy. And he had come forward with plans for industrial reconstruction which the Tory Party of his day thought too drastic and revolutionary.

In his address to the Conservative Political Centre the older Macmillan was obviously trying to explain things to the younger Macmillan. He said:

'It is just over twenty years since I was preparing my book, The Middle Way, for publication. It was the product of thought and experience of many years of study as a young man. Much that I wrote then is completely out of date. Many of the questions have been resolved in one way or the other, though some are still with us. But I do not feel on re-reading it, if I may say so without conceit, out of sympathy with the general approach. I still believe that it is along this line that the Tory tradition springs from the past and leads to the future, and that on the broad basis of this philosophy the future of our party can alone stand firmly. I will certainly try to practice it so long as I have any authority in the Party or the Government.'

But was the criticism that the young Macmillan had made of Britain in 1938 so out of date in 1958? Of course the statistics were out of date and the big army of unemployed of the pre-war years had dwindled and the worst poverty of those days had disappeared with the establishment of the Welfare State and measures placed on the Statute Book by the Labour Government which Macmillan had so bitterly opposed.

If there was not a big army of unemployed as there had been in the 1930's there were still the old age pensioners and the young Macmillan's arguments about minimum needs surely applied to them as much in 1958 as they did to the needs of the unemployed in 1938.

If Macmillan's 'Middle Way' arguments still held good and embodied the 'general approach' of a Tory Government, what had become of his ideas that public utility companies should be set up to distribute the basic foodstuffs to the people in the community that most needed them?

Instead of embarking on plans for cheapening milk and bread to the most needy Macmillan had taken away the bread and the milk subsidies, which meant increasing hardship on the poorest people.

Macmillan's arguments in *The Middle Way* all led to the conclusion that legislation must be introduced to bring about an improved industrial organization which would support a minimum and a rising standard of life for the working population. These plans inevitably involved large-scale interference with and compulsions on private capitalism to reorganize itself so that it could provide higher wages.

Had Macmillan proposed in 1958 many of the measures he had advocated twenty years before, his popularity among his Tory big business supporters would have disappeared overnight and they would have immediately begun a campaign to get rid of him. He had been accepted as a Tory Prime Minister just because they relied upon him not to interfere with private capitalism on the lines he had suggested twenty years before.

In *The Middle Way* Macmillan had been enthusiastic about trade unions. He had written:

'In any proposals that are advanced in regard to the more efficient organization of industry, what differentiates a democratic from a tyrannic system is the existence of trade unions, freely chosen by the workers themselves, and the presentation of the right of the worker to withhold his labour. I would rather fight against any reconstruction of industry, and tolerate inefficiency, than have any part in a policy of reconstruction that threatened to injure or impair, in any way, the freedom and rights which labour now possesses. I regard it as fundamentally important that, with every step we take in the tightening up of the efficiency of industry, an equal step forward should be taken in facilitating the development of the democratic factor in industry by recognition and encouragement of the workers' trade unions.

'In industries which had thus been reorganized, both in regard to their capital and their labour sides, it should not be difficult to find a method of bringing labour more and more into active partnership on the basis of a policy which sought to serve the common interests of both management and labour.'

Macmillan in his younger days had obviously been more enthusiastic about the trade unions than he was when he became Prime Minister. He didn't do much to give them encouragement then.

'We Conservatives,' said Macmillan, 'must believe above all in national unity. We are a Party at the roots of whose philosophy lies the conviction that we are all members of one nation and, whatever the faith or the doubt that may be in us, children of one God.'

But if the Tory Party was really a national party how could Macmillan explain the absence of anybody claiming to represent the trade unions or the Co-operative from it? Surely they were children of God too!

There was enough in *The Middle Way* to prevent it being re-issued as a political text-book for young Tories.

There was a whole chapter on 'Public Enterprise and Private Combination' which might lead any thoughtful young Tory who read it to wonder if public ownership or nationalization could be so wicked after all.

Indeed the young Macmillan had no objection to socialism or nationalization in principle. He was quite prepared to have some industries nationalized and ended up a chapter on 'Industrial Reconstruction' with the conclusion: 'The Socialist remedy should, on the other hand, be accepted in regard to the industries and services to which the analysis does apply; that is to say where it is obvious that private enterprise has exhausted its social usefulness, or where the general welfare of the economy requires that certain basic industries and services need now to be conducted in the light of broader social consideration than the profit motive provides.'

Any curious Conservative who chose to probe a little further into what Macmillan had advocated in *The Middle Way* would inevitably wonder why he had so bitterly attacked a Labour Government for doing what he had recommended. Indeed he had gone much further.

Macmillan may have been right when he said that 'the young fool has first to grow up to be an old fool to realize what a damn fool he was when he was a young fool'. But it is a pity that the young fool is not able to defend himself against the old fool. In our old age we can reflect on the follies of our youth but in youth we cannot foresee the follies of old age.

If we could, we could imagine what the young Macmillan might have replied to the old one. He might have said, 'Who would have thought that I would have become such a damn old fool? Who would have thought that I would have become the successor of Baldwin and Neville Chamberlain and Ramsay MacDonald, giving all the old evasive answers at the Dispatch

Box, dodging all the big issues, making the same old speeches, using the same old clichés, retailing the same old platitudes, doing the same old Parliamentary and political tricks?'

Whether this speech satisfied the perplexed old gentleman from Scotland, one does not know. But one old gentleman was far from satisfied with Macmillan's performances as Prime Minister.

'Yes,' said Lord Boyd Orr, 'I did know him in his young days when he used to study my books. Then I thought he was a fine young fellow with plenty of guts. But when he sent me his book *The Middle Way* I said "You can't stay in the middle of the road. You've got to go either Left or Right." And look where he is today! I heard him on the television the other night. Had to turn him off. Just blah-blah! Why do the politicians go like that?'

CHAPTER XVIII

MISSION TO RUSSIA

MACMILLAN'S visit to Russia in February 1959 aroused world-wide interest. Why was he going there? What did he hope to achieve?

Moscow received this strange and unexpected visitor from the West with all the ceremonial honours and with great cordiality. When he descended from the plane at the Moscow airport the Red Army Band played martial music and Khrushchev, the leading members of the Soviet Government and the Diplomatic Corps were there to greet him and there was friendly cheering as he reviewed the armed guard.

His white bearskin hat surprised and delighted everybody. Nothing quite like this had descended on Moscow before. The press said he had been given it by a Canadian friend but it was not the kind of thing worn in Russia. Every pair of eyes in the crowd at the airport was concentrated on this amazing white hat. Khrushchev read a long speech of welcome. He recalled that Macmillan had visited them before, thirty years ago, and that Russia and the world had changed a great deal since then. The Soviet Union wanted peace and was prepared for useful talks.

'We must understand each other better and make a contribution to world peace worthy of our two nations,' he said. It was three years since he had visited Britain. Relations between the two countries had been affected by the cold war but they regarded the British Prime Minister's visit as 'the thaw'. They welcomed the visit and would do everything they could to make it a success.

Macmillan was obviously impressed with the warmth of the welcome. The only British Prime Minister to visit the Soviet Union had been Sir Winston Churchill during the war. He was the first British Prime Minister to come in times of peace. There were three reasons why he had come. It was a return visit for the one paid by Khrushchev to Britain three years before and he was sorry he had not been able to come earlier. He hoped to see

Pilgrims' Progress

something of the Soviet Union, which he had first visited thirty years ago, to see the great changes which had taken place. Thirdly he hoped to have some serious discussion in the hope that it would lead to a better understanding. He concluded: 'Perhaps in this way our visit may help to alleviate some of the cares that at present bring anxiety to the world. That at least is my objective. Let us see if we can achieve it together.'

They went away to Stalin's old residence in the country and had long talks. Khrushchev, it was said, was not long before recalling the fact that in his broadcast talk to the British nation Macmillan had called for an Anglo-Russian Non-Aggression Pact and in indicating that Russia was prepared to agree to this and to sign one.

Macmillan evidently thought that this was going rather fast. He had clearly not anticipated these developments when he had made the speech. Certainly, he had not come there to sign a Non-Aggression Pact with the Soviet Union. He would have to consult his allies.

What exactly they said to one another was not disclosed but it seemed that Macmillan wished to talk in generalities and had not come there prepared for definite negotiations. It is quite possible that at some stage Khrushchev asked him why, if he was not in favour of a Non-Aggression Pact, he had made that speech.

When the two Prime Ministers were seen sitting together in the Royal Box at the Bolshoi Theatre, journalistic observers thought that they were both looking rather glum and that the cordiality between them had cooled off. It had been assumed that they were to travel together to Kiev but at the last moment Khrushchev had an attack of toothache and called it off. The British press declared that Khrushchev's toothache was a personal insult to Macmillan and it was suggested that Macmillan should cancel the arrangements to visit Kiev and Leningrad and return home. But when he arrived at Leningrad, Mikoyan had been sent specially from Moscow to meet him. Macmillan had not shown any sign of petulance or injured dignity and came out of the incident well, and so the situation eased and the talks with Khrushchev at Moscow were renewed.

Macmillan made many speeches proclaiming his desire for friendly relations with the Russians and proposed, and responded

[Associated Press]

WITH MOLOTOV IN VIENNA
At the signing of the Austrian Treaty of Independence

[Barratts]

WITH NEHRU
Commonwealth Prime Minister's Conference, 1961

[Barratts]

FACE TO FACE

Kremlin, February 1959

to, so many toasts that it seemed that he was running out of friendly platitudes.

His most remarkable speech at these convivial gatherings was, however, the one he delivered in proposing the health of Khrushchev at a reception in the British Embassy.

Addressing the Soviet Prime Minister he said:

'Already, Mr Prime Minister, I have realized how passionately you are devoted to the great work of building up the economy of the Soviet Union. Your immense grasp of detail on a mass of various topics I find impressive and fascinating.

'This is a truly constructive life's work which you have undertaken. The future before the Soviet people is one of expanding horizons. Across the steppes glows the furnace of industry beckoning to a promised land. This is no mirage which you see before you. It is sober reality. The rate and quality of your progress are indeed extraordinary and—so far as I know—unparalleled in history.

'Gentlemen, I give you the toast of the Soviet Union coupled with the health of the members of the Soviet Government.'

In his reply Khrushchev paid a generous tribute to Macmillan. He said:

'In the British Government you, Mr Macmillan, have always held most difficult posts. You dealt with finance and your activity in this post produced big results and was highly appreciated in your country. Your activity as Minister of Housing has also been worthily recognized and most highly appreciated. You also held such an important position as that of Foreign Secretary. You have made your contribution to the spirit of Geneva.'

The compliments certainly flowed that night. Some of the journalists wondered whether these exuberancies should be reported and went to get the hand-out at the British Embassy next day in order to check up.

But all the tributes to Khrushchev and the eulogy of the achievements of the USSR, even the reference to 'a promised land', were there in black and white in the official hand-out.

Some of them speculated how this would be received by the rank and file of the Conservative Party at home. Others wondered what would be the reactions in Paris, Bonn and Washington when the diplomats reported there.

Khrushchev's toothache had been completely cured before the Russians gave their farewell reception in the Kremlin. He was friendly and expansive. He returned, however, to the idea of a Non-Aggression Pact. Of this he said:

L

[Evening Standard]

Big Brothers are watching you

'We have proposed a treaty of non-aggression between the Soviet Union and Britain in the belief that this would be useful, not only to our own peoples, but also for strengthening world peace. Under this treaty both parties could undertake to refrain from attacking each other or to resort to the use of force against each other. It would be good to provide that our countries should not permit new foreign bases to be set up on our territories and that steps should be taken to scrap the existing foreign bases.

'We believe that whatever issues in dispute may arise between our countries should be settled in the spirit of mutual understanding by means of negotiations in accordance with the charter of the United Nations. We are convinced that this would be welcomed by the peoples of the Soviet Union and Britain. The establishment of good neighbourly relations and closer understanding would be useful not only to our own peoples, but to other peoples as well, because it would strengthen general security.'

Macmillan, in his speech in reply, side-stepped the proposal for a Non-Aggression Pact. He said:

'On one matter—your suggestion of a Non-Aggression Pact (it had originally been his)—I would just say as I told you earlier today. I am prepared to declare at once our agreement that:
(a) In all matters of dispute our countries should act in the spirit and letter of the United Nations Charter;
(b) Neither Government should seek unilaterally to prejudice the rights, obligations and vital interests of the other;

(c) On the basis of these principles our Governments agree that dis-
    putes should be settled by negotiation and not by force.
This in no way prejudices our firm resolution to stand by our defensive alliances until the happy time comes when the world can give
up these protective measures.'

The last sentence was obviously meant for Washington, Paris
and Bonn.

In his broadcast talk he had said:

'We could start by a solemn pact of non-aggression. This has been
done before. It would do no harm; it might do good.'

The Russians had invited him to start. They had accepted his
own proposal not only for a non-aggression pact but for a 'solemn
non-aggression pact'. It was he who had suggested it, not them.

One wondered what explanation he had given to Khrushchev
behind the scenes. Was it this that had given him the toothache?

He thanked the Russians for giving him the opportunities to
see Moscow, Kiev and Leningrad.

'All are beautiful in very different ways. All are rich in history and
tradition. But though I was interested in their past, it was not this
that impressed me most. What is really impressive is the work of
construction and economic development that is in evidence on all
sides. These achievements are even more notable when one remem-
bers the destruction of the war. All three of these great cities that I
visited suffered either by bombardment, siege or occupation. Now
there is little trace of war devastation. You, yourself, Mr Prime
Minister, played the leading part in the work of reconstruction and
recovery in the Ukraine.'

In Great Britain, too, he went on to say, we were proud of our
achievements in production and reconstruction since the war.
Britain was small in area and the population is dense, and as we
live by overseas trade we needed peace and prosperity in the
world.

He went on:

'However great the differences between us—and we must not under-
rate them—I remain convinced that our basic aim is identical—to
prevent the outbreak of a third world war. For that would make it
impossible for any of us to continue to build up the prosperity and
happiness of our peoples.
'We should all be involved in common ruin.'

Undoubtedly what he had seen in Moscow, Kiev and Leningrad had impressed for he had the advantage of having travelled

in Russia thirty years before, and everywhere he went he could notice the tremendous changes that had taken place.

The Russians certainly provided him with every possible opportunity to see everything that he wished to see.

He spent an afternoon at the big new University on the Lenin Hills. When he asked the Rector how many students were there he was told that there were over 10,000 students there and twice that number getting part-time and correspondence courses. All the students were learning English. He made several speeches, concluding with one in the great assembly hall which was crowded out with young men and women who had never seen a British Prime Minister before and were anxious to see what he was like. They applauded him enthusiastically and he was obviously moved by the warmth of his reception. He concluded his speech by saying:

'I have seen enough of your University to see how magnificently it has been equipped and how splendidly it has been designed. I am sure it will make a great contribution to the health and strength of the Soviet Union. Fortunately in this age of economic progress all nations can work together in friendly rivalry. We have lived through two world wars and I know how vital peace is to progress. Much of the trouble in the world is due to mutual misunderstanding and lack of knowledge. If my visit can make the slightest contribution to better understanding, my colleagues and I will be well satisfied. I shall never forget your friendly greetings and I will convey them to the youth of my country.'

The press photographers and television cameras followed him everywhere and the Russian papers gave him great publicity. He was taken about a hundred miles out of Moscow to see Dubna, the Institute for Nuclear Research, which is the Russian Harwell. An enthusiastic crowd of villagers clapped him as he arrived. They showed him five laboratories: Nuclear Problems, High Energy, Theoretical Physics, Neutron Physics and Nuclear Reactions. They left him in no doubt about Russian advances in nuclear science.

At Kiev there was a large and curious crowd at the airport. He had learnt a few words of Russian for the occasion and he went through the crowd shouting in Russian, 'I wish you success', 'I wish you success!'

From Kiev he went to visit a collective farm. The products of the farm were displayed in the village hall like in an English

flower show and he listened to an account of how the farm had
been built up again after the war, when its buildings had been
destroyed, its animals driven away and its population taken off
to slave labour in Germany. It helped him to understand the
Russian fear of the invader and their dread that it might happen
again.

In Leningrad he was received at the Frunze Naval College and
reviewed an armed guard of Russian sailors from the Red Fleet.

Admiral Bogdenko escorted him round the college and he
made a speech of thanks.

'For us islanders,' he said, 'the Royal Navy is a sacred and cherished
tradition. The friendship between the British and Russian fleets is of
long standing. The long record of co-operation between the British
and Russian Navies was cemented during the last war. I bring greetings to you from the British people and from one Service to another.'

[Evening Standard]
'They said they've never had it so good'

There were no tactless references to Russian submarines.
He was shown the new atomic ice-breaker *Lenin*, the first in the
world, of which the Russians were intensely proud, and in
returning through the city stopped to make an unexpected visit
to a big food store where he was mobbed by a friendly crowd of
Leningrad workers doing their week-end shopping.

There were more friendly interchanges with Mikoyan at
dinner. Everybody was again in a good mood. There were the
familiar passages which by now everybody knew. Macmillan
said:

'These talks, even if they could not—and were not intended to—lead
to any immediate solution, would be of great assistance in the

international discussions that lay ahead . . . But I have been struck by the universal approval with which I have been met during my short tour of the country when I have said that we both have a common interest in peace . . . I am confident we can and will work together to preserve peace.'

Mikoyan spoke about the tragic absurdity of atomic war. He said:

'Many various disputes and misunderstandings have accumulated between states. All this like a heavy load burdens mankind and creates the threat of another war. But the people don't want war. Nor does our Government want war. I think that the British Government does not want war either. In our conversations Eisenhower and Dulles declared to me that the American people did not want war either . . .

'Arguments go on in your country whether capitalism or socialism is better but the Labourites are not making atom bombs to throw at their political opponents, the Conservatives. States may also argue without the use of threats.'

Everybody agreed upon this. Nobody wanted a war.

With Khrushchev eager to sign a declaration in favour of the Non-Aggression Pact that Macmillan had advocated in his broadcast speech and Macmillan not prepared to sign anything that might cause a rift between Britain, America, France and West Germany, it had at one time been doubtful whether any agreement could be reached upon a joint communiqué as to what, if any, conclusions the two Prime Ministers had reached.

But finally a joint communiqué was signed which deserves its place in the museum of diplomatic obscurities.

Although they did not hold negotiations they had had discussions and a valuable exchange of views. They agreed 'that an advance towards a solution of the problem of disarmament would be a major contribution to the maintenance of peace', which was surely the most obvious of platitudes. It would help to increase international confidence and to reduce the burden of military expenditure. They agreed to continue their efforts to make progress in this field.

The document continued:

'Their common objective remains the ultimate prohibition of nuclear weapons and the application of nuclear energy solely to peaceful purposes. They recognized, however, the great importance of achieving agreement to stop nuclear tests under an effective system of international inspection and control. They reviewed the course of the work of the Geneva Conference on the discontinuance of nuclear

weapons tests and resolved to continue their efforts to reach a satisfactory agreement. They considered that such an agreement would
reduce tension, would eliminate the possible danger to health and life
resulting from nuclear weapons tests, and would help to avert the
further development of nuclear weapons.'

They had discussed Berlin and matters relating to Germany,
but they 'were unable to agree about the political and juridical
aspects of the problems involved.'

'At the same time they recognized that it was of great importance for
the maintenance and consolidation of peace and security in Europe
and throughout the world that these problems should be urgently
settled. They therefore acknowledged the need for early negotiations
between the interested Governments, to establish a basis for the
settlement of these differences. They considered that such negotiations could lay the foundations for a stable system of European
security. In this connection they agreed that further study could
usefully be made of the possibilities of increasing security by some
method of limitation of forces and weapons, both conventional and
nuclear, in an agreed area of Europe, coupled with an appropriate
system of inspection.

'In relation to all these matters the Prime Minister endorsed the
principle that differences between nations should be resolved by negotiations and not by force. They recognized that if such negotiations
were to succeed it was important that each side should make a
sincere endeavour to understand the point of view of the other. They
agreed that the present visit of the British Prime Minister and Foreign
Secretary to the Soviet Union had made a valuable contribution
towards such an understanding.'

On two particular questions of direct concern to the Governments of the United Kingdom and the Soviet Union they had
had discussions. They noted with approval the development of
cultural exchanges between the two countries and they agreed
that a United Kingdom Minister should visit the Soviet Union
in the near future to investigate the possibilities of increasing
trade.

Finally:

'The Prime Ministers expressed their confidence that the personal
contacts which had been established between the heads of Governments of the Soviet Union and of the United Kingdom would be
continued in the interests of the developments of friendship and
co-operation between the peoples of the two countries as well as in
the interests of preservation and consolidation of universal peace.'

The communiqué was signed with cordiality between the two

Prime Ministers and Khrushchev's toothache, whether actual or diplomatic, no longer seemed to trouble him.

Macmillan was given an opportunity to give an uncensored talk to the Russian viewing public over the TV. This he did in his best television style.

Many of the *Daily Mail* readers must have learned for the first time that television was popular in Russia and that there were millions of television sets there. Otherwise ten million people could hardly have listened to the Prime Minister's speech and seen what he was like.

He spoke for about twenty minutes about the British way of life, about how conditions in Britain had changed since Dickens wrote *Oliver Twist*, about the amount of money the British were spending on agricultural machinery and motor cars and houses and bicycles and washing machines, and the number of students at our Universities.

'In fact,' he declared, 'the British standard of life is the highest in Europe.'

He certainly put everything in the shop window. He talked about how our aircraft engineers had built the first turbo-prop airliner, how we had invented radar and penicillin.

Never was so much said about a country in Moscow in such a short time.

Then there was the spiritual side.

'The Gospel says man cannot live by bread alone. We believe that man has a spiritual destiny also. Every individual should have the freedom to develop his personality. On this foundation our whole political system is based. We hold that the State is for Man, not Man for the State.'

Certainly Macmillan had no reason for complaint that the Russians had not allowed him every facility to have his say and to put across to the Russian radio and TV public his point of view, and he had taken full advantage of it. They evidently were not afraid of the ordinary Russian hearing what he had to say.

The visit had received enormous publicity in Britain and had helped to give him the reputation of a man striving to reduce international tension and a man who was honestly and sincerely striving for peace.

He was cheered from both sides in the House of Commons on his return.

[Evening Standard]

'Do we have to ask Adenauer before I make the next move?'

Politically it had been a shrewd move. A General Election was approaching and the Conservative Party would be able to cash in on the visit and urge the electors to vote for Macmillan, the Prime Minister who was working for peace.

There had been considerable criticism of Macmillan's decision to visit Russia in Paris, Bonn and Washington and he had to make a round of visits to these capitals to explain what he had done. What had caused special concern was the reference in the Moscow communiqué to the possibility of a demilitarized zone in Europe which seemed too similar to the Rapacki Plan for disengagement which Russia favoured but which France, Germany and the United States rejected.

When Macmillan and Selwyn Lloyd arrived in Paris the Paris Correspondent of *The Times* said that they had been at pains to emphasize that their views about the possibility of disengagement in Europe did not include the creation of an unarmed and central vacuum. What they had in mind was not the Rapacki

Plan but the Eden proposals of 1955 which foresaw the limitation of armaments and military strength with inspection and control in an area to be determined.

He added: 'In spite of the official silence it seems clear enough that the British and French views of Russian intentions and the best way for the West to behave in regard to them are still not identical'.

The Correspondent of *The Times* further remarked that

'On the whole Macmillan's demonstration of solo diplomacy failed by a wide margin to rouse enthusiasm here. No responsible person in a position of authority ever gave much weight to the fear that Mr Macmillan might betray Western interests over Berlin or anything else, but in less responsible quarters such suspicions are freely expressed. M Francois Poncet, a former French Ambassador to Germany, in yesterday's *Figaro* implied a comparison between Mr Macmillan's trip to Moscow and Mr Chamberlain's to Munich. The same comparison is encountered even more crudely in other press comments and in private conversation the charge of British softness is now often heard.'

Another matter that displeased De Gaulle and the French Government was that Macmillan had now taken upon himself the 'leadership of the West'.

Dr Adenauer was, to put it mildly, not enthusiastic about the Moscow visit either and there was a lengthy meeting at Bonn where *The Times* said 'Mr Macmillan appears to have been tougher than was expected on the question of recognizing East Germany'. He had emphasized 'that something must be done, a

point which Dr Adenauer tends to be reluctant to face'. There had been a barrage of criticism from the American press. The *New York Times* found 'increasing irritation in official circles with the British Prime Minister's apparent assumption of a central role in dealing with the Russians. They reproach Mr Macmillan with being too ready to talk of solving military problems without taking into account the knotty political issues that must be dealt with concurrently.'

When Macmillan went to see President Eisenhower 'the President's attitude to Mr Macmillan's ideas changed from neutral to tepid'.

Macmillan at these meetings had stressed the importance of a Summit Conference. 'Macmillan,' said *Time*, 'has set into motion a march to the Summit that could be diverted only by complete Soviet obduracy . . . The basic problem is no longer one of getting to the Summit but of reconciling viewpoints so as to make it absolutely certain that the West presents a united front once the Summit is reached.'

Macmillan was desperately anxious to assure the Americans that he was not following a policy of appeasement with the Russians.

Time reported a meeting at the home of Vice-President Nixon which it described as 'one of the most interesting tea parties since Boston Harbour'. Among the guests were some of the most powerful and influential Senators in the USA, who closely questioned Macmillan on his Russian visit.

['Vicky'—*New Statesman*]

Time reported:

'He summed up his determination to achieve a Summit Conference in emotional terms: "I cannot go to the Queen and ask for approval of the evacuation of millions, many of them children, to far places of the Commonwealth until I have exhausted every other possibility."

'Some of the Americans had plain doubts about Britain's readiness to stand firm once a Summit Conference is held. Both Styles Bridges and John McCormack used the word appeasement. Macmillan bristled. "I am no Neville Chamberlain," he said, "and I want that thoroughly understood. I detest 'appeasement'. I will not tolerate such an approach to our present problems, even though I realize that a war could burn my homeland to a crisp as well as Russia, Germany and France."

'Some of the Americans were vastly relieved. Minnesota's Democratic Senator Hubert Humphrey praised Macmillan highly, added (while Republicans grumbled) that he was glad Macmillan had stepped into the foreign-policy vacancy left by the illness of John Foster Dulles. Massachusetts' Republican Senator Leverett Saltonstall felt much "encouraged" by what Macmillan had said. Some of the other Americans were less reassured; they shared with President Eisenhower the strong reluctance to hold a Summit Conference without first a Foreign Ministers' Conference that has made substantive progress. But at the very least, by the time Harold Macmillan left the Wesley Heights Tea Party to emplane for London next day, he had cleared up any confusion there might have been about where he stood.'

As *Time* remarked, 'Some of the Americans were vastly relieved' at Macmillan's indignant denial that he was in favour of an appeasement policy towards the Russians. What they were anxious about was that Macmillan should appease and reassure them.

He appeared to have been as successful in reassuring them as he had been in reassuring the Russians.

The Times (8.10.59), reporting a meeting at which he spoke on the eve of the General Election at Bromley, quoted him as saying that in going to Moscow he took a chance. 'I know that quite a lot of people here at home did not like it. The Germans did not like it at all and my friend Dr Adenauer reproved me. The French did not like it and President Eisenhower was uncertain.' He had tried an experiment in unilateral diplomacy. But the British people approved it and it helped him to win the General Election.

CHAPTER XIX

SELLING THE PRIME MINISTER

'THE ELECTION is the end of a long process,' said R. H. S. Crossman, and the Conservative campaign had been carefully planned long in advance of October 1959.

There had been the big advertisement campaign paid for by Big Business, expensive newspaper advertizing, poster displays and every means of mass publicity that the experts paid by the Conservative Head Office could think of. And this included a gigantic boost of Harold Macmillan whose portrait looked down on the British people from every possible hoarding from Land's End to John o' Groats.

The total cost of the Tory Party advertizing and poster campaign, between 1957 and 1959, was estimated by Butler and Rose in their book *The British General Election of 1959* (Macmillan, 30s) as at least £468,000.

The same authors tell us that 250,000 short recordings of a message from the Prime Minister were distributed through constituency associations.

Crossman had said that Macmillan was 'being sold to the country as though he were a detergent'.

In a debate in Parliament (5.11.58) Gordon Walker said that Colman, Prentis & Varley, the advertizing firm, had set itself to 'put over' the Prime Minister and to 'sell him' like the other branded goods it handles.

'The Prime Minister finds himself in rather curious company among the other accounts of Colman, Prentis & Varley. He finds himself rubbing shoulders with Chocolate Penguins, Lyons Ready-Mixes, Munchmallows, Payne's Poppets and Amplex.

'What I find particularly disturbing about this development is that the employment of a commercial advertizing firm to "sell" the Prime Minister and the Conservative Party and sell political ideas, as if they were packaged goods is bringing about in this country the worst sort of Americanization of our public life.'

In fact the vice-chairman of the Tory Party, Donald Kaberry, had been sent especially to America to study the publicity methods used in the American Presidential campaign.

No money was spared to give Macmillan the maximum amount of publicity during the Election. But it was only the culmination of a carefully calculated and well thought out publicity campaign. We are told by the authors of *The British General Election of 1959*:

'The public image which Mr Macmillan presented at the time of the Election had not been built up immediately.

'The rise in Mr Macmillan's popularity coincided with his first major television success, a carefully couched interview with Mr Ed. Murrow in May 1958. Shortly after this, the Gallup Poll had found that he was "doing a good job as Prime Minister", by late June the figure had grown to fifty per cent and it went on rising. The evidence linking his sharp jump in public favour to this television programme is suggestive, rather than conclusive. The Gallup Poll found that the party had gained twice as much support from television viewers as from non-viewers in the period between May and November 1958, but many other influences were also at work.

'The Prime Minister's flying visits to world capitals, beginning with his trip to Moscow in February 1959, served to publicize him as a statesman. Because he was acting dramatically and constructively in the cause of peace, the trips were the most effective kind of public relations. By August 1959 he had reached a peak of approval—sixty-seven per cent in the Gallup Poll. The Prime Minister's own flair for showmanship, which led him to step from the plane in Moscow wearing a white Russian fur hat, provided cartoonists with a welcome and instantly recognized symbol.'

Undoubtedly Macmillan did have a flair for showmanship. He had been developing it and exploiting it ever since he had returned to Parliament in 1946.

His final broadcast was carefully thought out in order to create the greatest possible impression. Butler and Rose tell us:

'The final Conservative broadcast, in which the Prime Minister was to be the principal spokesman, caused much agitation among party officials, and there were belated discussions, some of which leaked into the press, about the form it should take. A few days beforehand the matter was removed from the hands of the officials who had dealt with all the other broadcasts. On the advice of Mr Norman Collins, a leading figure in commercial television, Mr Macmillan agreed to do a solo performance. To ensure against any hitch in delivery, Mr Macmillan recorded the performance at an independent television studio on the afternoon of October 6th. The tape was handed over to the B.B.C., but the public were not told that they were watching a recorded broadcast. Standing up and walking from a map to a desk and then to a globe, he talked directly to the camera for fifteen minutes about the Election and the future of the country.'

'One section of the community,' Butler and Rose add, 'had already shown faith in a Conservative victory; under pressure from small investors, Stock Exchange prices rocketed upward.'

A graph showed the way the shares of four leading steel companies increased when it became known that Macmillan had won. His victory was immensely popular on the Stock Exchange.

During the Election campaign he travelled to many parts of the country and addressed seventy-four meetings and spoke to over 150,000 people. The theme of his many orations was usually the same, the 'wonderful record' of the Conservatives since they had been returned to power compared to the 'dismal failure' of the Socialist Government when it had been in power after the war.

At Glasgow he said that the electors' 'choice was between the path to progress and the road to ruin'.

At Tonbridge he declared: 'If a Labour Government is returned there will be another economic crisis, prices will go up, the pound will go "to pot" '.

At Swansea he said: 'Even if they do not nationalize the six hundred largest companies at once, as they intend to do with steel and road haulage, they threaten to put these in a strait-jacket of Whitehall control'.

There too he boasted about the strength of the British economy. 'There could be no dispute as to the strength of the British economy today. The pound is strong, prices are stable. We have full employment. Taxes are lower despite Britain's economy which is now sounder than at any time since the First World War.'

At Bromley on the eve of the poll he boasted: 'We are solvent, prosperous, paying our way in the world. We got rid of controls. We stopped nationalization. We gave people a chance to go ahead. They seized the opportunity and the whole nation has gone ahead.'

He returned over and over again to Gaitskell's Budget of 1951 when income tax had been cut and the charges imposed on the Health Services. This was what the Socialists would do again. And he attacked Gaitskell for proposing a capital gains tax and suggesting that businessmen's expense accounts should be examined.

In a personal message to every elector which the Tory candidates sent out with their Election addresses he said: 'Our policy can be simply stated: PROSPERITY AND PEACE. I do not remember any period in my lifetime when the economy has been so sound and the prosperity of our people at home so widely spread, but we must also do what we can to extend a generous helping hand to the Commonwealth family and others overseas.'

Undoubtedly his leadership of the Tory Party played a great part in sending it back to power with an increased majority.

'Record Dealings on the Stock Exchange' was the headline in the leading page of *The Times* next day. Underneath one read:

'It was a record day's business for stockbrokers. More than 22,000 separate transactions were marked—a new peak—and that figure was again considered to understate the total amount of business . . . Bank managers were also overwhelmed by orders from their customers. By the end of another strenuous day prices of industrial shares had reached another peak . . . Steel shares remained in the forefront of the advance. Several closed with rises of up to two shillings, making net gains of about six shillings in two days. Continental and United States orders continued to play their part in raising prices . . . By the close of the day there were large fresh gains in all the well-known shares such as Associated Cement, Courtaulds and Glaxo . . . Foreign banks continued to take it for granted that the Conservative Party would win. On the City Page we were told: "Buying on the scale witnessed in the stock markets yesterday could only have come from a supreme and unshakeable confidence in a Conservative victory. Brewery shares, armament shares, Courtaulds, I.C.I. all went up".'

When the final results were known next day the City was more jubilant still. *The Times* City Correspondent said:

'Members of the Stock Exchange with up to forty years' experience had never before witnessed such scenes as those which took place on the floor of the market as a veritable flood of buying orders broke all records.

'When business opened dealers in steel shares were forced to stand on benches to avoid being crushed by the rush of brokers waiting to deal . . . Records were broken with almost monotonous regularity. All the industrial shares reached new peaks.

'Freed of the re-nationalization threat steel shares soared to heights unexpected even in this week's remarkable trading. Dorman Long jumped more than 11s to 51s, South Durham rose nearly 10s to

49s 6d and Steel Company of Wales reached 43s with a gain of almost 7s. The popular industrial shares gained over 4s apiece.'

Certainly the Institute of Directors, the steel company magnates and Big Business generally could not complain that during the Election campaign Macmillan had not done his best for them. Big Business regarded its contribution to the Tory Party funds as an excellent investment. It was perfectly entitled to toast Macmillan at its victory celebrations on October 10th.

When he strode into his place in the House of Commons at the opening of the new Parliament, Macmillan was loudly cheered by his enthusiastic Tory followers. They were grateful to him for having led them to victory at the polls and for their seats. The Tories had now a majority of 100 in the Commons, a comfortable majority which would enable those who had other businesses to stay away altogether except when they were needed in the division lobbies on the occasions when there were three-line whips. It had not looked so good for the Tories since the war. There were a lot of young Tories, vetted and approved of by the Tory Head Office for their good looks and youthfulness which had helped to win the marginal seats. It was not like the Parliament when the Government benches were packed with 'hard-faced men who had done very well out of the war'. They might become so when they had settled down to Parliament and had picked up a few directorships. But they were now mostly young innocents who had told their working-class constituents that they had never had it so good and that Macmillan could be relied on to oppose any more nationalization and lead them into the new affluent society.

It looked as if Macmillan had a good five years before him before the next General Election, with no chance of being defeated in the House of Commons, and a united party behind him to do what he liked.

He could afford to be generous to the depleted Opposition in front of him and pose in Parliament as the elder statesman who had the mandate and the authority to speak for Britain in the councils of the world.

There would be no need for a great deal of new, contentious legislation. The landed interests, in the country and in the towns, had been well looked after in the previous Parliament. There was no longer any threat to the steel magnates and the question

M

of selling out what remained of the companies who had been nationalized at good prices for the speculators was only a matter of time. The new licensing laws would bring still greater profits to the brewers, the new laws on gambling would help the vested interests in bookmaking and in sport, and as rents went up the property owners and speculators in land values would have the time of their lives. It would be a good time for the moneyed interests in the City, who profited by high interest rates, and for the gentlemen on the Stock Exchange. They could breathe freely for the next five years, realizing that there would be no Socialist Chancellor of the Exchequer with ideas about a capital gains tax or introducing new clauses into the Finance Bill which would interfere too much with businessmen charging big expense accounts to reduce their income tax and super tax. The gentlemen who had put up the money for the Tories at the General Election might now with every justification murmur, 'For what we are about to receive may the Lord make us truly thankful', and add 'Thank God for Macmillan'.

All this, however, did not mean that the problems facing Britain could be solved as easily as winning a General Election. The post-Election boom on the Stock Exchange had hardly subsided when another financial and economic crisis loomed upon the horizon. One Tory M.P. thought that the Prime Minister had become too much absorbed in international problems and should devote more attention to Britain's economic problems. It was even suggested that he should become Chancellor of the Exchequer again when Heathcoat Amory retired. Harold Wilson protested strongly:

'One Honourable Gentleman wants to bring the Prime Minister back out of the misty stratosphere—in which of late he has been disporting himself with singularly little result—and get him to put in his oar here.

'May I say, and this cry comes from the heart, for heaven's sake spare us from that. The Prime Minister's year at the Treasury was, without exception, the most disastrous in our financial history . . . The economic problem is too serious for there to be put forward such frivolous suggestions as that. Every Hon. Member knows that for four years the Prime Minister's stock-in-trade has always been to deal with any problem by a rather elegant improvization, and always to seek to solve this year's problem by last year's gimmicks . . . The Hon. Member also made it very plain that there was concern on the other side of the House that the Prime Minister was not taking enough interest in economic affairs. I may tell the Hon. Member that that concern is not shared on this side of the Chamber.'

Wilson's fears were, however, not realized. Macmillan did not choose to return to the Exchequer.

Having reached the summit in Parliament the Prime Minister looked forward to another personal triumph in the wider world. He had been persistently advocating a Summit Meeting of the heads of governments of Britain, France, the United States and the Soviet Union, and heard with great relief when it was finally decided that the meeting was to be held in Paris. He had pioneered the way by his visit to Moscow. If agreement on the outstanding problems between East and West was achieved at the Summit Meeting then he would have achieved a great international success and his prestige not only in Britain but throughout the whole world would be immense and he would be known as the man who had paved the way for disarmament and world peace. The prospects were not too bad. Khrushchev had been on a long visit to the United States which had also helped to break the ice, and the relationship between Russia and America was better than it had been for years. When the announcement that the long-expected Summit Meeting would definitely be held in May 1960 the world gave a sigh of relief and waited expectantly. The shares of the leading American armament firms dropped and the financiers of Wall Street began to wonder what would happen if the Summit Conference was a success.

Then suddenly a bolt came from the blue. An American reconnaissance aircraft making its way high up in the air from an aerodrome in Pakistan to a base in Norway had been shot down in the very centre of the Soviet Union, near the town of Sverdlovsk. Khrushchev protested angrily and vehemently. It was against all international law and the first explanation given by the Americans that it was a plane that had got lost made things worse. The Americans had been caught out lying and the whole world soon knew that their explanations were false.

What Macmillan said about the news when it was conveyed to him is not known, but he must have realized that this was the end to his hopes. How could the Summit Conference be a success now? How could he blame the Russians if they reacted strongly? What would he have done if the Minister of Defence had rung him up at 10 Downing Street to tell him that a Russian

spy plane had been brought down just outside Coventry or
Oxford? Would he not have been forced to go to the House of
Commons and denounce the Russians indignantly and ask what
Khrushchev meant by allowing this? What would Eisenhower
have said if a Russian spy-plane had been brought down outside
Detroit?

Whether Macmillan protested vehemently across the Trans-
Atlantic wire one does not know, but he certainly did not do so
in the House of Commons. Much as he may have cursed the
Americans in private, in public he was the model of diplomatic
discretion. His great concern was lest the incident should prevent
the Summit Meeting in Paris.

When it was at last announced from the Kremlin that the
Russians were coming to the Summit after all, Macmillan must
have given a big sigh of relief. He would have an opportunity of
playing the negotiator and the mediator again.

He appears to have been hopeful when he first arrived in Paris,
but Khrushchev soon dashed his hopes to the ground. Khrushchev laid down terms which Eisenhower could not accept; he
wanted a full apology, a guarantee that U2 flights would cease
and that those responsible should be punished, terms that the
Americans could not accept. Khrushchev must have been under
pressure from his defence advisers too.

Macmillan moved to and fro, doing his best to argue, remon-
strate, conciliate. He was obviously doing his best to achieve the
impossible. The Summit Conference, which he had tried so hard
to get, turned out to be the greatest international fiasco since
the war. The Russians were obdurate and they could not be
dictated to. The West was obviously not in a position to dictate
to Khrushchev from a position of strength.

It was a crestfallen and chastened Macmillan who returned to
a House of Commons that could not but sympathize with him.
His great effort to achieve an international triumph had not
come off.

CHAPTER XX

WIND OF CHANGE IN AFRICA

WHEN he became Prime Minister Macmillan made up his mind that during his term of office he would visit as many of the countries of the Commonwealth as possible.

At the end of 1958 he had visited India, Pakistan, Ceylon, Australia and New Zealand and towards the end of 1959 he set out on a tour of Africa, visiting Ghana, Nigeria, the Federation of Rhodesia and Nyasaland, and the Union of South Africa.

His purpose in making these visits was not to negotiate or to settle any particular problems which there might be between the United Kingdom and the Commonwealth Governments. Those matters were better left to the men on the spot or to the Ministers with special responsibility for them. His idea was that the visits of Commonwealth Prime Ministers to a conference in London ought not to be just a one-way traffic.

He thought that a British Prime Minister should have at least a glimpse of the countries in the Commonwealth and a first-hand impression of what they were like and the problems that they faced. In this he was absolutely right and it is to his credit that he made these long journeys and took such pains to visit the Commonwealth countries to meet their leaders personally and to understand their point of view.

There was every evidence that the visits of the British Prime Minister were greatly appreciated. Macmillan at least had taken the trouble to visit them and they had their opportunities of meeting him and realizing that he was not just some remote and isolated mighty personage just looking at things from 10 Downing Street in London.

He told the House of Commons:

'I felt that the presence, even for a few weeks, of a British Prime Minister in office would be both a symbol of the links which bind the Commonwealth and a practical method of holding informal discussions on broad general issues such as are appropriate on a visit of this kind. I may add that it makes my work in London much easier and, I think, more fruitful, if I have some personal impression of the character of these countries, their problems and their ambitions. In addition one is able to have personal discussions in their own homes with the Prime Ministers and other Ministers concerned.'

He had now visited all the independent countries of the Commonwealth with the exception of Malaya (which was the first time a British Prime Minister had done so) and so had completed the task which he had set himself on assuming office. He said he would certainly not over-estimate the value of these visits nor claim that in a few weeks one can gain any expert knowledge of the problems of each country.

'Nevertheless,' he added, 'I hope that these journeys will at least have demonstrated the faith of Her Majesty's Government and people in the United Kingdom in the value of the Commonwealth as one of the greatest forces for peace and progress in the world today.'

In two years' time he was to be faced with the choice of fulfilling the promises he had made to the Commonwealth countries or joining the European Common Market. The Commonwealth Prime Ministers must have asked themselves then to what extent they were likely to be affected if Britain joined up with the Six in Europe. They had an idea that General de Gaulle and Dr Adenauer could not be expected to be as enthusiastic about the British Commonwealth as Macmillan was.

And when the time came when a decision was inevitable to what extent would he be prepared to sacrifice the Commonwealth to the Common Market?

In Ghana he had the opportunity of seeing 'the great economic, social and political progress' which was 'the culmination of many centuries of contact with the West'. Europeans were playing their part in this and he believed they would continue to do so in the future. He found 'a real sense of friendship for the British people in Ghana and a full understanding of the debt which Ghana owes to them'.

In Nigeria he was fortunate to be able to address the National Assembly on a historic date, the first meeting of the Parliament elected under the agreement with Britain. By the end of 1960 Nigeria was to reach the last stage in its progress towards independence. In area it was four times the size of the United Kingdom and in population the largest single country in Africa and the fourth largest in the British Commonwealth. He thought that Nigeria had a great future before it and the discovery of oil and the development of agriculture should give it a sound economic basis. He hoped and believed 'that the federal structure which has been devised will enable the three regions to work together in the development of a truly national spirit'.

In the Federation of Rhodesia and Nyasaland he was able to have talks with the Prime Minister of the Federation and his Cabinet, with the Prime Minister of Southern Rhodesia and his Ministers, with the Governor of Northern Rhodesia and his Council and also with the Governor of Nyasaland and his advisers, and with representatives of a large number of political and other groups, and 'was able to form at least some picture of the difficult problems as well as the impressive prospects of this immense country'. He was not able to see all the picture, of course, for Dr Banda, the leader of the Africans there, was still in jail. Much no doubt as he would have liked to, there was a limit to what British Prime Ministers visiting Africa could do. It would have been utterly unprecedented and undignified for British Prime Ministers to visit native leaders in jail. They would have to be released and become respectable and appear in London as V.I.P. guests of the British Government before a British Prime Minister could be expected to do that.

The Prime Minister made speeches in all the countries that he visited but the one which aroused the greatest interest in Africa and in many other parts of the world was the speech he delivered to the South African Parliament at Cape Town on February 3, 1960. This was indeed a difficult speech to make. He had come from territories where the population and the Governments were predominantly African and in the Union of South Africa a White Government was in control pursuing a policy of apartheid and race segregation which was bitterly resented throughout the rest of the African Continent. South Africa had been given its independence in 1910, nearly fifty years before. He had begun his journey by visiting Ghana, which has never had and never could have a white European resident population, but in South Africa there were three million Europeans, many of whom were descended from ancestors who had gone there three hundred years before. In a short time South Africa was to leave the Commonwealth and this was probably the last time that a British Prime Minister was to visit the country representing a fellow country in the Commonwealth and to be given an opportunity of addressing a South African Parliament. It was a long speech in which Macmillan first traced the history of South Africa and its relations with Britain and the way they had co-operated in two world wars and the close economic ties that had been built up between them in the previous half-century.

Britain had been mainly responsible for financing the industrial development of South Africa. Britain had always been South Africa's best customer and as her industries developed, he believed that this could continue. He paid a tribute to General Smuts and 'the inspiration which he had brought to Britain in her darkest hours', and to Dr Malan who in post-war years had greatly assisted in the recovery of the sterling area, and he said he recognized the part South Africa was playing in building up new industries in the Africa of today.

Then he began to strike a new note.

'Sir, as I have travelled round the Union I have found everywhere, as I expected, a deep preoccupation with what is happening in the rest of the African continent. I understand and sympathize with your interest in these events, and your anxiety about them. Ever since the break-up of the Roman Empire one of the constant facts of political life in Europe has been the emergence of independent nations. They have come into existence over the centuries in different forms, with different kinds of Government, but all have been inspired by a deep, keen feeling of nationalism which has grown as the nations have grown.

'In the twentieth century and especially since the end of the war, the processes which gave birth to the nation states of Europe have been repeated all over the world. We have seen the awakening of national consciousness in peoples who have for centuries lived in dependence upon some other power.

'Fifteen years ago this movement spread through Asia. Many countries there of different races and civilizations pressed their claim to an independent national life. Today the same thing is happening in Africa and the most striking of all the impressions I have formed since I left London a month ago is of the strength of this African national consciousness.

'In different places it takes different forms but it is happening everywhere.

'The wind of change is blowing through this continent and, whether we like it or not, this growth of national consciousness is a political fact.

'We must all accept it as a fact, and our national policies must take account of it.'

The South African Parliament had never heard anything quite like this before. He went on:

'Of course you understand this better than anyone. You are sprung from Europe, the home of nationalism, and here in Africa you have yourselves created a new nation.

'Indeed, in the history of our times yours will be recorded as the first of the African nationalisms, and this tide of national consciousness which is now rising in Africa is a fact for which you and we and the other nations of the western world are ultimately responsible. For its causes are to be found in the achievements of western civilization, in the pushing forward of the frontiers of knowledge, in the applying of science in the service of human needs, in the expanding of food production, in the speeding and multiplying of the means of communication, and perhaps, above all, the spread of education.

'As I have said, the growth of national consciousness in Africa is a political fact and we must accept it as such. That means, I would judge, that we must come to terms with it.

'I sincerely believe that if we cannot do so we may imperil the precarious balance between the East and West on which the peace of the world depends. The world today is divided into three main groups. First there are what we call the Western Powers. You in South Africa and we in Britain belong to this group, together with our friends and allies in other parts of the Commonwealth. In the United States of America and in Europe we call it the Free World. Secondly there are the Communists—Russia and her satellites in Europe and China whose population will rise by the end of the next ten years to the staggering total of 800,000,000. Thirdly, there are those parts of the world whose people are at present uncommitted either to Communism or to our Western ideas.

'In this context we think first of Asia and of Africa. As I see it the great issue in this second half of the twentieth century is whether the uncommitted peoples of Asia and Africa will swing to the East or to the West.

'Will they be drawn into the Communist camp?

'Or will the great experiments in self-government that are now being made in Asia and Africa, especially within the Commonwealth, prove so successful, and by their example so compelling, that the balance will come down in favour of freedom and order and justice?

'The struggle is joined and it is a struggle for the minds of men. What is now on trial is much more than our military strength or our diplomatic and administrative skill. It is our way of life. The uncommitted nations want to see before they choose.'

Could South Africa really be called the Free World? How much political freedom did the black population of South Africa have? He went on:

'What can we show them to help them choose right? Each of the independent members of the Commonwealth must answer that question for itself. It is a basic principle of our modern Commonwealth that we respect each other's sovereignty in matters of internal policy. At the same time we must recognize that in this shrinking world in which we live today the internal policies of one nation may have effects outside it. We may sometimes be tempted to say to each other "Mind your own business", but in these days I would myself expand the old saying so that it runs: "Mind your own business but mind how it affects my business, too".

'Let me be very frank with you, my friends. What Governments and Parliaments in the United Kingdom have done since the war in according independence to India, Pakistan, Ceylon, Malaya and Ghana, and what they will do for Nigeria and other countries now nearing independence, all this, though we take full and sole responsibility for it, we do in the belief that it is the only way to establish the future of the Commonwealth and of the Free World on sound foundations.

'All this of course is also of deep and close concern to you, for nothing we do in this small world can be done in a corner or remain hidden. What we do today in West, Central and East Africa becomes known tomorrow to everyone in the Union, whatever his language, colour or traditions. Let me assure you, in all friendliness, that we are well aware of this and that we have acted and will act with full knowledge of the responsibility we have to all our friends . . .

'Nevertheless I am sure you will agree that in our own areas of responsibility we must each do what we think right. What we think right derives from a long experience both of failure and success in the management of our own affairs. We have tried to learn and apply the lessons of our judgment of right and wrong.

'Our justice is rooted in the same soil as yours—in Christianity and in the rule of law as the basis of a free society.

'This experience of our own explains why it has been our aim in the countries for which we have borne responsibility, not only to raise the material standards of living, but also to create a society which respects the rights of individuals, a society in which men are given the opportunity to grow to their full stature—and that must in our view include the opportunity to have an increasing share in political power and responsibility, a society in which individual merit and individual merit alone is the criterion for a man's advancement, whether political or economic . . .

'I have thought you would wish me to state plainly and with full candour the policy for which we in Britain stand. It may well be that in trying to do our duty as we see it we shall sometimes make difficulties for you. If this proves to be so we shall regret it.

'But I know that even so you would not ask us to flinch from doing our duty.'

There was no ambiguity about this. It was not what the M.P.s of the South African Parliament had expected. Had the Prime Minister come there to lecture them?

'As a fellow member of the Commonwealth it is our earnest desire to give South Africa our support and encouragement, but I hope you won't mind my saying frankly that there are some aspects of your policies which make it impossible for us to do this without being false to our own deep convictions about the political destinies of free men to which in our own territories we are trying to give effect.

'I think we ought, as friends, to face together, without seeking to apportion credit or blame, the fact that in the world of today this difference of outlook lies between us.'

He went on to declare that he was speaking as a friend. He was also a Scot and the Scottish Church and the Dutch Church had been closely associated.

'But though I count myself a Scot my mother was an American, and the United States provides a valuable illustration of one of the main points which I have been trying to make in my remarks today. Its population, like yours, is a blend of many different strains and over the years most of those who have gone to North America have gone there in order to escape conditions in Europe which they found intolerable. The Pilgrim Fathers were fleeing from persecution as Puritans and the Marylanders from persecution as Roman Catholics. Throughout the nineteenth century a stream of immigrants flowed across the Atlantic to escape from poverty in their homelands, and in the twentieth century the United States have provided asylum for the victims of political oppression in Europe.

'Thus for the majority of its inhabitants America has been a place of refuge, or place to which people went because they wanted to get away from Europe. It is not surprising, therefore, that for so many years a main objective of American statesmen, supported by the American public, was to isolate themselves from Europe, and with their great material strength, and the vast resources open to them, this might have seemed an attractive and practicable course. Nevertheless in the two world wars of this century they have found themselves unable to stand aside. Twice their manpower in arms has streamed back across the Atlantic to shed its blood in those European struggles from which their ancestors thought they would escape by emigrating to the New World; and when the second war was over they were forced to recognize that in the small world of today isolationism is out of date and offers no assurance of security.

'The fact is that in this modern world no country, not even the greatest, can live for itself alone. Nearly two thousand years ago, when the whole of the civilized world was comprised within the confines of the Roman Empire, St Paul proclaimed one of the great truths of history—we are all members one of another. During this twentieth century that eternal truth has taken on a new and exciting significance.

It has always been impossible for the individual man to live in isolation from his fellows, in the home, the tribe, the village, or the city. Today it is impossible for nations to live in isolation from one another. What Dr John Donne said of individual men three hundred years ago is true today of my country, your country, and all the countries of the world:

"Any man's death diminishes me, because I am involved in Mankind. And therefore never send to know for whom the bell tolls; it tolls for thee."

All nations now are interdependent one upon another and this is generally realized throughout the western world. I hope in due course the countries of Communism will recognize it too.'

His audience was relieved when he went on to dissociate himself from the British movement that advocated the boycott of South African goods.

'I certainly do not believe in refusing to trade with people because you may happen to dislike the way they manage their internal affairs at home.

'Boycotts will never get you anywhere, and may I say in parenthesis that I deprecate the attempts that are being made today in Britain to organize the consumer boycott of South African goods. It has never been the practice, as far as I know, of any Government of the United Kingdom of whatever complexion to undertake or support campaigns of this kind designed to influence the internal politics of another Commonwealth country, and my colleagues in the United Kingdom deplore this proposed boycott and regard it as undesirable from every point of view.

'It can only have serious effects on Commonwealth relations, on trade, and lead to the ultimate detriment of others than those against whom it is aimed.'

It had been a long speech and he apologized for its length.

'In conclusion may I say this. I have spoken frankly about the differences between our two countries in their approach to one of the great current problems with which each has to deal within its own sphere of responsibility. These differences are well known. They are matters of public knowledge, indeed of public controversy, and I should have been less than honest if by remaining silent on them I had seemed to imply that they did not exist. But differences on one subject, important though it is, need not and should not impair our capacity to co-operate with one another in furthering the many practical interests which we share in common.

'The independent members of the Commonwealth do not always agree on every subject. It is not a condition of their association that they should do so. On the contrary the strength of our Commonwealth lies largely in the fact that it is a free association of independent sovereign states, each responsible for ordering its own affairs but co-operating in the pursuit of common aims and purposes in world affairs. Moreover these differences may be transitory. In time they may be resolved. Our duty is to see them in perspective against the background of our long association.

'Of this at any rate I am certain—those of us who by grace of the electorate are temporarily in charge of affairs in your country and in mine, we fleeting transient phantoms in the great stage of history, we have no right to sweep aside on this account the friendship that exists between our countries, for that is the legacy of history. It is not ours alone to deal with as we wish. To adapt a famous phrase, it belongs to those who are living, but it also belongs to those who are dead and to those who are yet unborn. We must face the differences, but let us try to see beyond them down the long vista of the future.

'I hope—indeed, I am confident—that in another fifty years we shall look back on the differences that exist between us now as matters of historical interest, for as time passes and one generation yields to another, human problems change and fade. Let us remember these truths. Let us resolve to build not to destroy, and let us remember always that weakness comes from division, strength from unity.'

It was certainly a courageous and historic speech. It reverberated throughout Africa. Wherever people could read they asked, 'When is the wind of change going to sweep through South Africa?' Dr Banda in prison in Nyasaland and Jomo Kenyatta in prison in Kenya wondered when the wind of change was going to reach them.

They had not long to wait.

CHAPTER XXI

CHANCELLOR OF OXFORD UNIVERSITY

In March 1960 he agreed to be nominated as Chancellor of Oxford University.

The Times came out for his opponent, Sir Oliver Franks. It thought that Macmillan had enough to do as Prime Minister. It said:

'To be either Prime Minister of England or Chancellor of Oxford University is each sufficient for any one man without his being also the other. However skilfully affairs are managed a single holder of two such posts may face a conflict of claims on time, on attention, on influence. . . . Appeals to precedent are irrelevant. The world of yesterday was a much less explosive, complex and dangerous proposition than the world of today. Even if the Chancellorship were nothing but a sinecure there is much to be said for a modern Prime Minister not holding it. As for the argument that now Mr Macmillan has entered the lists he cannot, because he is Prime Minister, be allowed to lose, that underlines for thinking people, surely, the undesirability of his victory. We hope the majority of Oxford M.A.s, whether existing, delapsed, or newly recruited, will elect Sir Oliver Franks.'

The result was:

Mr Macmillan	...	...	1,976
Sir Oliver Franks	...	...	1,697
	Majority	...	279

which was by no means an overwhelming victory. The result was announced in Latin and there 'was a ragged cheer'. When it was translated into English there were hurrahs and hand clapping for Mr Macmillan.

In the House of Commons Wedgwood Benn asked the Prime Minister what plans he had for restoring the University seats. He replied: 'None, but if the Hon. Member so wishes I will consult the Chancellors of the Ministries concerned.' [Laughter.] Wedgwood Benn then asked:

'Is the Chancellor [Laughter] aware that his reply will be received with great relief after the recent mediaeval frolics in the city of Oxford? May I also congratulate him on having proved by his own tremendous victory in a ballot held in Latin, open for all to see, that the Establishment has nothing to learn from the Electrical Trades Union.' [Laughter.]

Mr Macmillan: 'Except that on this occasion I think the Establishment were beaten.' [Renewed laughter.]

Sir Oliver Franks was Chairman of Lloyds Bank.

Harold Wilson asked to be allowed to express the wishes of the whole House that he would be a more successful Chancellor at Oxford than he was at the Treasury.

Mr Lipton asked him to bear in mind that the graduates of Oxford who took part in the election were so exhausted that they did not want to vote for anybody or anything for at least thirty-five years.

Mr Macmillan: 'I am particularly grateful to the Hon. Member and I will do my best to survive.'

At the end of July 1960 Macmillan reshuffled his Cabinet. Selwyn Lloyd left the Foreign Office to become Chancellor of the Exchequer and Lord Home was appointed to succeed him.

This was the first time for many years that a Foreign Secretary had been appointed who was not a Member of the House of Commons and there were strong protests by the Labour Opposition and also by the Liberals.

Macmillan had done what Eden did not think could be justified in the case of Lord Salisbury.

Gaitskell in recalling the Salisbury case mentioned that at the time Macmillan himself had been opposed to the Foreign Secretary being in the Lords. He based this on an article by Viscount Lambton, who had written:

'Mr Macmillan himself was one of the most stalwart supporters of this point of view and expounded it frequently to his friends. But then the question was whether he or Lord Salisbury should go to the Foreign Office.'

Gaitskell argued strongly that the appointment of Lord Home was a mistake and that in these democratic times it was essential that the Foreign Secretary should be in the Commons. He said:

'In our opinion it is essential that the Foreign Secretary should be in the House of Commons, so that through the elected Members of the House of Commons, he can be in constant touch with public opinion and so that he can be here in this Chamber exposed to criticism and questioning like any other Minister on the benches opposite. There is another reason which is also powerful. The Foreign Secretary should be in the House of Commons, because in representing our democracy abroad, his prestige must rest on his position at the heart of our democracy at home, in this Chamber.'

Gaitskell asked if other members of the Cabinet in the House of Commons were not qualified for the post. Why couldn't Butler have gone to the Foreign Office? In the past he had been Under-Secretary for Foreign Affairs. And what about the other members of the Front Bench.

Mr Clement Davies, for the Liberals, also criticized Macmillan for this appointment. He described it as 'a retrograde step'.

Both the Prime Minister and the Foreign Secretary ought to be answerable to the House of Commons for what they said and did elsewhere. 'There is no other place where they should do it. It is this House that is responsible to the people and it is to this House and this House alone that the Foreign Secretary should be answerable.'

Macmillan defended his appointment of Lord Home strongly and said:

'I will tell the House, simply, and I ask for its support. It is because, after watching his work for so many years in the Commonwealth Relations Office, I felt he was the best man for the job. I believe that Lord Home has the qualities which will make him a successful and widely respected Foreign Secretary.'

He thought it would be 'a very bad precedent to set to say that this or that Ministry should be forever debarred from going to a member of the House of Lords'.

He had, however, appointed Edward Heath as Lord Privy Seal, who would be a member of the Cabinet, to specially deal with Foreign Affairs in the House of Commons and argued that this met the situation.

He concluded by saying:

'If there is a Division, I should like to make it clear that, although I was, of course, aware that there would be some temporary difficulties and objections, I have made my choice in accordance with what I conceive to be my public duty.'

The matter was pressed to a division and the House approved of Macmillan's action by 332 votes to 220.

Macmillan had struck another blow for democracy.

CHAPTER XXII

SURRENDER TO AMERICA

WHEN Parliament reassembled in November 1960, Macmillan announced that the Government had decided to agree to an American Polaris submarine base at the Holy Loch in Scotland. This was yet another concession to America. When De Gaulle had refused to allow the American bombers to remain in France unless there was some measure of French control of their activities the British Government had obligingly allowed them to come here. De Gaulle had insisted that he was the Government of France and not the Americans. If there were to be bomber bases in France then they should be under the control of France and not of American strategists in the Pentagon in America.

Questioned in the House of Commons, Macmillan said that the American request for a base in Britain had been received at the end of 1959 and that he had discussed it with President Eisenhower at the meeting at Camp David in March 1960. Discussions had been going on since then 'on the technical and political aspects of the question and these had been finalized between the two Governments at the very end of October'. This had enabled him to make his statement at the earliest moment in the new session.

There were of course American air bases in Britain already, but the establishment of the Polaris base at Holy Loch meant a new departure. Macmillan refused to publish a White Paper on the negotiations which had been going on for ten months.

The Holy Loch was situated on the Clyde about twenty miles from Glasgow and there was an immediate outcry from Scotland. The Scottish Trade Union Congress, the Scottish Council of the Labour Party, the local authorities in the area sent their protests to the Prime Minister without avail. He had made his agreement with the Americans and no protests from the people in the locality could change it.

The decision to establish the Polaris base in Scotland raised once again the dangerous position in which the British people

N

YOUR QUEEN & Mr KENNEDY
NEED YOU

SALLON after
ALFRED LEETE

['Sallon'—*Daily Mirror*]

Kitchener poster up-to-date

had been placed as a result of Britain becoming the main base for
American strategy in Western Europe. In and around Glasgow
were more than two million people now placed in great danger
if a nuclear war developed and if the Russians were to attack the
base of the Polaris submarines whose destructive power had been
emphasized in the American press. An American admiral had
described the Polaris submarine as a 'city killer', and other
writers in the American press had given details of the submarine
which carried sixteen atomic missiles, each capable of destroying
a city. The people of Scotland remembered how British bombers

had gone out to destroy the German submarine bases in the last war. Now the West of Scotland had been placed in the front line in the event of a nuclear war. The whole of the West of Scotland could be devastated by one hydrogen bomb and if the Holy Loch were the base of the American Polaris submarines the area would be an inevitable target.

Questions were asked by a former First Lord of the Admiralty, John Dugdale, as to why Scotland had been chosen. He asked the Prime Minister 'whether, before agreeing to give the United States Government a base for the Polaris submarines in this country, he asked the United States Government what other countries had been approached for the lease of bases, and whether he asked what replies they had given'.

The Prime Minister answered some other questions but avoided this one, but Dugdale persisted in a supplementary:

'Is the Prime Minister aware that he has not answered my question. I asked him specifically whether any other country had been approached to give these facilities. Does he propose to answer that now?'

Macmillan then replied:

'The Americans asked us to provide this facility. We gladly agreed in the interests of both countries and of the whole Atlantic Alliance. The question whether other countries may have been asked to do the same thing does not appear to be relevant.'

But it surely was relevant. Had Norway, for example, with lochs much nearer the area where the Polaris submarines were supposed to operate, been approached and had Norway refused and why? And if Norway were not prepared to take the risk why had the Prime Minister agreed to the base in Scotland?

Then what control would the British Government exercise over the activities of the submarines based on the Holy Loch?

On December 17th the Norwegian Government announced that it had decided against the stockpiling of nuclear weapons in Norway and that 'it had taken this decision after a careful weighing up of all relevant considerations'.

In his statement Macmillan had said that 'wherever these submarines may be I am satisfied that no decision to use these missiles would ever be taken without the fullest possible consultation'. The key word in this assurance was the word 'possible'. When the report of what Macmillan had told the

House of Commons reached Washington there appeared to have been some misunderstanding and a statement was immediately issued emphasizing that control of Polaris submarines would remain with America. When Watkinson, the Minister of Defence, came to explain why there was some difference in the explanations he said: 'I think that the misunderstanding in America, in so far as I can track it down, occurred because some reports of his speech omitted the word "possible". [Hon. Members: 'Oh!'] Yes, and of course if that is omitted it becomes an absolute statement.'

If a mistake like this could lead to a misunderstanding between London and Washington couldn't some misunderstanding come about in a message between Washington and an American Polaris submarine operating in the Arctic? It illustrated the danger that Britain was involved in. The opposition to Polaris was not confined to Opposition M.P.s. *The Scottish Sunday Express* in a leading article called it 'The Humiliating Agreement' and said:

'Is there anyone in Britain this morning who does not feel a sense of shame at the mere words "Holy Loch"? For just think what the agreement for an American base there means. Britain's leaders have not only ceded the base to America. They have surrendered any right to ask what use it will be put to. They may not even be allowed to know where the submarines from Holy Loch will operate. A missile-carrying submarine could set out from the Clyde on a mission into Russian waters. It could involve Britain in the responsibility for war. But the first the British Cabinet would know about it would be when they saw the Russian protests in the newspapers.

'Would any tenth-rate banana state under American tutelage allow itself to be put into such a position of humiliation and danger? It may be said that President Eisenhower would never allow his Service chiefs to endanger Britain by irresponsible submarine tactics. The uncertainty makes it all the more urgent for the Cabinet to renounce the humiliating agreement.'

The announcement of the Polaris submarine base in Scotland certainly increased the international tension which Macmillan had set out to lessen. For the first time since his visit to Moscow he was sharply attacked by a prominent member of the Soviet Government.

On November 6th Koslov, the Vice-Chairman of the u.s.s.r. Council of Ministers, referred to Macmillan's announcement about the Polaris base in a speech at Moscow. He said:

'Some Western leaders, and in particular the British Prime Minister Mr Macmillan, have more than once spoken in favour of negotiations to relieve international tension. The latest steps of the British Government, however, compel us to question seriously the sincerity of Mr Macmillan's statement about the striving of the British Government to reduce international tension. Only a few days ago Mr Macmillan announced to Parliament the conclusion of an agreement between Britain and the United States under which the American Navy will get a base in Scotland near Glasgow, Britain's second biggest city, for submarines armed with missiles and nuclear weapons. The base is being created to serve as a point of departure of American atomic submarines equipped with nuclear missiles. The American military command plans to send these submarines to prowl near the sea boundaries of the Soviet Union. Who will fail to see that this is a case of a most dangerous adventure designed to worsen the international situation sharply and fraught with dangerous consequences to its American sponsors and their British allies.

'It is worth noting that Mr Macmillan negotiated the establishment of the base during his stay in the United States at the fifteenth session of the United Nations General Assembly which has been discussing disarmament as one of its main themes.

'With the Americans he discussed the question of the base. And with the Soviet delegation Mr Macmillan discussed the question of the need for negotiations to solve international questions ripe for settlement. Apparently the British Government is trying to move simultaneously in two diametrically opposed directions'.

The argument for the Polaris submarine was that it was part of the strategy of the nuclear deterrent. It could move about in Arctic waters and could not be destroyed because its exact location could not be detected. Later on when the Russians came to explode their megaton bombs in the Arctic the *Economist* explained that one of the military lessons of the tests was that the Russians might now be able to destroy a Polaris submarine without knowing its exact whereabouts with a bomb that could destroy submarines over a wide area. In the arms race one move follows another. It did not seem that by giving America a base on the Clyde Macmillan had helped to relieve international tension.

When he returned from his talks in Bermuda at the end of 1961 he talked about 'the terrible nuclear arms race'. It was not easy to see how a Polaris base in Scotland had helped to stop it.

Macmillan's policy of persistently yielding to America is, according to A. J. P. Taylor, the historian, the inevitable climax of a policy which Britain has been following for the past twenty years since the beginning of the last war. The appeasement of America by handing over the Holy Loch as a Polaris submarine base is just one instance of it.

'Why does Dr Adenauer, and even President de Gaulle, influence American policy where Mr Macmillan does not?' asked Taylor. 'They get their way,' he answers, 'by being independent. They have to be persuaded, won over by concessions, their interests deferred to.'

But in the case of the Polaris base the concessions were all on our side. It was in its way as great an act of appeasement by Macmillan as anything that Chamberlain agreed to at Munich.

Britain has no control over the Polaris submarines whose base is at Holy Loch when they embark upon their voyage towards the Arctic seas and their patrols in the region of the Russian coasts from which they would be able to fire their nuclear missiles to destroy Russian cities.

We know that it was a part of our own bomber strategy in the last war to destroy the German submarine bases. Now that the Polaris submarine base is in Scotland, Scotland will be regarded as one of the vital potential targets of the Russian rockets.

We have been placed in the maximum amount of danger with the minimum of defence. There were no indications given at all in the discussion that took place in Parliament about the Polaris Agreement that the question of the safety of the civil population of the West of Scotland was even considered.

CHAPTER XXIII

AMONG THE MILLIONAIRES

BRITISH Prime Ministers, Cabinet Ministers and members of the Government are supposed to give up any company directorships they may have when they take office. That is the recognized rule and convention. Out of office they resume their connections with big business and high finance. During the time of the Labour Government Anthony Eden was a bank director. Oliver Lyttelton, the Colonial Secretary in Churchill's Government, came into politics from big business and when he left politics he resumed the chairmanship of British Electrical Industries Ltd. His successor at the Colonial Office, Lennox-Boyd, when he was tired of being Colonial Secretary, was given a peerage and returned to the board of Guinness. Sir Walter Monckton was given a peerage and became the chairman of the Midland Bank. R. A. Butler out of office was closely associated with Courtaulds, the artificial silk combine. If the present Conservative Government were defeated at the next Election, its leading members would almost immediately be given directorships on the board of one of the big banks, or of the insurance companies.

If Selwyn Lloyd were no longer in office it is a safe guess that in a few months afterwards he would appear on the board of one of the big banks or one of the more prosperous insurance companies.

And if Harold Macmillan were no longer Prime Minister he could certainly go back to Macmillans.

The big Tory industrialists played a great part in financing the large-scale publicity and advertizing campaign which helped to win Macmillan the General Election of 1959.

In November 1961 Macmillan made a short week-end visit to Scotland to speak at a luncheon in Glasgow which had been arranged by the Central Office of the Conservative Party and to which had been invited many of the wealthy industrialists and financiers who were there to be swayed by the Prime Minister's eloquence into contributing substantial contributions to the Conservative Party funds.

Among them was Sir Hugh Fraser, the successful take-over bidder, who had been given a knighthood, and who had been successful in acquiring financial control over many of Britain's big drapery concerns.

It was said afterwards that Sir Hugh Fraser had been convinced that he had now not only taken over Harrods but Macmillans as well.

There was a lively interlude in the House of Commons when the Prime Minister was asked about this visit. 'Is the Prime Minister aware,' he was asked, 'that there is a strong public opinion in the West of Scotland that it is below the dignity of a British Prime Minister to travel to Scotland to get money for the Tory Party funds out of take-over bidders?'

He was obviously uncomfortable and his answer was evasive. He had as much right to express his views as anyone else. He refused to release the text of his speech. Tom Fraser asked if a report of the speech could be published and asserted that the Prime Minister's speech had been followed by an appeal from Sir Hugh Fraser to a great many men who had made huge sums of money in capital gains, on which they paid no tax, to be generous in their contributions to Tory Party funds.

'The speech,' said Macmillan, 'was made off the cuff, so no copy exists.'

It is not difficult to understand why the Prime Minister spoke off the cuff and did not want his speech to be reported.

The men who ultimately decided Macmillan's policy were the big business and financial tycoons who put up the money for the Tory Party funds.

They could say, as Bernard Shaw made Andrew Undershaft, the armaments king, say to the protesting politician in *Major Barbara*:

'The government of your country! I am the government of your country: I and Lazarus (his partner). Do you suppose that you and half-a-dozen amateurs like you, sitting in a row in that foolish gabble shop, can govern Undershaft and Lazarus? No, my friend: you will do what pays us. You will make war when it suits us, and keep peace when it doesn't. You will find out that trade requires certain measures when we have decided on those measures. When I want anything to keep my dividends up, you will discover that my want is a national need. When other people want something to keep my dividends down, you will call out the police and the military. And in return you shall have the support and applause of my newspapers and the delight of imagining that you are a great statesman.

'Government of your country! Be off with you, my boy, and play with your caucuses and leading articles and historic parties and great leaders and burning questions and the rest of your toys. I am going back to my counting-house to pay the piper and call the tune.'

Wealthy Scots businessmen could very well say, 'Of course Macmillan is one of us'.

In the *Sunday Express* of June 17th one of its leading writers, Robert Pitman, asked the question, 'Is Macmillan a millionaire?'

Prime Ministers these days cannot escape the glare of publicity or speculation about their private affairs. When Ramsay MacDonald was Prime Minister there was a major sensation when it was discovered that an old Scottish friend who was director of McVitie & Price had given MacDonald a gift of a batch of shares in his company in order to buy a motor car.

It is, however, taken for granted that Tory Prime Ministers are wealthy men who are not even dependent on their official salaries.

The question that was asked in the *Sunday Express* appears to have been fair political comment. It was certainly not reported to the Press Council as a breach of journalistic good taste.

Having asked the question 'Is Macmillan a millionaire?' the writer went on:

'Today the holiday-makers in the family cars on the Eastbourne road may catch a glimpse of one of those assets for themselves. Just past Haywards Heath, on the edge of Ashdown Forest, they may see a big country mansion tucked away beyond a high fence and a belt of trees.

'That is Mr Macmillan's home, Birch Grove.

'To most of the gazers the mansion among the trees—with its forty rooms and 800 acres of woods and grounds—may seem a fortune in itself . . .

'For the real facts about that ledger you must return from Birch Grove's woodlands to the Strand, to that big concrete wedge called Bush House.

'There in the blue-covered company records, sent up to you by lift from the vaults, you will find the key to the Prime Minister's private wealth. In those records you will find the only figures available to anyone outside the family about the Macmillan family trust.

'*What are the assets of the Macmillan Trust?*

'I will list them.

'First. The trust owns Macmillans, the publishers, holding all but 505 of the 370,000 £1 Ordinary shares.

'The value of that holding today? Well, let us send for the file on Macmillans.

'The figures inside the blue cover may astonish you. You will find that Macmillans not only has issued capital of £740,000, it has accumulated reserves of £1,289,000.

'A study of the balance sheet which has resulted from this plough-back policy reveals a flourishing, strongly based business which any enterprising City take-over man would be delighted to buy for £3,000,000.

'Secondly, the Macmillan Trust has benefited from a big trans-action which took place in 1951 when the controlling interest in the Macmillan Company of New York was sold to an American syndicate for £1,250,000.

'There are no records at Bush House to tell you what happened to all that money. But you can be sure that the bulk of it must be counted as an asset of the Macmillan Trust.

'Thirdly, the Macmillan Trust holds all but two of the shares in a company called Birch Grove Estates Ltd. One of the directors of the company is Lady Dorothy Macmillan, the Prime Minister's wife. Another is the Prime Minister's son, Mr. Maurice Macmillan.

'Birch Grove Estates not only owns £94,000 in Preference shares in Macmillans the publishers; it also owns Birch Grove, the Prime Minister's own home. So you can assume that the company's nominal capital of £89,500 in £1 shares is a very underplayed figure.

'Let us then add up the worth of the Macmillan Trust. It owns a publishing company with a value of perhaps £3,000,000. It has received unspecified proceeds from the £1,250,000 sale of the Mac-millan Company of New York. It owns Birch Grove Estates Ltd.

'Inevitably you must come to the conclusion that the trust itself is worth £4,000,000 at the least.

'There are other Macmillans, of course. There are the descendants of Frederick and George. There is also Arthur Macmillan, now a retired barrister of sixty-nine, a brother of Daniel and Harold.

'They could all have a claim on the Macmillan millions. But let us remember that those millions are built largely round the firm of Macmillans. And since 1936 the firm has been run by two men, Daniel and Harold.

'Who can doubt, then, that these two have the dominant interest in the trust? Who can doubt that—however we may apportion his share—Harold Macmillan is effectively a millionaire?

'Millionaire Macmillan! What a contrast that presents with the usual image of a remote, Trollope-reading figure.

'And the contrast becomes even sharper when we pay attention to one further fact—to the actual estate left by his father.

'What was the inherited fortune on which the present Macmillan millions are based?

'The answer is striking.

'When he died in 1936 Maurice Crawford Macmillan left an estate of £112,000.

'It is possible of course that he had made earlier provisions against death duties. And it is certain that the two other elder Macmillans who died in the same year left a substantial contribution to the family riches.

'But, whatever allowances are made for items like that, it becomes obvious that the enterprise and business sense of Daniel and Harold Macmillan have enormously increased the Macmillan inheritance.'

The article went on to speculate on the profits from publishing.

The writer had, however, forgotten that at one time Macmillan was a director of the Great Western Railway. When the Labour Government nationalized the railways they bought him out and compensated him. When he went north to visit Lord Home in Scotland a conscientious ticket collector at a country station insisted on seeing his ticket. He proudly produced the medallion of an ex-railway director who is entitled to free travel on British railways.

CHAPTER XXIV

CRITICS ON THE RIGHT

NOBODY emerged from the Tory back benchers to challenge Macmillan in the same way that he had challenged Baldwin and Neville Chamberlain in the years before the war. There was no Left wing in the Tory Party to attack him for supporting the vested interests or for not introducing more progressive legislation.

But he had his critics on the Right. After his resignation from the Government over the release of Makarios, Lord Salisbury continued to attack the Government for yielding to the forces of nationalism in Africa and for going forward too quickly there.

In a debate in the House of Lords on March 17, 1961, Lord Salisbury sneered at Macleod, then the Colonial Secretary, as 'being too clever by half' and carrying on negotiations in Rhodesia with the 'technique of a bridge player'. Macleod had been the bridge correspondent of a Sunday paper before entering Parliament. The Prime Minister, he said, had given Sir Roy Welensky a guarantee that the subject of secession from the Federation would be outside the terms of the reference to the Monckton Commission but had meant something else. That was 'an unfortunate episode' which had created suspicion and distrust in Rhodesia.

There was strong support in the Tory Party for Sir Roy Welensky and Lord Salisbury spoke for influential people on the Tory benches both in the House of Commons and the House of Lords. By placing himself at the head of the African Lobby Lord Salisbury was in a strong tactical position for making difficulties for Macmillan. He remained a powerful and influential figure behind the scenes.

Lord Salisbury himself had to meet a vigorous and surprise attack from Lord Alexander, the leader of the Labour Peers, and there was a lively interlude which disturbed the normal serenity of the House of Lords and enlivened the Official Report.

Viscount Alexander: The noble Marquis who spoke so feelingly yesterday, said he was speaking for the majority of the white population in the Rhodesias. Perhaps he did not remember that since 1957 he has also been a director of the British South Africa Company. [In previous years this company had paid dividends of thirty and forty per cent.]

Lord Salisbury: My Lords, I really think it is an abominable charge that I am allowing financial interests to interfere with my judgment. I hope the noble Viscount will withdraw that at once.

Lord Alexander: I am not making any charge at all.

Lord Salisbury: You are making a charge.

Lord Alexander: I said you spoke yesterday on behalf of the majority of people in the white minority in Africa. On the other hand, the noble Marquis must not be a law unto himself. As a rule every noble Peer who speaks upon these matters in which he has a financial interest declares it at the beginning of his speech. That is all I have to say.

Lord Salisbury: I think that is much too much.

Lord Alexander: On that point there is nothing whatsoever to withdraw.

Later Lord Salisbury announced that he had resigned from the directorship of the British South Africa Company.

His opposition to Macmillan's policy, however, continued.

Lord Salisbury was also a director of the Westminster Bank and had some influence in financial as well as political circles.

Criticism from this quarter was the sort of criticism that Macmillan could not ignore.

On March 10, 1961, Lord Salisbury made an attack on the Macmillan Government in a letter resigning from the presidency of the Hertford Constituency Conservative Association. He strongly disapproved of the Government's policy in Africa. He wrote: 'As you know I have been for some time growing more and more out of sympathy with Government policy over the future of Africa. They seem to be embarking upon a course fraught with danger both for our fellow countrymen and many thousands of loyal Africans in the territories for which we are responsible in those parts of the world.'

When what was known as the Katanga Lobby revolted some time later, Macmillan yielded. Although he frequently and dramatically declared that he repudiated a policy of appeasement and would never be associated with it he knew when political appeasement was expedient. He had no doubts about the real powers behind the scenes in the Tory Party.

Macmillan's most consistent and most persistent critic in the House of Commons was Lord Lambton, the Tory M.P. for Berwick-on-Tweed, who made repeated outspoken attacks on him in Parliament, in public and in the columns of the Beaverbrook press.

Lord Lambton certainly did not hesitate to attack Macmillan.

When Macmillan appointed Harold Watkinson to be Minister of Defence in 1959, Lambton wrote in the *Evening Standard* (17.11.59) that it was an appointment 'which had caused considerable surprise' and argued that Macmillan had got into the habit of appointing Ministers on whom he could rely to faithfully carry out his own policies. He continued:

'The consensus of opinion is that Mr Macmillan has put him there so that he himself can influence the Ministry of Defence as effectively as he does the Foreign Office. If this is so, the dangerous precedent has been established of a concentration of power greater than that was even held by Sir Winston Churchill.'

Lord Lambton was one of the Tory M.P.s who was an early critic of Macmillan's defence policy.

He wrote in the same article:

' "Far called, our Navies melt away." So, prophetically, wrote Kipling in 1897. If you insert the words Armies and Air Forces after Navies you get our effective military strength in 1959. At the moment, the increasing inadequacy of our military power is not understood. It will probably take a crisis to shake the country out of its ostrich-like attitude into a realisation of our weakness.'

Lord Lambton agreed with those who said that Macmillan was ready to do anything to please the Americans.

He wrote in the *Sunday Express* (18.6.60):

'Shortly after Macmillan became Prime Minister, he decided to woo America at any price. The result was the Bermuda Conference. It involved our sacrificing our independence, our foreign policy, our everything to please the Americans.'

He concluded by saying:

'There is a terrible end to a novel of Balzac which relates how a fireman seizes control of a train and unconscious of everything except speed, sends it flying through the night regardless of stops or in blissful ignorance of the end of the line, while oblivious behind him a troopload of soldiers sang patriotic songs. I will make no comparison.'

On November 6, 1960, Lord Lambton expressed the view that Sir Anthony Eden was watching 'with grim despair the brilliant solo act of Mr Macmillan'.

CHAPTER XXV

FIVE YEARS AS PREMIER

ON JANUARY 10, 1962, Harold Macmillan completed his fifth year as British Prime Minister, and the political commentators remarked that of peace-time Prime Ministers in this century only Asquith, Ramsay MacDonald (in two different Governments) and Lord Attlee stayed in office for a longer period, and some of them went on to speculate that in the event of his winning the next General Election he might well break the century record.

The estimates of Macmillan of course varied according to the politics of the commentators. All of them had to admit, however, that he had lasted longer than anybody had prophesied when he had taken office after the Suez disaster of 1956.

In an editorial *The Guardian* said:

'Mr Macmillan's skill in staying in power should, in fact, be the starting point of any appraisal of his record. Whatever else may be said of him, no one can deny that he is a consummate political artist —and it is often forgotten that without the political sensitivity which he so clearly possesses no political leader, however great his other gifts, can even hope to reach the heights.

'But sensitive political antennae, although an indispensable part of a successful Prime Minister's equipment, are not the only part. To rank as a great national leader a Prime Minister must also possess a sense of history and a firm commitment to some principle or set of principles. On the first of these two counts Mr Macmillan's record is a good deal better than most of his critics would admit. Future historians will surely see his Prime Ministership as the period when Britain at last awoke from her dreams of grandeur and came to terms with her new role as part of a developing union of Europe.

'Mr Macmillan's first task as Prime Minister was to rescue the country from the consequences of Suez. It is true, of course, that he had been as deeply implicated in that folly as the rest of the Eden Cabinet. Nevertheless, it cannot be denied that his policy in the months immediately after the Suez fiasco was more successful than anyone had dared to hope. One lesson of Suez was that Britain can no longer behave as an independent Great Power, except by courtesy of the United States. For a man of Mr Macmillan's generation that must have been a painful lesson; but there is little doubt that he learned it.

'The implications of that lesson were spelled out by the failure of Blue Streak, the failure of Mr Macmillan's attempt to act as honest broker between Russia and the United States, and the failure of the Government's economic policies. Together these led to one conclusion : Britain could not hope for real influence in world affairs, or for continuous economic growth at home, unless she came to terms with the Common Market. Here, again, a purist could criticize Mr Macmillan for moving too slowly; but bearing in mind the party he leads, and the far worse record of the official Opposition, the wonder is that he had the courage to move so fast.'

The article concluded :

'Mr Macmillan's real failure lies not in his reluctance to adjust to the facts of international life but in his refusal to hold out any ideal to his country. The true motto of his Administration is that of the nineteenth-century French politician Guizot: "Get rich". The material prosperity which this country has begun to experience in the last five years has meant a great increase in happiness and human dignity, and it would be humbug to pretend otherwise. But under Mr Macmillan's leadership the Government has failed to suggest, or even perhaps to realize, that prosperity cannot be regarded in purely individual terms. It is pointless to make individuals more prosperous at the cost of impoverishing society. A Conservative Government, it might be objected, can do nothing else. But there is no warrant in the history of the British Conservative Party for believing that its principles can never amount to more than the proposition that £5,000 a year is better than £1,000.'

At the other extreme of the British press the *Sunday Pictorial* listed Macmillan's broken Election pledges and the black spots in the record of his Government.

' "We want our people to have ample opportunity, not drab equality," he said in January 1957.

'Unemployment that month was 383,000. In December 1961 it was 389,297.

'Our industries would be revitalized, he promised.

'But today we share only one-sixth of the world's manufactured exports whereas once we had one-quarter.

'In his 1959 Election Manifesto, Macmillan said: "I don't remember a period in our lives when the economy has been so sound and the prosperity of the people so good."

'It was the signal for prices to go up, up, up. And for additional charges to be slapped on the Health Service.

'In 1959 he pledged: "We shall give all our support to the work of conciliation and mediation which the United Nations is well fitted to carry out".

'His Foreign Secretary, Lord Home, recently launched a vicious attack at the very foundations of U.N.

'He delayed and delayed the inevitable granting of Cyprus her freedom. He argued that the Greeks and the Turks would butcher each other in a civil war.

'Macmillan sent his Foreign Secretary to Portugal on a "mission of friendship" at the time its dictator, Salazar, was horrifying the world by burning, torturing and killing men, women and children in Angola.

'Macmillan haughtily dismissed the Berlin crisis. "It is all got up by the press," he said.

'There was a period when, under Iain Macleod, we had a wise Colonial policy. But when the chips were down over Northern Rhodesia, Macmillan would not back Macleod.

'Macmillan launched the Pay Pause without consulting the T.U.C. And apparently without thinking very deeply about it at all.

'Within days the whole of Britain blew it the biggest raspberry.

'As a reward for wickedly misleading the country over a "massacre plot" in Nyasaland, he protected the then Colonial Secretary, Lennox-Boyd—who is now a peer.

'At first he evaded questions about American planes flying over Britain armed with H-bombs.

'Finally the truth was dragged out of him word by word by Labour M.P.s.'

The writer accused Macmillan of being contemptuous of Parliament and British public opinion.

'Macmillan's disdain for Parliament and the public is constantly shown. Few are his major speeches in the Commons or on the television and the radio.

'He appears to live in a small world of his own. A world where we find six Old Etonians in his Cabinet. He also went to Eton.

'Harold Wilson has said of him: "These Edwardian posturings at race meetings and on ducal grouse moors might have been all right in more spacious easy times, but not today when this Government lives on borrowed money and borrowed time".

'He has perfected the art of talking for hours and saying nothing.

'His favourite sort of public utterance: "We must be neither foolishly swift nor obstinately slow."

'What does it mean?

'He has, however, produced one piece of philosophy everyone can understand: "The prize of success is great: but so is the penalty of failure".

'Almost cruelly his son, Maurice Macmillan, M.P., answers his father: "I feel the country and industry have looked in vain for economic leadership from the Government," he said.'

o

In the *Daily Express* Lord Altrincham wrote:

'How should his performance be rated? "Performance" is the word. Like most successful politicians, Mr Macmillan is a consummate actor. He has fooled the Old Guard of the Tory Party more effectively than any leader since Disraeli. He has also fooled the Labour Party.

'His technique has been to look and sound old-fashioned—to be admired (or ridiculed, according to taste) as a casual, supercilious English grandee, when in fact he is yet another radical adventurer from the Celtic fringe.

'Of course, he has a strong sense of history—only fools ignore the past—but he is thoroughly modern-minded. He is the least conservative Prime Minister since the war.

'Like Disraeli, he was a rebel in his youth. No Tory M.P. in the 'thirties—not even Churchill—was more fiercely antagonistic to the official party leadership.

'Now he controls the machine himself and exploits the blind loyalty and petty ambition of men whom he must secretly despise.

'He is not at all squeamish about the use of his immense patronage.

'But the aims are not cynical. He is a patriot and a humanitarian. The image of him as a plutocrat who neither understands nor really cares about the under-privileged masses is a grotesque caricature.

'Macmillan's handling of foreign affairs is open to much sharper criticism than his home policy. He has shed, since 1957, many of the illusions which seduced him into the deceitful folly of Suez. But he has continued to seek prestige without strength.

'In a period of nuclear stalemate, conventional forces have come back into their own. But Macmillan has reduced the British Army to such a low point that British diplomacy is fatally weakened.

'National Service was sacrificed for votes—or at best for economic advantages which have failed to materialize.

'The last five years have been the best years of his life. It is unlikely that he will be in any hurry to retire, though he will tease his would-be successors with hints of impending retirement.

'And it is safe to predict that he will accept no earldom unless, meanwhile, he has changed the law under which peers are disfranchized and disqualified from standing for the House of Commons.

'He will not want his son Maurice to share the fate of Lord Hailsham and Mr Wedgwood Benn.'

In an editorial article headed 'Five Years Hard' the *Daily Herald* said:

'Mr Macmillan celebrates his fifth anniversary as Prime Minister. He has worn well.

'His early years as Prime Minister were successful because luck—particularly the luck of the international terms of trade—was on his side. And because he was able to present a convincing Tory image to the Party while pursuing the liberal policies which events compelled and which pleased the electorate.

'All this was done with a good deal of skill in the political arts and in role-playing.

'The most important statement of his political life was the phrase "You never had it so good". It was a signal to the Tory Party to stop groaning about working-class gains, to take pride in them and to cash in on the benefits they could bring to the Party at the polls.

'For the past year Mr Macmillan's reputation has been on the downgrade. World conditions are no longer on his side. The countries of Western Europe are setting the pace today, and Britain is lagging. And to bring Britain up to date means upsetting recent Tory tradition—even the adoption of planning.

'At the last Conservative Conference Mr Macmillan spoke jestingly of his departure. "I do not want to live," he said, " 'after my flame lacks oil, to be the snuff of younger spirits'."

'Mr Macmillan's oil is perilously low. But Prime Ministers can seldom choose the time of their departure. The succession is not resolved. He must struggle on: and the way things are going the chances of getting out at a moment when all looks well in the nation's affairs appears to be slim indeed.'

The *Daily Mail* said that 'Macmillan's qualities are what the age demands'.

'These five years have been a time of confusion and uncertainty in a world built upon shifting sands. They demand the ability in statesmen to watch and wait and seize the flying opportunity.

'It is this which Mr Macmillan possesses in more than ordinary measure. He is not one who "rides in the whirlwind and directs the storm", as Chamberlain and Eden tried to do.

'He takes in a reef or two, runs before the tempest, and then makes for port. It can be said of him that he allows events to carry him to the point of maximum advantage.

'Suez was the last British attempt at "gunboat diplomacy", and Mr Macmillan's task was—for want of a better term—to move the country and his party and Government to the Left. The measure of his success was the 1959 Election.'

The *Daily Mail* thought that Macmillan fulfilled the role of the Ancient Mariner admirably.

It continued:

'But first he sensed that after the screaming weeks of argument and abuse, after the shocks and excitements of Suez, rest and quiet were needed. These he provided in the months when it was thought he was a mere cipher—or a "caretaker" Prime Minister.

'One clue to his thought and action came with the famous "wind of change" speech in Africa which recognized the inevitability of colonial transition. Note the metaphor with its image of gradualness.

'His approach to the Common Market was an act of courage. But there were months in which he did nothing, for he was once more allowing a situation to ripen.

'So it was with the recent Berlin crisis. To have rushed hot-foot into negotiation, as many demanded, would have been to suit Russia's book. A similar careful diplomacy led to the Summit of 1960, but that broke down and gave Mr Macmillan his biggest disappointment.'

It thought, however, that Macmillan's tendency to want to see which way the wind was blowing had its disadvantages.

'Britain has become much more prosperous since 1957, but the Government's failure to tackle recurrent economic crises at the roots is probably the failure of the Prime Minister to take drastic action at unpropitious moments.

'Defence is a mess—but so is the science of war, in that weapons become obsolescent almost before they leave the laboratories. Perhaps here also Mr Macmillan is waiting for some shape to emerge before he makes hard-and-fast decisions.

'Barring unexpected events his Premiership is by no means over, and the time has not arrived to assess his place as a head of our affairs.

'But he is certainly among the cleverest politicians Downing Street has seen this century—and he may yet rank among the outstanding Prime Ministers.'

The *Daily Mail* didn't quite know how to assess him. So like Macmillan it decided it would be better to 'watch and wait'.

In a quite different type of article in *Time and Tide*, Henry Fairlie began by saying 'Macmillan is an extravagantly plain man. This may seem to be a gratuitous paradox, but it is in fact only if we see him as such that all the other paradoxes in his character can be explained. There is very little that is remarkable about him, except the total effect; and how far that effect is genuine and how far it is artificial, a disguise in armour, it is difficult for his contemporaries to judge.'

This writer found Macmillan a complex and puzzling personality, a man of great industry and persistency, and an adroit and astute politician.

'Today when one listens to Macmillan converse about politics, one is listening to a man of not more than ordinary intellectual capacity sensitively explore the common moods and attitudes of ordinary people. He starts always with the Walpolian adage that what people want is prosperity at home and peace abroad. To him these are the clear objects of all political action . . .

'The common opinion is God. He is, in this sense, the most democratic of politicians. *Vox Populi* is *Vox Dei*, to be heeded, if possible anticipated, gratified at whatever price and adored at Election time.

'That is his strength and his weakness. He can calculate the hopes, fears, moods and attitudes of ordinary people with almost precise skill and by satisfying them he holds their support.

'But this inevitably means that to their common opinion he opposes only his own common estimate of them. He vulgarizes his own opinions, his own feelings and his own hopes, so that they will accord with theirs, and it is the essential vulgarity of his political leadership which contrasts so noticeably with the privately civilized, educated and reflective being which he clearly was, and perhaps privately still is.

'The vulgarity is sometimes not even veneered. "There ain't gonna be no war" (after the failure of the Geneva Conference). "They have never had it so good" (still meaning what it has been taken to mean, in spite of his tendentious re-interpretation of it at the Guildhall in November); these were not accidents, not lapses. This is how his mind works as a democratic leader.

The writer's estimate is that Macmillan, in spite of all his pretensions, is really not such a superior person as he seems to be.

'He is, as I said at the beginning, a plain man. If he were not where he is, it would be hard to think of any remarkable feature about him. This may appear to beg the whole question, but in fact it could not be said of most Prime Ministers.

'He is a man of almost no real quality, of mind, of opinion, or temper.

'If this seems too sweeping, I would only ask: "Is there one rough intellectual proposition which he has put to us in the whole of the past five years, when it was essential that we should think (above all *think*) clearly about our position in the world. Is there one strenuous and not flabby sentiment which he has inspired in us? Can anyone pretend that this country is as morally and spiritually alert as when he took office in 1957? . . .

'What the people want, he alone can divine; and what they want they shall be given. To some this may appear to be majestically democratic; but in practice it is as old as the Caesars. It is no different from Julius Caesar's habit of returning from his earlier triumphs to curry favour with the mob by organizing more extravagant games than any of his predecessors and rivals.'

This must have been the only way that Macmillan resembled Julius Caesar.

Having written about how Macmillan resembles Julius Caesar, Henry Fairlie goes on to say how he differs from Abraham Lincoln.

'This was not the practice of the greatest of all democratic leaders, Abraham Lincoln. If he had adopted the methods of Macmillan, there would have been no United States, the Southern states today would probably be organized like any other South or Central American dictatorship, and the leadership of the West would certainly not rest on the united, strong, energetic, generous, liberal and dignified democracy which all but the wilfully blind can recognize in America.

' "Let the grass grow in the streets though it may," proclaimed Lincoln, thus asserting once and for all that there are sacrifices of its ease and comfort which the present must sometimes make to secure its future.

'Macmillan is prevented by his attention to common opinion from ever making such a plea, for it implies that the common attitudes of the present, which are nearly always short-sightedly selfish, must be allowed to govern his own.'

Had the Tory Party had the slightest suspicion that Harold Macmillan might turn out to be another Abraham Lincoln he certainly would have been the last person they would have accepted as a leader. They did not want anybody like that.

This candid critic sums up:

'But let us look finally at his face. It is an extravagantly plain one. There is nothing remarkable about it, except his eyes, which are paler than one would expect from his pictures, and which have that unnerving quality, common in men of action, of appearing self-absorbed and yet penetrating at the same time.

'For the rest, the moustache, the hair, the cranium, the jaw, the teeth even, in spite of the cartoonists' exaggerations of them, are undistinguished, except by the fact of his office and well-tended age.

'He is the ham version of a plain man, and the plain man enjoys the reassuring reflection.

'On the day of his appointment, five years ago, I asked someone who knew him what he thought. "He's got in ten years too late," was the reply. Perhaps this is the answer. Perhaps the keen-eyed man of 1945 would have reacted differently to his opportunities.

'But, now that he has got it, and in the circumstances in which he got it, we find ourselves led by an aged cynic, who has learned too much of the shallows of human nature, and locked himself out from the depths of the human heart and the human understanding, determined to live, after a life of such ceaseless activity, according to the motto of the statesman who has abdicated: *quieta non movere*. Being interpreted, it is R.I.P. There, if his leadership continues, we may end.'

This must have been the harshest judgment of any of the commentators who wrote about him on this occasion. It was rather soon to write R.I.P. about Macmillan. 'The first thing about obituaries is make sure your man is dead,' wrote Bernard Shaw when he was asked to write an obituary notice of Mussolini on the first occasion when Mussolini was reported to have been executed. Shaw's caution was justified. Mussolini survived for a while. Macmillan's political fortunes have several times seemed to be at a low ebb, but he has recovered. He has shown great capacities of resiliency and staging a come-back.

The R.I.P. seemed a little premature.

CHAPTER XXVI

THE PARTY LEADER

IT IS certainly difficult to imagine anyone less like Abraham Lincoln than Harold Macmillan. But if he does not follow in Abraham Lincoln's footsteps he at least quotes from him. 'As Abraham Lincoln observed,' he told the Annual Conference of the Conservative Trade Unionists in London on March 19, 1960, 'you can fool all of the people some of the time; and some of the people all of the time; but you cannot fool all the people all of the time.' However, there is no doubt about it that Harold Macmillan did his best and if he did not succeed entirely, has had a fair measure of success.

At this conference of the Conservative Trade Unionists he was addressing an audience that was prepared to be fooled, indeed was there to be fooled.

But even if they were not all fooled they were certainly flattered.

He recalled that a year before he had not been able to attend but had sent them an inspiring message which had read:

'You who serve in the front line may at times feel isolated and out-numbered and may seem at times to be fighting a hard and often unrewarding battle. But do not forget that you are but the spearhead of a larger army, and an army that is winning.'

He thought that the General Election had shown the truth of that. 'I suppose that more trade unionists had voted Conservative than ever before and I would like to thank you for your part in bringing it about.'

They were certainly entitled to his thanks. So were the employers and big business men who had put up the money for the mass publicity and advertizing campaign that had helped so much to win the Election for the Conservative Party.

The Conservative trade unionists had, however, got precious little more than thanks. They had certainly not been given any of the safe Tory seats. If Harold Macmillan had been enthusiastic about getting Conservative trade unionists into Parliament what

had he done about it? How many *bona fide* Conservative trade
unionists had been adopted for Conservative seats by the Conservative Party constituency organizations? One wonders if
Harold Macmillan had even made an effort to get more Conservative trade unionists as Parliamentary candidates in seats where
there was any chance of them winning.

Of course there are no trade unions affiliated to the Conservative Party and no trade union organizations can nominate
candidates.

When Macmillan formed his Cabinet he chose the old
Etonians. There was not one Conservative trade unionist among
them. Even the Minister of Labour is an old Etonian.

True, large numbers of trade unionists were persuaded to vote
for Macmillan but nobody believes that trade unionists influence
or inspire the Conservative Party.

On the contrary, the Conservative Party is the party of the
employers. It resolutely refuses to disclose its balance sheet
because that would show quite clearly the contributions of the
big capitalist concerns that put up the money for the Conservative Party and its propaganda and no doubt did so for the conference of the Conservative Trade Unionists.

Macmillan went on to tell his audience:

'This great gathering is a striking contradiction of the idea that there
is something incompatible between Conservatism and trade unionism.
That is false historically, false theoretically and false practically.
Conservatism has always been sympathetic towards the right of
workers to organise. For example, the repeal of the laws which pro-
hibited associations either of workers or employers was the result of
a Commission set up by the Government of a Conservative, Lord
Liverpool. That was in 1824. But do not let us dwell too long on
historical memories. It would be unkind to remind modern Liberals
of the attitude taken towards trade unions in the days of their early
triumphs after the Reform Bill of 1832 and to contrast it with the
more far-seeing attitude of the Conservative Disraeli.'

We have been told that Macmillan is 'an avid reader of
history'. One wonders what kind of history! If he had read any
history of British trade unionism he must have known that it is
a history of long struggle between workers fighting for higher
wages, a shorter working day and better working conditions
against Tory employers.

If he had read the history of the Great Western Railway, of

which he was a director, he would have known that the Tory
directors of that company refused to recognize the railwaymen's
trade union and only did so as a result of the railwaymen's strike
in 1910. Macmillan must surely know that for a century the
Tory Party Members in the House of Commons regarded the
trade unions as their natural enemies. One has only to watch
how Tory M.P.s react in any industrial dispute to realize that
most of them still do so today. If the trade unions are powerful
today it is not due to any assistance that they have received from
Conservative Governments but because of their own efforts and
of generations of struggle.

Either Macmillan was showing a total ignorance of elementary
history, which one would hardly expect from the Chancellor of
the University of Oxford, or he was just saying anything that
would be likely to be accepted without question from an
ignorant and ineffectual audience.

He went on to tell the conference:

'I believe that your importance to the Conservative Party cannot be
over-estimated. We need your help in explaining the policy and ideas
of Conservatism on the shop floor. We need your advice on the
aspirations and views of trade unionists. Both these activities are at
times not unattended with difficulties. But I do assure you that I and
my colleagues are grateful to you for your untiring efforts. Do not
let up on any of these fronts, and remember that it is the votes of
Conservative trade unionists which put the Conservative Party in
office and which alone can keep them there. Without them we should
be a permanent minority, and I tremble to think what the state of
the country might be on that event.'

Obviously Macmillan wanted the Conservative trade unionists,
who had been paid out of the Party funds to attend this bogus
'conference', to act as Tory canvassers. But there their usefulness
to him ended. What sort of advice did he think they were likely
to give him on the aspirations and the views of trade unionists?

Indeed did he ever really think of treating them seriously as
genuine representatives of the trade unions? When he really
wanted to get any advice from the trade union movement he
sent for the T.U.C.; when he wanted the help of the trade unions
on the National Economic and Development Council which was
to plan the future development of the country? Not at all. He
ignored them. They were represented by the Conservative
nominees of big business.

Nobody knew better than Macmillan that their function was not to give him advice but to take orders from the Tory Head Office.

He went on to talk about how enthusiastic the Conservative Government were about 'full employment'. The Conservatives had only started to use the phrase 'full employment' in recent years. Why, he himself, in his pre-war days had been eloquent in the House of Commons on the way the Tories had neglected unemployment and had no constructive policy for dealing with unemployment. We could only get full employment if prices did not rise and if there was no inflation. Yet his Government had been responsible for increased wage demands because the workers needed extra wages to pay the increased rents that had been imposed on them by the Rent Act.

One wonders where the Conservative trade unionists were when the Tory Government introduced the Rent Act? Did Macmillan seek any advice from the Conservative trade unionists, or any trade unionists, then?

The picture Macmillan gave to the gullible Conservative trade unionists was that of a country whose production was steadily increasing as the results of the drive and energy of a Conservative Government.

Did he not know how shaky the economy was? Two years later he had to explain to the leaders of the trade unions that the country couldn't afford to give underpaid railwaymen and bus drivers and post office workers a rise?

After ten years without planning he had set up an organization to plan because unplanned British capitalism had brought us into an economic and financial crisis. He had said when he returned to the House of Commons after the 1945 Election that he felt like Rip Van Winkle. For ten years Rip Van Winkle had gone to sleep again. He only woke up to realize that British economy must be planned when the reverberations of economic crisis could no longer be ignored and when he was forced to wake up.

The speech that he delivered to the Conservative trade unionists was the typical speech that he was accustomed to deliver to Tory Party conferences and gatherings of all kinds. Undoubtedly the Tory Party had every reason to be grateful to him. He was their soothsayer-in-chief.

He could be relied upon to give pep talks to young Tories and soothing syrup to the Tory women's conferences that wanted more flogging and hanging. He was there to dish out the slobbering sentiment and the appropriate sob-stuff, to get the cheap laugh by some topical illusion in the manner of the music hall and wireless comedian and to pad it out with conventional platitudes and clichés and the half-truths which were likely to be appreciated by his audiences.

Tom Jones, who was for many years the Secretary to the Cabinet, was asked in 1931 to suggest a speaker to put the point of view of the Young Conservatives in America. Harold Macmillan was on the list and Jones wrote of him: Harold Macmillan belongs to the famous publishing firm and is married to a daughter of the Duke of Devonshire, is quite able, but I think, rather pedestrian'. He recommended Walter Elliot instead.

Anybody who studied the speeches of Macmillan at any of these Conservative gatherings will understand exactly what Jones meant.

Anybody who had been used to hearing Winston Churchill address Conservative Party gatherings could not help but realise that after him Macmillan was a complete anti-climax. Churchill had a superb platform manner and a wonderful command of the English language of which he was a master. Speeches to these gatherings were always great occasions in which he developed some political theme, elaborated it in a historical background, and concluded with a resounding peroration.

Macmillan is not an orator, and is acutely conscious of it. There are passages in these party speeches which are not just uninspiring; they are deadly dull. A party leader should inspire his audiences, especially his supporters, at conferences and mass gatherings. Reading the verbatim reports of these speeches in the official hand-outs of the Conservative Central Office (an exhausting task) one finds it difficult to find any really striking, memorable or quotable sentences.

Indeed, reading them one wondered whether Macmillan did not really despise his audience, play down to them and amuse them because he had no serious message to give them. Churchill was usually worth listening to and reading, even when one violently disagreed with him. A collection of Churchill speeches, when he was Prime Minister, make an interesting and readable

volume, but a collection of Macmillan's speeches as Prime
Minister would be unbearable. Not even Macmillans would
publish it.

It was not difficult for the London actor who so successfully
impersonated Macmillan to get suitable material. It was nearly
always the same theme, the wickedness of the Socialist Government, from which the country had been rescued in time by the
bold brave Conservatives who had been so successful in achieving
such miracles in a country where 'you've never had it so good'
with slab after slab of platitudes and long-drawn-out, laboured
argument as tedious to read as it must have been unbearable to
listen to.

Genuine oratory must come from deep emotion. There must
be life and humour and wit in it. Macmillan's speeches at Conservative Party gatherings have all the look as if the speaker had
spent the night before in studying the Conservative Party
Weekly Speakers' notes. There were nearly always panegyrics
on the wonderful record of the legislation that the Conservative
Party had produced throughout the centuries. Nobody listening,
for example, to Macmillan speaking to the National Conference
of the Young Conservatives in London on February 25, 1961,
would ever have thought that the Conservative Party had been
anything but the party of progress. Here he is in full swing.

'Some things are not so good. We must strive to improve them. And
what is bad must be eradicated. All this is not some new sort of Conservative policy hastily put together under the necessity of appealing
to a mass electorate. It has been the policy of our party for generations. We have a long and proud record of legislation dealing with
working conditions in factory, mine and field, with health and
housing, with the care of the elderly and the widening of educational
opportunity for the young. It is a record to which we are adding new
chapters in this latest spell of office. Today, for instance, we are
engaged in a massive drive to clear the slums. There have only been
two such drives in the whole of our history, both of them under
Conservative Ministers.'

It would have been difficult to pack so much misleading half-
truth into one short paragraph. If Macmillan had really believed
all this, what did all those pre-war speeches attacking the Conservative Government mean? Was he giving his audience any
credit for intelligence or for any knowledge of the history of
Britain in the nineteenth century at all? How much enthusiasm

for clearing away the slums did the Tories show before the Labour Party arrived on the scene. He assumed that the young Tories knew nothing of how bitterly the Tories had attacked even the legislation of the Liberal Government in the years before the First World War.

He explained why as a young man he did not join the Liberal Party or the Labour Party.

He said:

'Some of us had traditional Liberal connections, but we found the Liberal Party shattered and split. Some of us felt an instinctive sympathy with the new emerging Labour Party. For at that time it was still a party based upon a sincere if often a confused faith. It tried to represent the underdog, the poor, the oppressed. It protested against the inequalities of life and conditions of the day. It was in those days, or at least appeared on the surface to be, in the nature of a crusade. But when one looked below the surface you could see that it had already been inoculated with the fatal poison of Marxist Socialism, so un-English, so contrary to nature and to commonsense. So we found our home in the Conservative Party.'

It was rather a curious explanation of why he had not joined the Labour Party. It must have taken a very good microscope to have discovered the poison of Marxist Socialism in the Labour Party of those days.

His objection to Marxist Socialism was that it was 'un-English'. He might have objected to the New Testament for the same reason. And if Marx was un-English what was Macmillan's favourite political prophet Disraeli? Disraeli was surely as un-English as Karl Marx. One wonders how much of Karl Marx Macmillan had ever read. He clearly had not succeeded in getting as far as Marx's chapters on the history of the Industrial Revolution in Britain or he could hardly have acquired his ideas about the Conservative Party being in the van of progress during the nineteenth century. But if, as he had said earlier in his speech, the Conservative Party 'had such a long and proud record' and had a philosophy that had guided it for generations, why had Macmillan earlier been wondering whether he should join the Labour Party?

Perhaps it is unkind for anyone to critically examine a speech delivered to a mass meeting of Young Conservatives. Was this just another case of Macmillan underestimating the intelligence of his audience? Or did he think that after all the Young

Conservatives should not be treated too seriously. Were they not just like the Conservative Trade Unionists, brought there by the Conservative Head Office as potential future voters or as useful canvassers on election day? If he had such faith in them why was he against giving them the vote at nineteen? Or were they just another collection of people whom he could politically exploit?

Perhaps it would be merciful not to examine in too much detail Macmillan's speeches to the mass meetings of Conservative Women at the Albert Hall.

He had, however, a historic announcement to make at the mass rally on June 25, 1959. 'The latest example of the storming of male preserves,' he told them, 'is the creation of life peeresses. They are now making their mark in the House of Lords.'

He spoke enthusiastically about what the Government was doing for women on the housing front. The Minister for Housing, Mr Brooke, 'had got an assurance that where a woman applicant for a loan is in a regular job, the general policy of the building societies will be to treat her exactly the same way as a man'.

He might have added that she should have the privilege of paying the same high rate of interest on the loan as well.

But he had nothing at all to say on the subject that was worrying millions of housewives in London, the rise in rents that was coming as a result of the Government's Rent Act. Macmillan knew what subjects to avoid. It would have been quite inappropriate to discuss the Rent Act at a mass meeting at the Albert Hall. It might have damped down the enthusiasm. That was not what these demonstrations were for.

It should not be thought, however, that Macmillan's speeches at these Tory gatherings were not enthusiastically received. He was their leader, the Great MacWonder, the dear old Grandfather Politician, who spoke to them heart to heart. It never dawned on them to ask whether these speeches were silly or cynical. He filled the bill. He could get the Tory Party the votes.

CHAPTER XXVII

SICK MAN OF EUROPE

IN JULY 1961 it was obvious that the country, to use the description of ex-Chancellor Peter Thorneycroft, had 'slithered' into another financial and economic crisis, and on July 25th the Chancellor of the Exchequer, Selwyn Lloyd, appeared at the Dispatch Box to make the expected statement.

Since the Budget, he said, home demand had continued to increase and was likely to increase even more than was then foreseen.

'There are labour shortages in most areas. Investment is rising strongly. The building industry already has more demand upon it than it can satisfy and parts of the engineering industry are coming under increasing pressure.

'Simultaneously with the increase of pressure on our domestic resources, we are faced with a critical external situation. This is the third successive year in which our overall balance of payments has been in deficit and this is, clearly, not a situation which can be allowed to continue.'

This was a very different picture from the one that Macmillan had painted at the General Election.

There had been heavy withdrawals of short-term balances and British reserves of gold dollars had fallen by about £164 million during the previous six months. The Government had come to the conclusion that:

'First we should maintain investment in productive industry with a view to the long-term growth of the economy. At the same time we must make ourselves more competitive. Both are vital for a long-term improvement in the balance of payments.

'Secondly, we must see that public expenditure is brought under better control.

'Thirdly, we must take action designed to protect our position in the immediate future.'

He dealt first of all with the growth in the economy.

For years the Tories had been jeering at the very word planning. Now a Conservative Chancellor told them:

'The controversial matter of planning at once arises. I am not frightened of the word.'

The Tory M.P.s behind him certainly were. The time had come for co-ordinating planning activities and he intended to discuss urgently with both sides of industry procedures for putting together those various processes of consultation and forecasting with a view to better co-ordination of ideas and plans.

This was the Treasury verbiage for explaining that the economy must be planned and that the uncontrolled free-for-all capitalist economy had to be controlled at last.

He referred first of all to profits. In his next Budget he intended bringing forward 'measures designed to impose a clear liability to tax over a wider field than at present'. He had rejected Labour's demand for taxing capital gains during the Budget Debate a few months earlier. Now he was reconsidering it. He was considering dealing with speculation and other methods of tax avoidance.

As for wages, 'there must be a pause until productivity has caught up and there is room for further advances'.

He would be compelled to reduce public expenditure. The Government was going to look at the level of agricultural support and expenditure by local authorities would have to be considerably reduced.

The Government could not agree to the rise in teachers' salaries as agreed by the Burnham Committee. Government expenditure overseas would have to be reduced, the programme of the Ministry of Defence would be reviewed. The expenditure of £80 million a year in Europe in connection with NATO commitments, and especially the £65 million on the maintenance of forces in Germany could not be allowed to continue. He had come to the conclusion 'that the strain upon our balance of payments caused by this expenditure cannot be allowed to continue in the next financial year'.

With his approval the Bank of England had announced a rise in the Bank Rate from five per cent to seven per cent. He had agreed to this because of the need to restrain credit internally and partly because of the unsettled international situation.

There was to be an increase in purchase tax and Customs and Excise duties equivalent to ten per cent of the existing rates, and

P

there would be a substantial drawing by the Government from the International Monetary Fund.

These were the Government's proposals for dealing with the financial and economic crisis and they came in for heavy criticism in the two days' debate that followed on an Opposition vote of censure.

Harold Wilson said that the charge against the Chancellor was that 'this long-awaited, long-heralded, much-trumpeted July "Budget" is monstrously unjust'.

He recalled that during the Election the Prime Minister had proclaimed:

'Today, the British economy is sounder than at any time since the First World War. Sterling has been re-established in a sound and respected currency. Our balance of payments is strong.'

Wilson declared that Macmillan was the man who bore a heavier responsibility either for misdirected policies or for the inculcation of this climate of national complacency.

'I suppose it must seem to him years since he strutted on to the platform of that 1958 Conservative Conference as the mighty Wurlitzer organ throbbed to the strains of "Mr Wonderful, that's you" and then called his troops to the forthcoming Election battle with a speech which was an orgy of self-satisfaction and boasted that our economy was in such fine shape. The Right Hon. Gentleman, who pledged himself on television, on becoming Prime Minister, to "make Britain great", has so imperilled and squandered our economic security that we are in danger of earning for ourselves the gibe which the Czar Nicholas addressed to the dying Ottoman Empire: "The Sick Man of Europe". That is his contribution.

'This is a hard thing to say but it is not imagination. One of the leading German periodicals has an article in this week's issue headed "The Sick Man of Europe". . . . I am not running Britain down. Fundamentally, as the whole House knows, our latent virility, vigour, skill, ingenuity and inventiveness are such that instead of presenting this image of sickness, we could present an image to the world of bounding energy and enterprise.

'All that is lacking is the leadership and inspiration, the call for service and sacrifice which this administration is unable to give.'

Macmillan had a difficult task in replying to this debate but he did his best.

Before he had begun Julian Snow had shouted 'For God's sake go', which was hardly an encouragement. He defended himself against Harold Wilson's charge that he had deluded the country about the real economic situation of the country. When he had made the speech about the favourable balance of payments in September 1959 there had been a surplus for the three preceding six-month periods and at the time his optimism had been justified. But now there had been setbacks. Abroad British assets had suffered from nationalization and there had been an unexpected drop in earnings as a result of the lower world price of oil. His object was 'not merely to steer the country through these immediate difficulties but to make it possible to develop long-term policies which would maintain a sound basis for the continuing prosperity of the country'. He filled in the time with his customary gibes about what the Opposition had done when they were in power. 'They were years of shortages, high taxation and soaring prices and of a Government torn, hopelessly, divided and torn by bitter strife.' This was of course a caricature. Shortages there had been, for we had just emerged from a ruinous war, but the Labour Government had not been so torn by bitter strife until the rearmament programme.

But the House had heard this tale from Macmillan so many times that it had long been tiresome. It was his usual alibi. It was ten years away from the Labour Government now.

He ended by saying that the economic situation 'with which we are confronted must neither be minimized nor exaggerated. It is marginal but it is vital. [He had become an expert in using the clichés and phrases which cancelled each other out.] To resolve our difficulties is well within our power. It requires common sense and a practical assessment of our own interests. What I call our duty to ourselves. It requires imagination and an honourable acceptance of our obligations to less happy peoples and our duty towards our neighbours. It requires an effort of restraint and unity on a national scale. But I cannot believe that a nation which has survived such times and such fearful dangers in the past will fail to rise to its duty today.'

He had glossed over the failure of the Government as well as he could. If platitudes and clichés could solve the economic problems that faced Britain, Macmillan would not be found wanting. But the facts spoke for themselves.

CHAPTER XXVIII

RETURN TO PLANNING

MOST of those who wrote comments on the occasion of the fifth anniversary of Macmillan's Premiership agreed on his ability and dexterity as a politician and on his achievement in restoring the political prestige of the Tory Party after the Suez adventure.

Nobody could deny this. The Tories had every reason to be grateful to him for this and for the successful way he had led them to victory at the General Election of 1959. But what is good for the Tory Party is not necessarily good for Britain or for the world.

And after five years of Macmillan's Premiership one was justified in looking at the condition of Britain and her place in the modern world.

What had Macmillan been able to achieve during this time that was likely to make his reputation as one of Britain's great Prime Ministers? He had not only been Prime Minister but he had been in the Cabinet for a decade and had occupied many of the most important positions in it.

Whenever he was in difficulties in debate in the House of Commons he invariably returned to the theme of how much better things were under the Tories than under the Labour Government which had preceded it. Whenever he had gaps to fill up in his winding up speeches in reply to vote of censure debates he pointed his finger across to the Opposition Front Bench and asked, 'What did they do? What happened under the Socialists?' This enabled him to get away with a lot at many awkward moments and invariably brought cheers from the back benchers behind him. But ten years afterwards this was wearing very thin. It was a long way from 1951 and the Tories had been in office for ten years themselves and had every opportunity to show how much better they could run the country than the Labour Government. To what extent had they succeeded?

It must be remembered, too, the circumstances under which the Labour Government had taken office. It had come into power in 1945 at the end of the most destructive war in history. Churchill, himself, towards the end of the war had outlined the tremendous tasks that any Government would have to face when peace came. One often wondered when the Tories were attacking the Attlee Government between 1945 and 1951 what they would have done had Churchill and his followers won the General Election of 1945. Indeed what would or what could Macmillan have done had he become Prime Minister five years earlier? We do know, however, what an anti-Socialist Government, with the Tories dominating it, had done after the First World War. Indeed Macmillan himself had testified to the complete failure of the Tory Governments that had been in power between the wars to produce any constructive policy for dealing with the problems of unemployment and poverty.

Macmillan always attacked Labour as if the Labour Government had ruined a prosperous country. He did not allow for the fact that Labour had come into power in a Britain shattered by war.

There is no reason to believe that if the Tories had been returned to power in 1945 that they would have done better then than after the First World War. For they were fundamentally a capitalist party mainly concerned with protecting the vested interests of the capitalist and the landlord classes, whether in opposition or in power.

Had Macmillan been in power in 1945 could he have faced the problems of rebuilding industry with any measure of success, except on very much the same lines as the Labour Government did between 1945 and 1951?

Could a Tory Government have removed controls and rationing immediately war had ended? How would it have faced the problems of getting transport going again and the coal mines working to provide the fuel for the industry changing over from war to peace?

Something obviously had to be done about the railways, the coal mines, electricity and transport, and Labour's answer was reorganisation under public ownership—nationalization.

Had the Tories won in 1945 they would have been forced themselves to carry out drastic reorganization of these key industries on lines not very dissimilar from those which were carried out by the Labour Government. The railways had been virtually nationalized during the war. How could any Government that wished to have anything like a working transport system at all have gone back to pre-war private ownership? In any case it could not have done this without big State subsidies. Railways were nationalized in most countries of Europe before the war. Churchill himself had advocated nationalization of railways twenty years before and Gladstone had supported it even in his time.

Had Harold Macmillan been Prime Minister in 1945 he would have had to nationalize the railways too.

Then there were the coal mines. The Reid Committee had recommended nationalization and it would have been a choice between nationalization and reorganization under trustification with national subsidies which would also have meant a large measure of State control. The same applied to the electricity and gas industries which, before the war, Macmillan had agreed should be run under public ownership or on public utility lines.

Indeed if nationalization had failed so hopelessly, why had the Tories not denationalized everything that the Labour Government had nationalized?

Nobody is in such a weak position to sneer at nationalization and suggest that it has been a hopeless failure than Macmillan. His only success on the home front was his drive for 300,000 houses a year, which was only possible by using the local authorities to speed up municipal house building on the lines which a Labour Government had begun.

When house building was handed over to private ownership and public enterprise damped down, the number of houses built decreased.

The Tories were opposed to the nationalized Health Service and the establishment of the Welfare State. They disliked it but could not do away with it because they feared the unpopularity and the electoral consequences that would follow. The modern Tory, unlike the Tories of half a century ago, must accept ideas like old age pensions and full employment and better social insurance because they would not win General Elections if they were opposed to them.

In spite of any mistakes that it made, the Labour Government of 1945 to 1951 was the best Government this country has ever had.

It was not its Socialist policies that brought the Labour Government down but the rise in prices and the financial crisis that came with the war in Korea and the rearmament programme which had nothing to do with Socialism and which the Tories supported.

That is why Macmillan's innumerable references to the failures and incompetence of the Socialist Government are so hollow and superficial.

For ten years it was hardly possible for anyone from the Socialist benches to refer to planning and controls without somebody jeering from the Tory side. Nobody played up to this prejudice and ignorance more than Macmillan, though he was in a position to know better than anyone.

So with the return of the Tories to power we had a decade of the free-for-all, no controls, the unplanned economy, the paradise for the speculator and the take-over bidder which has inevitably and ultimately landed Britain into economic and financial crises.

In concluding the debate on the economic situation on July 27, 1961, Macmillan remarked almost casually:

'As regards the structure of our economy and guidance, what is ordinarily called planning, I have little to add to what my Right Hon. Friends have said yesterday and today. I can only say that I have nothing against planning. I once wrote a book about it. I was happy to see when I was re-reading it the other day that nearly everything I had recommended has since been done. However, if more is needed to meet changing conditions it will have my support, but we must be sure that it is the kind of planning which suits our political and industrial habits and institutions.'

One can only ask who had done so many of the things that Macmillan had recommended in his pre-war days—the much-maligned Labour Government of 1945-51, and in the teeth of Macmillan himself.

Nothing could better illustrate the attitude of the Macmillan Government to controls and planning than a statement issued by Dr Charles Hill, the Minister of Housing, on January 15, 1962. It read:

'The Government are not at present contemplating the introduction of building controls so that workers can be diverted from constructing large blocks of offices to more essential projects, such as houses for the homeless.

'Such a plan has not yet come before either the Cabinet or any Cabinet committee, and no decision has been taken. Drastic steps of this kind seem improbable, but Dr Charles Hill, Minister of Housing, is believed to be disturbed by the problem of the homeless, particularly in parts of London. If other steps fail, some diversion of labour to housing would seem to be a possibility in due course, but extensive redirection of building forces is unlikely.'

It was quite true that he had advocated planning before the war. But he had forgotten about it for over twenty years. It was Rip Van Winkle waking from a long sleep again.

Ten years after Macmillan went to the Ministry of Health and Housing to accomplish his miracles on the housing front 'the Minister of Health is believed to be disturbed by the problem of the homeless, particularly in parts of London'.

The Minister is 'believed to be disturbed', and 'if other steps fail some diversion of labour in housing would seem to be a possibility in due course'. But just in case the building speculating fraternity is disturbed, as well as the Minister, they are assured that 'extensive redirection of building forces is unlikely'.

Why was it necessary to issue this statement at all? Because it was obvious that workers who are more needed to build houses for the homeless were employed on constructing large blocks of offices.

This was five years after Macmillan became Prime Minister, and six years after Eden had suggested that office building needed to be cut down.

Indeed after five years of Macmillan's Premiership the housing situation in London had become so bad that a special service for the homeless of London was being held at Southwark Cathedral.

Anybody could see in the centre of London the new skyscraper blocks of offices. On the banks of the Thames they towered over the Houses of Parliament and over County Hall. But London was as chronically overcrowded as ever and rents had soared as a result of the Tory Government's Rent Act.

Macmillan had been supposed to have made a great success of housing. Hadn't he been responsible for achieving the record target of 300,000 houses a year? But the housing drive had slowed down. Nobody looking carefully at the state of London five years after he had been Prime Minister would argue that the Government record on housing was now anything to boast about.

High rates of interest had slowed down the house-building activities of local authorities and as the Minister of Health had admitted, the building workers were being employed on building luxury offices for big business while the homeless were waiting in the housing queue.

Five years after Macmillan had been in power there was greater industrial discontent than there had been since the war, as the result of the Government's insistence on the Pay Pause. The Post Office workers were carrying out a go-slow policy and the workers in the Civil Service were following their example. Other workers were lining up with their demands and the relations between the Government and the T.U.C. were severely strained. These were the inevitable results of the financial and economic crisis.

In the by-elections the Tory vote had slumped. The 'You've never had it so good' slogan did not carry any conviction now and the Macwonder legend no longer worked. The Tories were comforted by the forecast that before the next Election Britain would be in the Common Market and that there would be a trade boom and a wave of prosperity, but there were doubts about that. Could Macmillan win another General Election for them? They were not quite so confident now.

On the fifth anniversary of the day on which he had become Prime Minister Macmillan returned from a visit to Dr Adenauer.

Dr Adenauer had at one time been dismissed by the British from his post as Lord Mayor of Cologne. Perhaps he was now wondering when the British were going to sack Macmillan for the same reason.

Even the *Daily Mail* had admitted that Defence was 'in a mess'. Macmillan, it was said, had been to tell Dr Adenauer that Britain could no longer afford to keep such a big British Army in Germany and Dr Adenauer's remedy was to spend more money buying arms from Britain. Fifteen years after she had been defeated and her economy destroyed Germany had so far recovered that she was in a position to lend Britain money to help her out of her difficulties.

Indeed Britain was so hard up that she was glad to borrow money to tide things over from neutral Switzerland.

During the ten years that the Tories had been in power we had spent over £16,000,000,000 on defence but nobody could say how Britain could be defended in a nuclear war. A few hydrogen bombs delivered by rockets and Britain could be destroyed. We had become just a satellite of America with Kennedy looking upon Macmillan very much in the same way as Khrushchev looked upon Walter Ulbricht. A section of military opinion in America appeared to look upon Britain just as an island base in Western Europe which was expendable. America, it was said, had insisted that Britain should go into the Common Market and become economically a part of Europe for defence purposes. The old days of a proud, independent Britain seemed to be over. Once in the Common Market the days of British sovereignty would be over. The power of the House of Commons would be transferred to some super-national committee meeting in Brussels or Paris or Bonn, with the British Parliament being about as important in deciding vital matters affecting our lives as a county council or a district council.

One writer in the Beaverbrook Press, John Junor, even wrote an article on Macmillan entitled 'The Last Prime Minister'. He was not thinking of a Britain destroyed in a nuclear war but of a Britain where the British Prime Minister had so little prestige and power that he no longer mattered very much.

All this, however, is in the future, a matter of speculation. Harold Macmillan as a politician has certainly played a considerable part in the events which had led to Britain being described as 'The Sick Man of Europe'.

CHAPTER XXIX

COMMON MARKET OR COMMONWEALTH?

ON JULY 31st, shortly before the House rose for the Summer Recess, the Prime Minister rose after Question Time and announced that he wished to make a statement on the policy of Her Majesty's Government towards the European Economic Community. It was one of the most important and significant statements Macmillan was to make as Prime Minister. The Government had decided to make an application to join the Common Market. It had not been unexpected and a crowded House listened carefully to every word. It was a historic occasion.

He said:

'The future relations between the European Economic Community, the United Kingdom, the Commonwealth and the rest of Europe are clearly matters of capital importance in the life of our country and, indeed, of all the countries of the Free World.

'This is a political as well as an economic issue. Although the Treaty of Rome is concerned with economic matters it has an important political objective, namely, to promote unity and stability in Europe which is so essential a factor in the struggle for freedom and progress throughout the world. In this modern world the tendency towards larger groups of nations acting together in the common interest leads to greater unity and thus adds to our strength in the struggle for freedom.

'I believe that it is both our duty and our interest to contribute towards that strength by securing the closest possible unity within Europe.'

But there were reservations. There was the Commonwealth. If a closer relationship between Europe 'would disrupt the long-standing and historic ties between the United Kingdom and the Commonwealth then the loss would be the greater than the gain'.

'On the economic side, a community comprising, as members or in association, the countries of Free Europe, could have a very rapid expanding economy, supplying, as eventually it would, a single market of approaching 300 million people. This rapidly expanding economy could, in turn, lead to an increased demand for products from other parts of the world and so help to expand world trade and improve the prospects of the less developed areas of the world.'

At the same time the Government was concerned to protect the interests of the Commonwealth and British agriculture.

'No British Government could join the European Economic Community without prior negotiation with a view to meeting the needs of the Commonwealth countries, of our European Free Trade Association partners, and of British agriculture consistently with the broad principles and purpose which have inspired the concept of European unity and which are embodied in the Rome Treaty.'

The Government therefore had come to the conclusion that it would be right to make a formal application under Article 237 of the Treaty for negotiations with a view to joining the Community 'if satisfactory arrangements can be made to meet the special needs of the United Kingdom, of the Commonwealth and of the European Free Trade Association'.

That was the big 'if'.

How could Britain go into this European Community and keep up its association with the Commonwealth and protect British agriculture at the same time? At some time, at some point, the House of Commons would be faced with a decision in which it would have to make its choice. Meanwhile the Government wanted approval of its decision to open negotiations.

Gaitskell, for the Labour Party, was non-committal but it soon became obvious that Macmillan was faced with trouble from the Tory side.

Anthony Fell, the young Right-wing Tory from Yarmouth, broke out impetuously:

'Is the Prime Minister aware that he has made a shocking statement full of political double talk? [Hon. Members: 'Nonsense!'] Is he aware that it had the effect on one former supporter that he now thinks that the Prime Minister is a national disaster?'

Macmillan rose angrily and tried to wave his critic down. Fell refused to give way and continued:

'I can be told to sit down by the Speaker, but not by the Prime Minister.

'Is the Prime Minister aware that this decision to gamble with British sovereignty in Europe, when 650 million people of the British Commonwealth depend upon his faith and leadership, is the most disastrous thing that any Prime Minister has done for many generations past? I would say to the Prime Minister——'

Tory M.P.s supporting the Prime Minister shouted 'Sit down', but he went on:

'I would ask the Prime Minister to believe, despite his laughs and smirks and the smirks of other Right Hon. Gentlemen on the Government Front Bench, that there are those British people who believe that it is impossible under the Treaty of Rome, except an entirely new Treaty of Rome, an entirely scrapped Treaty of Rome, to protect British agriculture, the British Commonwealth and the E.F.T.A. countries. Therefore, for these reasons I suggest that the best service that the Prime Minister could do to the country would be to resign.'

Macmillan rose, pale and angry, and said acidly:

'The Hon. Gentleman has stated a point of view which he will, no doubt, repeat in debate. Meanwhile I can only say that I think he has maximized his support.'

It looked as if the Tory Whips had assured the Government that it could rely on their docile supporters behind them to back them in the division lobby if it came to a vote.

There were other dissentient voices, two ex-Ministers, Turton and Walker-Smith, and other Tory M.P.s concerned with the possible effect on agriculture, and they expressed their doubts in the two-day debate that followed. But the Whips were on, there were some abstainers on the Government side and the official Labour Party was also able to abstain. The five Labour M.P.s from whom the Labour Whip had been withdrawn voted against the Government, as did Fell. Macmillan had easily won the first round. This was, however, only the first round, there were others to follow.

Outside, however, the opposition to Britain's proposed entry into the Common Market was stronger. Lord Beaverbrook and his papers thought this was the first step towards betraying the Commonwealth and as time went on Labour began to be more critical and have its doubts.

Outbursts by impulsive back bench M.P.s do not, however, worry Macmillan. He knows how to assess them. They do not seriously threaten his position. He can turn the tables on them by some appropriate rebuke or retort if necessary and come out of the incident with dignity. When he first hinted at going into the Common Market Lord Hinchingbrooke asked superiorly if he remembered what happened to the last Prime Minister who went to negotiate at Godesberg. 'Yes,' said Macmillan, 'and I remember where I was then—and where the noble lord was,' and turned the laugh against Hinchingbrooke.

It was, however, a more serious matter when Tory back benchers let it be known that they were against the Government sending bombs to the United Nations forces in the Congo. About a hundred of them signed a motion and there were indications at the 1922 Committee that they had influential support inside the Tory Party.

There were strong financial interests involved in Katanga and these were able to constitute a pressure group which could not be ignored. Macmillan had pledged the Tories at the General Election to give the utmost support to the United Nations, but the Cabinet yielded to the Katanga Lobby. It was an awkward debate for Macmillan but he brazened it out and when the Opposition motion was defeated he was loudly cheered by back benchers and turned to bow to them as he left the Chamber. He had staved off a crisis within the Tory Party by refusing to stand by the United Nations at a difficult moment in its history. Macmillan, as an astute Tory Party politician, knows when to crack the whip and when to obey the whip in awkward situations. At one time he had stood out for principle against the Tory Party machine in the House. Then he was the young idealist. Now he had become the hardened politician. He had at one time scorned appeasement, but appeasement of his Tory followers in the House had become necessary in order for him to maintain his grip on power.

CHAPTER XXX

RUSSIAN TESTS AND CHRISTMAS ISLAND

SPEAKING in the debate on the Queen's Speech on October 31, 1961, Macmillan indignantly denounced the action of the Soviet Government in leaving the Geneva Nuclear Test Conference and in resuming nuclear tests in the Arctic. The Soviet Government, he declared, had come to 'a wanton decision to pollute the air for what appeared to be more a political than a military purpose'. Arrangements had been made to set up 'a comprehensive system of sampling milk throughout the country' so that 'the position could be closely watched, day by day, both on a national and a regional basis'. Processed milk would be made available for infants under one year old should this prove necessary. The longer term results of the Russian tests would 'give anxiety in every part of the world'. He would not weary the House 'by trying to find new expressions with which to condemn the cynicism and brutality of what the Russians have done'.

The House was interested in what the American and British Governments were going to do now. After all their indignant denunciations of the Russian Government were they going to do precisely the same thing? Were they too going to pollute the air and poison the milk?

Macmillan was obviously uneasy as he went on to discuss this situation. Dr Jekyll was having his usual struggle with Mr Hyde.

He went on:

'First of all, both we and our American friends are very conscious of two duties, both grave and, to some extent, I fear, conflicting. We have a duty, all of us, to think of the dangers to the health of mankind, including children yet unborn, which may arise to a greater or lesser degree from the continuance of any large-scale atmospheric nuclear tests. At the same time, we have a duty to maintain the balance of power in the world, to ensure that the deterrent still deters and that the security of free men is not overthrown because an aggressor suddenly becomes possessed of an overwhelming advantage. Both of these duties place a very heavy moral responsibility on the Heads of Government of the nuclear Powers.'

From the Opposition benches below the gangway came the interruption:

'That is what Mr Khrushchev says.'

He replied:

'We did not test for three years. We did not start after 1958.

'I say, therefore, that these duties are, to some extent, conflicting, but they at least enable us to draw certain definite conclusions. First of all, we have a duty to work for an agreement which will put an end to nuclear tests under proper control. No one can say that we have not honestly and honourably worked for that, as the Hon. Member for South Ayrshire (Mr Emrys Hughes) knows. Both the American Government and the British Government are ready at any time to resume talks now suspended, for a nuclear test agreement, or to begin talks anywhere else which seem likely to lead to a similar result. That is our first conclusion on which we stand.

'Secondly, we are clear that we will not make tests for terroristic or retaliatory purposes [*Interruption*]. Ask Mr Khrushchev for his views. I am giving ours. We will not make tests merely because the Russians have done so—terroristic or retaliatory—which I call a kind of political testing.

'Thirdly, if tests must be conducted for good military or scientific reasons, if possible they will be made underground where there is no danger of pollution. I have specifically in mind the possible need to ensure the safety in peace and the effectiveness in operation of weapons either newly in service or under development, or the study of new techniques—most probably of a defensive kind—whose production might revolutionise the nuclear balance.

'We cannot risk putting the West in a position of permanent military inferiority, but if it proves technically necessary that any such tests should take place in the atmosphere, they will, of course, be on a very minor scale, the smallest possible, pending the conclusion of an effective agreement for the abolition of all tests.

'There is a great distinction between underground and atmospheric testing. We have kept off both for three years and underground tests themselves would be regrettable because they would mark, even temporarily, the breakdown of the policy to which so much patient service has been given by our negotiators, to which so much devoted effort has been attached and on which we based such great hope. But they have no ill effects on the health of the world.

'Atmospheric tests, however, are in a different category and I hope that it will not prove necessary for the Americans or ourselves to make atmospheric tests, however small. Certainly we have no plans for such tests in the near future. Nevertheless, I must be quite clear and frank with the House. If I were convinced that a particular atmospheric test was necessary in order to maintain the balance of the deterrent and to preserve freedom in the world, Britain would be bound either to co-operate in, or support, its conduct.'

In short, in order to maintain the military balance of power he was, too, quite prepared to conduct tests which might pollute the air and poison the milk.

He went on:

'I would ask how this principle would be applied, and I think it must rest upon the sincere judgment of those who are charged with this heavy responsibility, after doing their best to weigh the technical information at their disposal. I can assure the House that it is in this spirit that the British and American Governments intend to work.'

Then he went off at a tangent to discuss the proposals for extending National Service and later returned, uneasily, to the question of nuclear explosions.

Hansard reports what follows:

'I have dealt with two of the great issues which the House has mostly in its mind, issues raised by the Russian explosions, the deterioration of the position, and I have tried to explain the policy which Her Majesty's Government will follow and which I think will inspire the American Government.'

Mr Emrys Hughes: May I ask the Prime Minister one question? I am obliged to him for giving way. He is arguing about the balance of power. Is he arguing that, in order to preserve the balance of power, we should be prepared to conduct tests and be prepared to poison and pollute the atmosphere and poison the milk? If so, what is the difference, the broad general difference, between his argument and Mr Khrushchev's?

The Prime Minister: There is a very great difference. These tests have put into the atmosphere, for no military purpose, free-dropping bombs, sometimes at just 10,000 or 12,000 feet, and these tests, not to test a weapon and for no military purpose, have put into the atmosphere as much as has been put there over the whole period since testing began. I am saying that, if there were some new weapon, if there were some anti-missile missile, or if it were a matter of perfecting the safety of a weapon, and it was necessary—it being not possible to get results by an underground test—to make, perhaps, a kiloton test or a test of that category, unwilling as we should be, we should not shrink from it. We should be wrong to shrink from it because if we did we should be handing ourselves and the whole free world which we must defend to be trampled on by the Russians.

Mr Emrys Hughes: Poisoning the milk.

The Prime Minister: It would not poison any milk, because of the amount of material we should use. The Hon. Gentleman and his Friends—I fear that they represent quite a considerable part of the

Q

country—are so pro-Russian that they hate the name and thought of England.

Mr Emrys Hughes: We are speaking for humanity.

The Prime Minister: The Hon. Gentleman and his Friends poison quite a lot of their own friends. The Right Hon. Gentleman the Leader of the Opposition did well to throw them out.'

The interruptions had at least served the purpose of making him drop the humbug. Dr Jekyll had disappeared completely now, it was all Mr Hyde.

Macmillan's argument from the military point of view was understandable. But in the light of the conclusion all the preamble about the 'cynicism and brutality' of the Russians was so much hypocrisy. To maintain the balance of power, he argued, we must be prepared to be as brutal and as cynical as the Russians.

He had realized that he could no longer pose as being more humane or more Christian than they. And this realization had made him resort to smearing his critics in the Bottomley and McCarthy style.

He was obviously preparing the way for the time when he would appear at the Despatch Box to announce that somewhere in the world the Americans, with his consent and approval, were going to do what he had condemned the Russians for doing in the Arctic.

Indeed that time was to come very soon. In December he paid one of his periodic visits to meet President Kennedy at Bermuda and reports appeared in the American press that Macmillan had been asked to allow the Americans to carry out nuclear test explosions at Christmas Island in the Pacific.

Nothing was said in the official communiqué. He returned to Britain just before Christmas. It was the peace and goodwill season. It would be inappropriate to tell the world about this until later.

The American magazine *News Week* (8.1.62) asked 'Why the delay?' and explained:

'One reason is political. Edward R. Murrow's United States Information Agency, for example, has made capital of the fact that Moscow first spread the poisonous seeds of radioactivity after a three-year respite.'

Another reason, it was explained, was that there had been

protests from the Marshall Islands where the Americans had previously tested.

In the Marshall Islands eighty-two natives had suffered from radioactive fall out after an H-bomb had been set off there in March 1954.

'Though no natives died,' *News Week* said, 'from the 175 roentgens of radiation which most of them had received (450 to 600 is considered a fatal dose) and no long-term deleterious effects have appeared so far under careful U.S. supervision, the Marshallese don't want any more tests on their islands. Thus the pressure has built to the point where the problems involved in using the Marshall Islands outweigh all other considerations.' *News Week* continued:

'There are other islands in the ocean, of course, and many belong to the U.S., but most of them are populated, or close to populated areas. As a result, the U.S. has turned to its allies. President Kennedy, in his recent talks in Bermuda with Prime Minister Harold Macmillan, asked about the availability of Christmas Island, a thirty-five-mile-long, palm-fringed island 1,200 miles south of Hawaii. Britain conducted nine weapons tests there in 1957 and 1958, and the base has been kept up ever since. But, despite a statement issued from Bermuda agreeing that 'preparations should be made for atmospheric testing', British permission to use the island apparently has not been granted. The British, it was understood, do not want to become directly involved in nuclear testing unless it is necessary.'

It looked as if Macmillan had his hesitations. But a month later they had been overcome.

On February 8th he rose in the House of Commons to make the anticipated statement. He prefaced it with the news that the United States had agreed to make available to Britain facilities for an underground nuclear test in Nevada. He added:

'At Bermuda, we also dscussed the question of atmospheric tests about which the House, I think rightly, feels a more lively concern. President Kennedy explained that in accordance with his statement on November 1st he felt it militarily necessary now to make preparations for a limited series of atmospheric tests for specific purposes. In the world of ballistic missiles offensive power remains far ahead of defensive power, and we know that some most formidable practical problems stand in the way of devising a defence against missiles. Yet, while the arms race continues, we dare not fall behind in the struggle between offensive and defensive capabilities, with their increasingly complex systems of counter-measures and counter-counter-measures. We must bear in mind the claims, true or false, made by Russian

military leaders at the time of their nuclear test series last autumn
that they have solved the problem of destroying ballistic missiles in
flight. As I said in the debate on 31st October, I conceive that "we
have a duty to maintain the balance of power in the world . . . and
to ensure that the security of free men is not overthrown because an
aggressor suddenly becomes possessed of an overwhelming advantage".

'I felt myself bound to accept, therefore, the military and scientific
arguments in favour of preparations for a resumption of tests [Hon.
Members: 'Shame'.] and when President Kennedy asked for the use
of facilities at Christmas Island for them, Her Majesty's Government
thought it right to agree. Accordingly, an agreement is being discussed in Washington at the moment under which Her Majesty's
Government will allow the United States the use of facilities at
Christmas Island for a limited period and for a specific programme of
tests with which we shall of course be associated.'

He then read the statement that was also being issued at the
same time at Washington and proceeded:

'While our two Governments have reluctantly accepted the need to
prepare for further tests, both President Kennedy and I were deeply
distressed at this necessity and at the future position in the world if
a halt cannot be called to the nuclear arms race. When I was in
Bermuda I made this point strongly to the President, who was very
receptive, and accordingly, on my return after consulting my colleagues, I made a definite proposal to President Kennedy that the
Western Powers should make another determined effort to reach
some agreement with the Soviet Union on the question of disarmament. We have already agreed to join in the work of the Committee
of Eighteen which meets in Geneva on March 14th, and I believe that
this will offer an opportunity for renewed serious discussions.

'I am glad to say that President Kennedy very much welcomed the
idea of trying to give special impetus and effectiveness to this conference. Accordingly, the two Governments have today communi-
cated with the Soviet Government, and have invited them to send
their Foreign Minister to a tripartite meeting to assemble before the
Geneva meeting and to begin this meeting also at the level of Foreign
Ministers. I have addressed a personal letter to Mr Khrushchev
appealing to him to agree to this proposal and President Kennedy has
done the same. It is our hope that a preliminary meeting of Foreign
Ministers may reach broad agreement on the type of work which
could be studied in the Committee of Eighteen and that the presence
of Foreign Ministers at the start of the meetings of the Committee
will give an impetus to its work.

There were numerous questions from the Opposition side of
the House. One of the most pertinent comments came from Jo
Grimond, the Liberal leader. He asked:

'Is the Prime Minister aware that he has made a profoundly depressing announcement to the House? [Hon. Members: 'Oh'.] If Hon.
Members opposite do not think it is depressing I am astonished.
Many of us who support deterrence are horrified in case it develops
a sort of competitive momentum of its own and it becomes impossible
ever to stop these tests.'

On his return from Bermuda he had talked about 'the terrible
nuclear arms race'. But he himself, by agreeing to the Polaris
submarines being based on Britain, had taken an action which
had accelerated the arms race.

The Polaris submarines were supposed to be the last word in
nuclear strategy, to which, we were told, the Russians could
have no answer. Moving about under the sea they could not be
detected nor destroyed like a missile base on land.

Yet there was a connection between the Polaris submarine and
the Russian experimental explosions of megaton bombs.

It was explained in *The Economist* in an article 'Megaton
Motives' on October 28, 1961.

Discussing the military uses of the Russian explosions we
were told:

'The usefulness of a big warhead is that by increasing the area of
devastation it diminishes the need for accuracy in the rocket that
carries it. This may be particularly important in the case of the
Russian rockets designed to destroy American missiles kept in underground emplacements, like the Minuteman and some Titans. The
Russians have claimed that rockets can be made extremely accurate,
and American experiments have tended to confirm that a missile can
be put down within a mile or so of its target after a 5,000-mile run.
Even so it might take two or three five-megaton warheads to guarantee the destruction of the underground emplacement.

'If the Russians have found that their rockets are slow in coming
off the assembly line, and if a fifty-ton megaton warhead compact
enough to fit into existing rockets is successfully tested, they may
have decided that the bigger bang represents an economy . . .

'The suspicion that rockets are being produced more slowly than
they would like is strengthened by the fact that the Americans have
recently reduced their estimate of the number of missiles the Russians
have ready for firing from one hundred to sixty.

'On the same grounds, the big warhead might be used against
prowling Polaris submarines, if their general whereabouts, but not
their exact position, were known to Soviet intelligence; the extra
hull-cracking pressure produced by the biggest explosion might make
a difference between a hit and a miss.'

Every Polaris submarine, we had been told, carried missiles

which could destroy a dozen cities. The Russians could justify their tests on the ground that it was necessary to have bigger bombs in order to destroy the Polaris submarines. The Polaris submarines were testing and rehearsing with their 'city killer' missiles all the time.

Having approved of the Polaris, Macmillan was obviously not in a strong position to strike moral attitudes about the wickedness of the Russians.

Macmillan was obviously taken aback when from behind him came an unexpected question from a Conservative, Mr Tiley, who asked:

'While supporting my Right Hon. Friend in the policy he is pursuing may I ask whether it would not be a good thing if we changed the name of the island?'

He replied:

'It was because that thought, curiously enough, was in my mind, and because of the deep feeling which we all have, that President Kennedy and I decided to make another effort to see whether what we call this sterile competition could be brought to an end.'

Mr Tiley might have asked if it would not be appropriate if the name of the ocean should be changed at the same time.

Undoubtedly there was something supremely ironical in agreeing to the testing of megaton bombs on an island which had been named after the founder of the Christian religion.

One wondered what he had told Kennedy when this thought came to him at the meeting in Bermuda. After meeting the Pope, Macmillan had given a talk over the Rome television in which he had said: 'We are all God's children. Why should we destroy ourselves?'

Could he have said at Bermuda: 'What sort of Christians are we, Kennedy, to be here talking about using Christmas Island for exploding a H-bomb?'

CHAPTER XXXI

THE BEGINNING OF THE END

EARLY in 1962 Macmillan gave one of his political broadcasts
which while it pleased his television audience fans also brought
criticism from quarters which had not hitherto been critical of
him. In reporting the speech the *Daily Telegraph* said that 'the
Prime Minister, who will be sixty-eight on Saturday, looked
about twenty years younger in his television broadcast. At all
events, this was the impression of many political observers who
have seen him regularly at Westminster.'

What had happened to rejuvenate him? Was the international situation any brighter or were there signs that the
economic crisis was disappearing. Or was it really a triumph for
the television make-up experts who could do for a politician
what the powder and paint experts of the theatre could do at
Christmas to make a rather middle-aged lady into a handsome
principal boy?

The technique of the fireside heart-to-heart talk, filmed four
hours before the event at Admiralty House, was the same as that
which had been so successful on the eve of the General Election.

Yet it seemed not to have impressed so many people. It certainly had not greatly impressed the correspondent of the
Sunday Telegraph who was more candid about it and wrote
irreverently about 'Mr Macmillan's favourite bedside manner
which gives so falsely optimistic a picture of the patients' prospects and so misleading a picture of the doctor's anxieties'. All
this might have been said of the General Election TV broadcasts
too. Only it was now being said prominently in a paper that
normally supported the Government.

The following week the same correspondent reported a meeting at Oxford at which the Prime Minister delivered a speech
in which 'there was no intellectual content at all, no grand
themes for the undergraduates to remember, only the mournful
picture of a rather tired, silver-haired gentleman with nothing
to say and no particular interest in saying it well'.

In *The Observer* (February 4th) there was a statistical examination of the number of TV viewers who had switched off before the end of the speech. This could not but be read with interest by the advertizing experts.

The success or failure of a Prime Minister's appeal can now be estimated by T.A.M. (Television Audience Management) based on the statistical sampling of 950 homes which can see both results:

The writer of *The Observer article*, Mark Arnold Foster, gave a fascinating account of how this technique of assessing the Prime Minister's talk worked out:

'Examined minute by minute the Prime Minister's audience was seen to dwindle from the occupants of 7,767,000 houses when he began to 6,529,000 houses by the time he had finished . . .

'Over on Channel 1 about 100,000 sets were switched off when the Prime Minister said "Now what about abroad?" About 336,000 had left him by the time he started on new emerging countries in Africa and Asia; another 100,000 began to quit when he began to talk about his meeting with President Kennedy ("We discussed this at length when President Kennedy and I met just before Christmas . . . "), after which his T.A.M. rating stayed steady for some minutes.

'It was not until he told viewers "We have not done badly; we have done quite well; but we have not done quite well enough" that the final decline began. By peroration time ("It's a test of our determination to play this role in the world . . . ") only 2,251,000 sets were tuned in to him on the B.B.C. channel—1,357,000 fewer than had been with him when he started.'

In these days when General Elections can be won or lost by television appearances the experts could hardly have failed to note what was happening. Macmillan was losing his capacity of appeal and persuasion to sufficient of a percentage of the population to make politically minded calculating financial gentlemen speculate whether at the next General Election he would be able to bring it off for them again.

These doubts were also reflected in moderately worded speculative articles that appeared even in papers that loyally supported the Tory Government and Macmillan, like the *Sunday Times* which devoted a main feature middle page article to the subject 'How real is the Tory Revolt?' and summed up by saying:

'It has to be accepted, however, that whether there is a recovery or not, another Macmillan administration after the next Election now seems quite unlikely.'

This followed an examination of the views of the Tory M.P.s.
It said:

'When Conservative Members came back they did so in an uneasy
state of mind, whether they belonged to the Left, the Right or the
solid Centre. The ten days since they returned has plunged them
into a far worse state of depression. The Party does not know what
its economic policy is meant to be; it can see the effects in terms of
strikes, but it does not feel that there is a competent long-term
purpose.'

The problems that Macmillan had dodged for five years were
still unsolved. Evasions and improvisations no longer worked.

A blunt if not a tactful and rather premature notice to quit
came in a speech at the beginning of February from Sir Harry
Legge-Bourke, the Tory back bencher from the Isle of Ely. He
was bold enough to say what many Tory back benchers were
thinking.

He described Macmillan as 'one who had reached the conclusion that mankind is condemned to eventual self destruction'
and continued:

' "There have been moments when I have sensed that the Prime
Minister sees little hope for the future, and yet at other times he
tends to play down the difficulties and presents the problems with
which we are confronted as though they were comparatively easy
and trivial."

'He hoped that the Prime Minister would remain an optimist.
"But," he added, "it is no good being optimistic one day, pessimistic
the next and indecisive in between. That can only lead to the
impression in the public mind that there is indecision, uncertainty,
and lack of direction."

'Men like Mr Macmillan who fought in World War I, were in
politics between the two wars, and had heavy responsibility in the
Second World War, can justifiably be excused were they now to feel
exhausted.

' "It is no condemnation of those men if we should now say to
them 'Thank you for what you have done. Thank you for what you
have tried to do. The time is coming for you now to hand over those
responsibilities to men whose good fortune it is not to have had to
bear for so many grievous years the burdens you have borne.'

' "We must all put the country first, and the country today needs
unflagging vigour, undaunted hope, infallible faith, and the forward
look."

'In an obvious reference to the Prime Minister's TV appearance,
Sir Harry said: "This is no time for cosy fireside chats. It is time for
someone to thump a table a little, to bring home to every man,

woman and child in this country the realities of the situation and the responsibility of every one of us." '

Of course he was immediately disowned and repudiated by other Tory M.P.s but the impression created by his speech remained.

Nobody of course expected Macmillan to retire as a result of this attack. The *Sunday Times* prophesied that the initial reaction would be another 'stiffening of loyalty' but added significantly:

'On the other hand the Conservative Party has the business of trying to win the next General Election. It persuaded Sir Winston Churchill to retire in order to win the Election of 1955; it will consider Mr Macmillan's position in the light of 1963.'

They would not stab him in the back. They would delicately suggest that the time had come for him to say with dignity, 'Now lettest thou thy servant depart in peace', so that they too could reply with dignity, 'Well done thou good and faithful servant, you can have an earldom and a seat in the House of Lords and you will have the time and leisure to write your memoirs'.

Macmillan has told the House of Commons that he does not intend to write his memoirs 'even if I can find a publisher'. One doubts if he could resist the temptation. He could certainly throw a lot of light on what happened in British politics in the years when he was Prime Minister.

In these days it has become the convention that ex-Prime Ministers and Cabinet Ministers and generals and others who have been at the centre of things to devote their leisure time to writing their autobiographies, which, even if they are not very lively or inspiring, yet provide very useful material for the historians. Even if Macmillan's autobiography were not so exciting as Churchill's it could surely be as interesting as those of Attlee and Eden. He could certainly make a formidable volume of answering the questions which he did not answer or evaded when he was Prime Minister. It would be very interesting, for example, if he would tell us the real inside story of Suez which marked the end of a volume in our Imperial history. Then there is obviously a lot more to tell about his visit to Russia, what he told Khrushchev and Mikoyan and what they told him. He must have met more of the important European and

American political personalities of the post-war years than most contemporary politicians.

Obviously, too, he could tell us more about himself and what he really thought about people and events in his day and generation. How and why did the keen young reformer of the 'thirties turn out to be the conventional politician of the later years, the Prime Minister who became the defender and the spokesman and the hope in politics of the vested interests that he had in his younger days so vigorously attacked? Why did he fail to use the opportunities that were presented to him at a time when great and imaginative leadership was so urgently needed in the world?

He really should write his memoirs, if only as a guide and as an awful warning to other politicians who may follow him in Downing Street.

INDEX

INDEX

GEORGE ALLEN & UNWIN LTD
London : 40 Museum Street, W.C.1

Auckland : 24 Wyndham Street
Bombay : 15 Graham Road, Ballard Estate, Bombay 1
Buenos Aires : Escritorio 454-459, Florida 165
Calcutta : 17 Chittaranjan Avenue, Calcutta 13
Cape Town : 109 Long Street
Hong Kong : F1/12 Mirador Mansions, Kowloon
Ibadan : P.O. Box 62
Karachi : Karachi Chambers, McLeod Road
Madras : Mohan Mansions, 38c Mount Road, Madras 6
Mexico : Villalongin 32-10, Piso, Mexico 5, D.F.
Nairobi : P.O. Box 12446
New Delhi : 13-14 Asaf-Ali Road, New Delhi 1
São Paulo : Avenida 9 De Julho 1138-Ap. 51
Singapore : 36c Prinsep Street, Singapore 7
Sydney, N.S.W. : Bradbury House, 55 York Street
Toronto : 91 Wellington Street West